Creative Practice in Highe Education

This must-read book considers the ways in which creativity can inspire new ideas, invigorate teaching in the adult learning space, and motivate professionals and learners alike. Written by a diverse group of international collaborators, this book empowers readers to embrace creative practices that are considered innovative, engaging, and impactful for adult learners at different levels.

Drawing from a range of theoretical perspectives, contemporary research, and the lived experiences of the contributing authors, this edited volume offers readers a rich collection of pedagogical ideas and practical examples to apply within their professional practice. Chapters are divided into three key sections:

- *Engaging experiences*, such as large lectures, learning beyond the classroom, innovative technologies, and creative approaches to self-reflection.
- *Engaging groups*, including an exploration of communities within a range of educational, research, and geographical contexts.
- *Engaging tools* for learning, for example, poetry, digital portfolios, and innovations in providing feedback.

An essential read for anyone working in adult education, this book highlights how practitioners may engage adult learners in creative ways within universities, with implications for further education and other adult education institutions.

Simon Brownhill is a Senior Lecturer in Education at the University of Bristol, UK.

Creative Practice in Higher Education

Engaging Adult Learners through Theory and Pedagogy

Edited by Simon Brownhill

Routledge
Taylor & Francis Group

LONDON AND NEW YORK

Designed cover image: Getty Images

First published 2025
by Routledge
4 Park Square, Milton Park, Abingdon, Oxon OX14 4RN

and by Routledge
605 Third Avenue, New York, NY 10158

Routledge is an imprint of the Taylor & Francis Group, an informa business

British Library Cataloguing-in-Publication Data
A catalogue record for this book is available from the British Library

ISBN: 978-1-032-63354-1 (hbk)
ISBN: 978-1-032-63477-7 (pbk)
ISBN: 978-1-032-63353-4 (ebk)

DOI: 10.4324/9781032633534

Typeset in ITC Galliard Pro
by KnowledgeWorks Global Ltd.

In short: The RC for TLC @ SoE, UoB.

In long: The Research Centre for Teaching, Learning and Curriculum at the School of Education, University of Bristol.

Contents

Figures

Tables

About the editor and contributors

The editor

Simon Brownhill is Senior Lecturer in Education (*Teaching and Learning*) at the School of Education, University of Bristol. As the Pathway Lead for Teaching and Learning on the MSc Education programme, his teaching commitments are focussed on directing units that are linked to creativity, learning, and assessment. Simon also supervises a suite of research students at both master's and doctoral levels (EdD and PhD). He is a founding co-director of the Research Centre for Teaching, Learning and Curriculum (TLC) in the School of Education and serves as a key English member of the Editorial Board for *Pedagogical Dialogue*, an information and methodical journal for educators in Kazakhstan. With 20 years of experience working in Higher Education institutions in England (including the University of Derby and the University of Cambridge), Simon was a former Assistant Head Teacher of the Early Years (3 to 6), actively working as a class teacher in a number of educational settings in Derby/Derbyshire. He is co-author of the award-winning book *Men in Early Years Settings: Building a Mixed Gender Workforce* (2019, Jessica Kingsley Publishers).

The contributors

Alison Oldfield is Lecturer and Director of Master's programmes at the School of Education, University of Bristol.

Antonia Yu is a doctoral candidate (EdD) at the School of Education, University of Bristol, with research interests in communities of practice and teacher professional development.

Eugene Li is Lecturer at The Hong Kong University of Science and Technology for the Center of Language Education.

Ibrahim Berksoy is an academic manager at the University of the West of England Bristol's International College.

Janet Orchard is Associate Professor and Director of Postgraduate Research at the School of Education, University of Bristol.

Lucy Kelly is Associate Professor in Education at the School of Education, University of Bristol.

Maria Tsapali is Lecturer of Psychology in Education at the School of Education, University of Bristol.

Mark Neild is Associate Professor in Innovation and Entrepreneurship at the Centre for Innovation, University of Bristol.

Michelle Graffagnino is Senior Lecturer in Secondary Geography Education at the School of Education, University of Bristol, teaching on the PGCE and other master's programmes.

Nicola Warren-Lee is Subject Lead for the Secondary Geography PGCE at the School of Education, University of Bristol.

Nurul Nakiah Abdullah is a doctoral candidate (PhD) at the School of Education, University of Bristol.

Rachel Helme is a part-time Lecturer on the Secondary Mathematics PGCE course at the School of Education, University of Bristol.

Acknowledgements

It is with heartfelt thanks that the following individuals and organisations are recognised:

- Harriet, Lucy W., and Annie who initially expressed interest in what became this collaborative edited book.
- The reviewers of our book proposal who took the time to offer us constructive feedback.
- The School of Education at the University of Bristol for giving Simon four months of Study Leave to work on editing the book together.
- All at Routledge for their diligent efforts in putting us in print, especially Sarah Hyde and Lauren Redhead.
- And finally to all of our 'creatively brave' readers who take just one idea and utilise it within their own practice.

Thank you all very much indeed.

SPB (editor)

Glossary of terms

21st Century skills A suite of skills, abilities, and learning dispositions identified as requirements for success in the workplace and a rapidly changing, digital society. Also referred to as *Employability skills* and *Transferability skills*.

Action learning sets A structured approach which a small group of individuals use to address complicated issues.

Active learning An approach to instruction in which students are actively engaged in the learning process.

Adaptive motivation In the context of teachers and teaching, this refers to factors such as self-efficacy for teaching, valuing of teaching work, and mastery orientation towards teaching.

Adult learner Defined as any learner who is 18+ years old. Synonyms include *Student, Undergraduate*, and *Postgraduate*.

Affective learning A process of acquiring knowledge, skills, and attitudes through emotional engagement.

Andragogy The theory, methods, and activities involved in teaching adult learners.

(Generative) Artificial intelligence A type of technology which uses models that generate images, text, videos, and other media in response to inputted prompts.

Assessment Refers to the process of defining, selecting, designing, collecting, analysing, interpreting, and using information to increase students' learning and development.

Assessment *for* learning See *Formative assessment*.

Assessment *of* learning See *Summative assessment*.

Assistive technology Any products or systems that support and assist individuals with disabilities.

Audience response systems A tool that combines wireless hardware and presentation software to increase interaction between a lecturer and a group of students in the classroom.

Augmented reality A partially immersive, interactive experience that combines the real-world and computer-generated 3D content.

'Autobio' poetic structure A shortened form of 'Autobiographical' – this is a poetic structure that supports the writer to create a poem by self about self.

Autodidactic learning Learning that takes place without the direct supervision of a teacher, i.e., self-learning.

Blackout poetry Also known as erasure or redated poetry – the method involves the process of redating text such as literature or transcripts, using the final, unredacted words to create a poem.

Brain break An activity or short period of time that takes an individual away from hard mental work and allows their brain and body to reset.

ChatGPT A natural language processing chatbot driven by generative AI that allows the user to have human-like conversations to complete various tasks, e.g., composing emails, essays, and code.

Co-creation A transdisciplinary process in which members of different communities of practice work together to create new knowledge that would not have emerged within one's practice alone.

Cognition The mental action or process of acquiring knowledge and understanding through thought, experience, and the senses.

Community of practice A group of people who share a concern or a passion for something they do and learn how to do it better as they interact regularly.

Constructivism A learning theory which claims that learners construct knowledge rather than just passively taking in information.

Craftivism The use of crafts (think sewing) to try to achieve political or social change.

Creative learning A specific form of learning that involves creative expression in the context of academic learning.

Creative teaching An approach to teaching to make learning more interesting and effective by using imaginative approaches in the classroom. Also known as *Teaching creatively*.

Critical thinking The act of making reasoned judgements based on the interpretation, understanding, application, and synthesis of evidence gathered from one's reading, observation, and experimentation.

Decolonisation In the context of education, this refers to the process in which curricula and research that preserve the Europe-centred, colonial lens is rethought, reframed, and reconstructed.

Dialogic feedback Refers to the learning about and from feedback that takes place through dialogue between two or more individuals.

Digital divide The gap between people who have access to digital technologies such as the internet, smartphones, and tablets, and those who do not.

Digital portfolio A collection of digital artefacts which articulate experiences, achievements, reflections, and learning. Also referred to as an *E-portfolio* and a *Student learning portfolio*.

Digital technologies Refers to online resources, learning management systems, programmes, app(lication)s, and tools – think laptops, tablets, and smartphones – that are used to support learning and teaching.

Direct communication Use of the spoken word to explicitly and plainly say what an individual is thinking.

Early career researcher An individual who is within eight years of their doctoral award or within six years of their first academic appointment.

Early primary Refers to the 3–7 age range (early years foundation stage [3–5] and infants [5–7]).

Embodied learning A form of learning in which learners are holistically engaged and intertwined in their social and material surroundings.

Embodied stories Stories that convey deep and rich insights into a person's experience, engaging with both meaning and emotional responses.

Emergence A creative process using complex interactions between distributed actors to produce ideas which could not have been predicted from constituent parts.

Emotion A feeling which can be caused by the situation an individual is in or those they are with.

Everyday concepts Instinctive behaviour that is so natural to individuals that it is very hard to explain why or how to others.

Feedback literacy The understanding, capacities, and dispositions needed to make sense of information and use it to enhance work or learning strategies.

Feedback Information given to a learner about their performance in relation to set learning goals or outcomes.

Feed-forward Comments that target the improvement of an ongoing action or behaviour as opposed to commenting on actions and behaviour from the past (*Feedback*).

Fine motor Associated with skills – the ability to make movements using the small muscles in one's hands and wrists.

Flipped classroom An instructional approach where students are introduced to the learning materials before class, then use class time to enhance their understanding through peer discussion and problem-solving activities led by educators.

Flipped learning A style of learning which focuses on student engagement and active learning.

Flow A state of complete immersion in an activity.

Folk pedagogies The personal beliefs that educators have about how others' minds work, which lead to the ways in which teaching is enacted.

Formative assessment A form of assessment which is used to monitor student learning and provide ongoing feedback to both students and staff. Also known as *Assessment* for *Learning*.

Found poetry Poetry that is created by an individual using the words of others, e.g., from literature or participant transcripts.

Gamified platforms   Learning portals or development tools for educational content that incorporate various gaming elements to enhance the learning experience.

General primary   Refers to the 5–11 age range (primary: infants [5–7] and juniors [7–11]).

Global North   Refers to the richest and most industrialised countries, which, geographically, are mainly located in the northern part of the world.

Growth goals   Goals that are personally set to enable oneself to reach their full potential.

Hackathon   An event, typically lasting several days, where people come together to collaborate to solve a problem or identify new opportunities. The word is a combination of 'hack' and 'marathon', i.e., a marathon for hackers.

Haiku   An unrhymed poem consisting of 17 syllables, these being arranged in three lines of 5, 7, and 5 syllables, respectively.

Headteacher   An individual who is in charge of a school. Also referred to as a *Principal*.

Heterogeneous   Made up of different things or people; mixed, not the same kind.

High-stakes assessment   Refers to examinations or assessments (typically summative) that have significant consequences for students, lecturers, and the institutions involved.

Icebreaker   A game or activity that is used to introduce people to one another so that they feel more relaxed together.

Imposter syndrome   A pattern of self-doubt and persistent fear of being exposed as a fraud, often despite evidence of competence.

Indirect communication   Use of body language, gestures, and facial expressions to share one's thoughts, feelings, and intentions with others.

Instruction   The act or practice of teaching.

Intersubjectivity   The intersection between the different culturally mediated cognitive meanings that people ascribe to phenomena.

Journalling   The act of keeping a record of one's own personal thoughts, feelings, insights, and ideas.

Learning style   Refers to an individual's preferred way to absorb, process, comprehend, and retain information.

Lecture   A talk that is given by someone in order to teach others about a particular subject.

Lecturer   Someone who teaches at a university. Synonyms include *Instructor*, *Educator*, and *Teaching tutor*.

Lyrical first-person stories   Stories, narrated from a first-person viewpoint, which may play with rhythm and rhyme to convey a personal experience.

Maladaptive motivation   In the context of teachers and teaching, this refers to factors such as anxiety, uncertain control, and performance avoidance.

Meme An image, an idea, or a video that is very quickly spread on the internet.

Mental warm-ups A type of pre-learning routine or activity that is undertaken before engaging in a learning episode.

Metacognition Put simply, this refers to thinking about one's thinking. It recognises the processes used to plan, monitor, and assess one's understanding and performance.

Metaphor A figure of speech in which a word or phrase is applied to an object or action to which it is not literally applicable, such as 'You are the black sheep of the family'.

Mindset Refers to a particular way of thinking, a set of beliefs, attitudes, and perspectives that shape how an individual interprets and responds to the world around them.

Multimedia The use of a combination of different media such as words, pictures, and sounds for delivering messages.

Multimodal(ities) Refers to the use of textual, aural, linguistic, spatial, and visual resources to compose and communicate information.

Narrative Refers to the stories, accounts, or personal experiences that are shared by individuals in interviews or diaries, for example.

Neuroplasticity Refers to the brain's ability to change and adapt due to experience.

Operational level Refers to practices which are executed on a day-to-day basis.

Pedagogy The method and practice of teaching.

Permacrisis Extended periods of insecurity and instability.

Personalised learning An educational approach that aims to customise learning in response to the strengths, needs, skills, and interests of each student.

Philosophy for children An approach to teaching and learning in which children take part in philosophical enquiry.

Philosophy for teachers An approach which promotes the development of teachers' mindfulness about learning, teaching, and philosophies of education.

Phrases A group of words that together hold meaning, e.g., 'I am a maths teacher'.

Poetic enquiry The use of poetry in various forms within qualitative research practices.

Poetic structures A term used to describe devices or sets of guidance that support an author to create a poem. Other authors may use this term to talk about the final product, for example, the structure of a poem.

Poeticity Sometimes called *poetic function*, poeticity relates to the quality of language use, considering verbal structures that draw attention to the meaning of the message, e.g., the repetition of related metaphors.

Poetry   A literary work in which the expression of feelings and ideas is given intensity using a distinctive style and rhythm.

Postgraduate   An adult learner (student) who has been awarded a degree and is studying at a university for an advanced degree (think master's and doctorate).

Professional development   Refers to the advancement of skills, traits, and competencies that contribute to an individual's success in the workplace.

Professional learning community   A group of educators that meets regularly, shares expertise, and works collaboratively to improve teaching skills and the academic performance of students.

Prose   Written language in ordinary form as opposed to poetry, for example.

Radical creativity   Refers to the generation of ideas that are completely outside one's previous experience.

Reflection   A process which helps an individual gain insight into their professional practice by thinking analytically about any element of it.

Reflection-*for*-action   Refers to thinking about future endeavours, with the intention of improving or changing one's thoughts, actions, and practice.

Reflection-*in*-action   Refers to the active evaluation of one's thoughts, actions, and practices during action.

Reflection-*on*-action   Refers to the evaluation of one's thoughts, actions, and practices after action.

Rhyme   Words which have or end with a sound that corresponds to another, e.g., *cat* and *hat*.

Rhythm   A strong, regular repeated pattern of movement or sound.

Rote memorisation   Refers to the process of learning through repetition, with new knowledge being remembered but not necessarily understood. Also known as *Rote learning*.

Self-efficacy   An individual's belief in their ability to complete a task or achieve a goal.

Self-reflective journal   A means of recording – in written or digital form – ideas, personal thoughts, and experiences, as well as reflections and insights of an individual.

Self-regulation   The ability to regulate one's own emotions, thoughts, and behaviour.

Simulations   A model of a real activity, created for training purposes or to solve a problem.

Situated cognition   The difficulty people face with trying to imagine creative concepts that are completely outside of their previous culture and experience.

Sonnet   A rigid method of poetry. Usually defined as a 14-line poem.

Stealth assessment   Refers to evidence-based assessments that are woven directly and invisibly into the fabric of the learning environment, such as well-designed games.

Student   See *Adult learner*.

Student teacher   An individual who is training to teach in schools. Also known as *Trainee teacher or Teacher trainee.*

Summative assessment   A form of assessment which evaluates student learning at the end of a learning experience/module or unit/year by comparing it against a set of standards or benchmarks. Also known as *Assessment of Learning.*

Surface learning   A type of learning in which students uncritically accept new facts and ideas and attempt to store them as isolated, unconnected items.

Syntax   Pertains to the arrangement of words and phrases.

Tactical level   Refers to procedures which are deployed to support the execution of day-to-day activities.

Teach-Back   A method by which individuals describe information they have been given, using their own words, to confirm understanding of said information.

Teacher educator   A university-based individual who supports the development of student teachers.

Teaching for creativity   Forms of teaching that are intended to develop the creative thinking or behaviours of adult learners.

Tertiary level   Refers to universities or higher education. Can be used to describe learners, institutions, and qualifications.

Thematic analysis   A popular method of identifying, analysing, and interpreting qualitative data patterns.

Transmission   The process by which information, knowledge, ideas, and skills are taught to others through purposeful, conscious telling, demonstration, and guidance (think teacher-centred teaching).

Undergraduate   An adult learner (student) who is studying for their first degree at a university.

Uni-directional   In the context of teaching, this refers to the one-way transmission of information from lecturer to student (think in a lecture hall).

Value line   A visual way to gauge learners' opinions by asking them to physically line up according to how strongly they agree or disagree with a statement or a proposition.

Verse   Writing that is arranged with a metrical rhythm, typically having a rhyme (note: the use of 'rhyme' is contested in Chapter 9).

Virtual reality   A computer-generated environment with scenes and objects that appear to be real, placing users in a fully immersive, virtual environment with minimal external stimuli.

Vocalisations   A sound that is produced by the voice.

Voice   To express an opinion, attitude, point of view, or perspective. Finding one's voice often refers to gaining the confidence to express an opinion, for example.

Wellbeing   Refers to a state of being healthy, happy, and comfortable, both physically and mentally.

Abbreviations and acronyms

5WH	What? Why? When? Where? Who? How?
AE	Adult education
AfL	Assessment *for* learning
(Gen)AI	(Generative) Artificial intelligence
aka	as known as
AL	Adult learning
ALDinHE	Association for Learning Development in Higher Education
AoL	Assessment *of* learning
AR	Augmented reality
AT	Assistive tool(s)
AU	Athabasca University
Becta	British Educational Communications and Technology Agency
BERA	British Educational Research Association
CAIE	Cambridge Assessment International Education
CAS	Complex adaptive system
CASEL	Collaborative for Academic, Social, and Emotional Learning
CCE	Climate change education
ChatGPT	Chat Generative Pre-trained Transformer
CHCB	Confucian Heritage Cultural Background
CL	Creative learning
CLOCC	Continent, lines of latitude, oceans and seas, country, compass rose
CoP	Community of practice
COVID-19	Coronavirus Disease 2019
CPD	Continuing Professional Development
CT	Creative Teaching. Also known as *Teaching Creatively* (TC)
DfE	Department for Education
DfEE	Department for Education and Employment
DOI	Digital object identifier
DRS	Design Research Society
E&PDE	Engineering and Product Design Education

EAL	English as an Additional Language
EBI	Even Better If
ECR	Early Career Researcher
EdD	Doctor of Education
ESL	English as a Second Language
FE	Further education
GCSE	General Certificate of Secondary Education
GSASTC	Graduate School of Arts and Sciences Teaching Center
HE	Higher Education
HEI	Higher Education Institution
HGSE	Harvard Graduate School of Education
ICT	Information communication technology/ies
IPD	Initial professional development
ITE	Initial Teacher Education
ITT	Initial Teacher Training (previously known as ITE)
JISC	Joint Information Systems Committee
L&T	Learning and Teaching. Also known as *Teaching and Learning* (T&L)
MD	Maryland
MIT	Massachusetts Institute of Technology
MOOC	Massive open online course
n.d.	No date (date unknown)
NACCCE	National Advisory Committee on Creative and Cultural Education
NCCA	National Council for Curriculum and Assessment
NJ	New Jersey
NOAA	National Oceanic and Atmospheric Administration
OAJELS	Open Access Journal of Education and Language Studies
OECD	Organisation for Economic Co-operation and Development
P4C	Philosophy for Children
P4T	Philosophy for Teachers
PGCE	Postgraduate Certificate in Education
PGR	Postgraduate researcher
PGT	Postgraduate taught
PhD	Doctor of Philosophy
PILES	Physical, intellectual, language, emotional, social
PLC	Professional learning community
PNAS	Proceedings of the National Academy of Sciences of the United States of America
PSHE	Personal, social, health and economic education
QR	Quick response
SEDA	Staff and Educational Development Association
SEL	Social and emotional learning
SMART	Specific, measurable, attainable, realistic, and time bound

SRHE	Society for Research into Higher Education
STA	Senior Teaching Associate
TA	Thematic analysis
TEA	Trend, example, anomaly
TESOL	Teaching English to speakers of other languages
TfC	Teaching for creativity
TTS	Text-to-speech
TUS: MMW	Technological University of the Shannon: Midlands Midwest
TV	Television
UAE	United Arab Emirates
UCET	Universities' Council for the Education of Teachers
UK	United Kingdom
US(A)	United States (of America)
VARK	Visual, auditory, reading/writing, kinaesthetic
VR	Virtual reality
WHO	World Health Organisation
WWW	What Went Well

Introduction

Simon Brownhill

*In May 2024, Dr. Simon Brownhill, the book's editor, sat down in front of a small mirror and undertook an individual, 30-minute, face-to-image interview with … himself! The text below is an edited transcript of the questions which were asked by the interviewer (**SIMON**) and the oral responses that were made by the interviewee (Simon). For reader ease, no pseudonyms are offered in the edited transcript.*

SIMON: Okay, let's start with a challenge! In no more than ten words, can you summarise what this edited book is all about?

Simon: Can I offer ten key words instead? [**SIMON** sighs and reluctantly says 'Yes'. *Simon* proceeds to verbally reel these off; for ease of presentation, these are offered in Table 0.1].

When readers look at these key words, they are likely to note that most of them are drawn from the title of our[1] edited book – this is purposeful because they truly reflect not just *what* our book is all about but also *who* it is all about (adult learners) and *where* it is all about (the tertiary sector, i.e., Higher Education [HE] institutions).

SIMON: Why do you think that there is a need for this edited book?

Simon: Well, I recently came across an EdCast (a podcast about education from Harvard Graduate School of Education [HGSE]) which claimed HE to be 'one of the few industries that has changed little in the past few decades' (Anderson, 2023). In it, Brian Rosenberg, a visiting Professor at the institution, was described as emphasising the 'urgent need to transform higher education but too many structures and practices are keeping colleges and universities stuck in the past' (Anderson, 2023). Our edited book is mindful of HE serving as a more 'traditional academic sector' (our words), with

---

1 **SIMON** note: Before the interview, *Simon* was very clear that this edited book was a collective effort and so was keen to refer to the volume as 'our book' and not 'his book'.

DOI: 10.4324/9781032633534-1

Table 0.1 Key words associated with *Creative Practice in Higher Education: Engaging Adult Learners through Theory and Pedagogy*

Key words				
Creativity	Practice	Higher Education	Engagement	Adult learners
Theory	Pedagogy	Learning	Teaching	Innovation

contributing authors implicitly recognising its resistance to change. However, our edited book strives to empower readers by showing them how creativity can be used in an impactful way to stimulate new thinking, energise professional practice and situated learning, and inspire instructors/educators and the learners they work with.

The need for our edited book has also been motivated by a long-term desire to galvanise impactful adult learners by sufficiently *engaging* them in their learning – making it pleasurable or enjoyable – thus challenging those approaches that are didactic, written, and individual in nature (Gouthro, 2019). Our collective and varied experiences in the HE sector underpin our passion for change in the ways that adults are creatively:

- introduced to new ideas and concepts for critique,
- challenged to learn new knowledge, skills, understanding, and attitudes in exciting ways and for particular audiences, and
- assessed.

Through illustrative examples of 'lived' (real) and notional practice, this academically informed professional book reflects on a wealth of relevant and applied strategies, 'creative touches' (see Chapter 1), and learning and teaching approaches. Embraceable by both academics and education professionals, our edited book strives to positively respond to the pressing demand for the HE sector to meet the complex needs of today's learners within an ever-changing educational climate that mandates stimulation, engagement, and agency.

SIMON: Before I move on to the next question, what do you mean by 'creativity', 'engagement', and 'adult learners', as per the title of this edited book?

Simon: I'll start with 'adult learners' if I may? We are aware that it can be difficult to describe or define these. Hansman and Mott (2010, p. 13) argue that '[r]ace, class, gender, sexual orientation, ability, age, and other elements of human difference all influence who adult learners are and the learning activities in which they engage'. However, for the purposes of our edited book, we define 'adult learners' as anyone who is 18 years old or over and engages with learning that is attributed to the tertiary sector. This typically relates to students who are studying for their undergraduate degree at university and mature students (25 years old+) who are studying for a postgraduate degree (master's or doctorate). We recognise that there are many students who do not fall within our 'typical' reference point above; however, wordage limitations prevent us from considering all students and all variations, learning-wise.

In terms of 'engagement', we initially favoured the thinking of Cohen-Mansfield et al. (2011, p. 860) who describe it as an 'act of being occupied or involved with an external stimulus, which includes concrete objects, activities, and other persons'. However, we felt that this did not fully reflect our understanding of 'engagement' as it failed to consider internal stimuli which we saw as including thoughts, feelings, ideas, and emotions. As such, we subscribe to the definition proposed by Shuck and Wollard (2010, p. 103) who see it as being a 'cognitive, emotional, and behavioural state' that is directed towards identified outcomes. As a former Early Years teacher, I personally remain ever mindful of the five main areas of child development: physical, intellectual, language, emotional, and social. The acronym PILES is helpful as it recognises engagement domains which our edited book strives to stimulate in adult learners. For example, in Nicola's chapter (Chapter 5), there is clear evidence in 'Example 2: Craftivism' (pp. 88–91) of student teachers and pupils

a *physically* engaging with reclaimed and recycled waste,
b *intellectually* engaging with concepts of and anxieties connected to climate change, and
c *socially* engaging with each other in an informal way.

In terms of 'creativity', we knew that this would be particularly difficult to define, a fact recognised by Puryear and Lamb (2020, p. 206) who assert that this 'remains an Achilles heel of creativity research'. Indeed, by surveying articles from business, education, psychology, and creativity journals (n = 600), the researchers found the following:

> small but notable improvements in the reporting of explicit definitions and field-specific trends addressing creativity in contexts. There were also strong suggestions … that elements present in creativity conceptions are strongly field-specific. Although … encouraging, issues regarding congruence across and within fields persist even on core elements such as novelty and usefulness.
>
> (Puryear and Lamb, 2020, p. 206)

We recognise the lack of creativity 'coherence and transparency' (Puryear and Lamb, 2020, p. 206), definition-wise, as being an issue, but we know we did not have the capacity, wordage-wise, to critically engage in this heated discussion. In an effort to alleviate 'coherence and transparency' concerns within the context of our edited book, we all subscribe to the standard definition of creativity, as presented by Runco and Jaeger (2012, p. 92): 'Creativity requires both originality and effectiveness'. We are mindful of the numerous critiques and criticisms of this as a definition (see Abraham, 2023; Dow, 2022; Walia, 2019), but for us, it is valuable in recognising two criteria of creativity:

- *Originality*: whether labelled as 'unusual, novel, or unique' (Runco & Jaeger, 2012, p. 92), all authors in this edited book have strived to offer illustrative examples of practice that are not 'commonplace, mundane, or conventional' (Runco & Jaeger, 2012, p. 92) in HE (see Chapter 9, for example).
- *Effectiveness*: whether taking 'the form of (and be label[l]ed as) *usefulness, fit*, or *appropriateness*' (Runco & Jaeger, 2012, p. 92; original emphasis), all authors in this edited book have strived to offer illustrative examples of practice that are quality-based, and are deemed to be suitable or proper *in the circumstances* (see Chapter 6, for example).

The criteria above serve as a valuable yet unspoken baseline from which different authors 'springboard off' into their respective chapters, clarifying their own interpretations and understandings of creativity – informed by academic thinking – which are of relevance to their chapter content. With this in mind, we took the decision to not offer 'creativity' in the *Glossary of Terms* to avoid hours of turbulent discussion and debate.

SIMON: What would you say is the current context this edited book finds itself in?

Simon: Well, I have already hinted at this in my response to one of your earlier questions. The HE landscape is one which El-Azar (2022) describes as 'failing on both counts of quality and access' due to the fact that in 'most countries, higher education is inaccessible to the socio-economically underprivileged [and] certifies knowledge rather than nurtures learning' (El-Azar, 2022). Our edited book focuses its attention on the latter point, arguing that learning and teaching in academia is subject to change, this being clearly evident during and post the COVID-19 pandemic. Guàrdia et al. (2021, p. 166) acknowledge that there are 'huge variations in quality, acceptance, completion, and learning' in universities across the globe; subsequently, this fuels a serious need for professionals and academic institutions to creatively consider ways to improve pedagogical methods and the experiences of students (AKA adult learners) in the sector. We see our edited book as positively contributing to discussions relating to this critical topic.

In our background desk research that fuelled our proposal for this edited book, it was troubling to read that 'trust in higher education is crumbling' (Watkins, 2018) in contexts such as America and England, this resulting in many voices 'sound[ing] the alarm for reform' (Watkins, 2018) in relation to research, student experience, and value-for-money. With adult learners being more discerning, non-conventional, wanting to make a difference, and being less willing to be told what to do, we became increasingly aware that universities across the globe are constantly seeking out new and innovative ways to build trust and secure educational achievement by *re-engaging* learners in their classrooms (Pham et al., 2022). We believe that our edited book offers a much-needed 'space' for discussion about both change and creativity in the 21st century. The knowledge that we share in each chapter in relation to the ways that people can creatively learn and educate others is designed to promote more innovative and stimulating approaches for application in the HE learning space.

SIMON: Can you give me a brief overview of the book and a statement of its aim?

Simon: I'm not sure it will be brief, but I'll try! The HE arena has long been deemed to be a space in which adult learning is facilitated through traditionally rigid and cumbersome academic structures (Jonasson, 1999). As the demand increases for academic 'flexibility, diversity [and] innovation' (Jonasson, 1999, p. 235), it is critical that the tertiary sector positively responds and adapts to the demands for change to remain both relevant and successful.

Our edited book locates itself in the heart of this discussion by considering ways in which creativity can inspire new thoughts, invigorate teaching in the university learning space, motivate professionals, and, most importantly, excite adult learners in *wanting* to learn. Driven by the voices of a passionate writing group of collaborators – both research- and practice-informed; with a variety of international backgrounds – our edited book aims to empower readers to embrace creative practices that are innovative, engaging, and impactful for adult learners at different levels.

We have organised our edited book into three main sections:

- *Engaging experiences* (at the university level),
- *Engaging groups* (of specific adult learners), and
- *Engaging tools.*

I could describe each of the chapters, but I am reminded of Bruner's (1962, p. 18) description of how creativity requires 'effective surprise', so instead, I hope to *stun* the reader with the presentation of an informative table [*Simon* quickly sketches this out on a piece of paper; this is replicated in Table 0.2].

SIMON: Who would you say this edited book is written for?

Simon: Oh, that's easy to answer. Our edited book has been written with a primary and a secondary readership in mind. Each contributing author had

Table 0.2 The three main sections of *Creative Practice in Higher Education: Engaging Adult Learners through Theory and Pedagogy* and their associated main content.

Engaging experiences	Engaging groups	Engaging tools
Large Lectures	Student Teachers	Poetic Methods
Environment	Part-Time Distance Postgraduate Researchers	Digital Portfolios
Technology	Student Innovators	Feedback
Self-Reflective Journals	Adult Asian Learners (aged between 18 and 24)	

access to a table [*Simon* brings this up on his laptop screen; see Table 0.3] that helped them to remember who we wanted to target, readership-wise, when writing our respective chapters.

SIMON: Do you think your edited book has an international appeal? If so, why, and in which countries?

Simon: Definitely. The scope of our edited book invites readers from across the globe to explore a range of refreshing conceptualisations of creativity and consider how these are translatable through innovative practice within a suite of international contexts such as Hong Kong, Turkey, Greece, and Malaysia, for example. We see this as a particular strength of our edited book, especially given that our collective author 'voice' combines those of established

Table 0.3 The primary and secondary readership of *Creative Practice in Higher Education: Engaging Adult Learners through Theory and Pedagogy*.

Primary readership	Secondary readership
Academic staff in Higher Education, e.g., lecturers, researchers, professors, and teaching tutors (those with a background in education, pedagogy, and/or research)	Education policy makers (those with a background in policy with (some) understanding of educational matters)
Adult learners, e.g., those who are seeking knowledge, skills, and professional/academic qualifications	Beginning (student) teachers, such as those who are undertaking a Post Graduate Certificate in Education (those who are learning to teach/work with adult learners – FE and HE)
Course writers and adult education trainers	
Teachers in Further Education (FE) colleges (those with a background in pedagogical practices)	

Table 0.4 Professional groups, scholarly societies, and other organisations (examples) with an anticipated interest in *Creative Practice in Higher Education: Engaging Adult Learners through Theory and Pedagogy.*

Professional groups	Scholarly societies	Other organisations
Association for Learning Development in Higher Education (ALDinHE)	Society for Research into Higher Education (SRHE)	Universities across the globe
National Education Association	International Association of University Professors and Lecturers	Colleges (tertiary) across the globe
Staff and Educational Development Association (SEDA)	British Educational Research Association (BERA) – Special Interest Group: Creativities in Education	Adult education centres across the globe

UK academics with educators and contemporary investigators in the field, e.g., postgraduate researchers (PGRs) with international backgrounds.

SIMON: Who do you think are likely to have a particular interest in this edited book?

Simon: That's a good question. Again, when we sat down to put together our proposal for this edited book, the publishers asked us this very question! On reflection, we still think that there are a number of professional groups, scholarly societies, or other organisations who would have a particular interest in this edited book [*Simon* brings up another table on his laptop screen; see Table 0.4].

SIMON: In some of your other books, you have offered readers a 'health warning' – something that they need to be mindful of before they engage with the book content. Is there one for this edited book?

Simon: Yes – it relates to how long our edited book will remain up-to-date for. Given that things in HE appear to move at a glacial pace (Rogoff, 2018), we collectively feel that this edited book will remain up-to-date for at least 10 years. The demand for subsequent editions of our edited book will ultimately be fuelled by both new thinking in the HE sector and innovative professional practices. We believe creativity and change to be a 'constant' in education and, for the reasons I have just mentioned, this edited book has a decade's lifespan of applicability in line with the theories and principles that are discussed within and underpin it. We are particularly mindful of the fact that discussions related to technology and digital literacy are likely to date more quickly – this is unavoidable due to the rapid rate of change in these specific areas (see Chapter 3).

SIMON: Is there anything readers should know before they start reading the book?

Simon: Sure. I'll offer these in verbal bullet point form for ease of transcription:

- All of the chapters have a small number of *aims* which give direction to the chapter content (see Chapter 8, for example). All of the chapters offer *Concluding comments* by way of bringing each chapter to a satisfactory close (see Chapter 10, for example).
- All of the chapters offer readers *Suggested further reading* that links to the content of the chapter (see Chapter 2, for example). There are actually two texts I am reading at the moment which I suggest readers have a look at as further reading for this book as a whole:

  - Brown, N., Ince, A., and Ramlackhan, K. (Eds.) (2024). *Creativity in Education: International Perspectives*. London: UCL Press. [Online]. https://www.uclpress.co.uk/products/177625
  - Greenberg, S. S. (2021). *Creative Acts for Curious People: How to Think, Create and Lead in Unconventional Ways*. Dublin: Penguin Business.

- Many of the chapters offer descriptive *Case Studies* by way of exemplifying quality practice. Select chapters offer *Examples*, with others offering *Scenarios* (see Chapter 4, for example).
- Virtually all of the chapters use *Tables* and *Figures* to 'vary the visual' for the reader (see Chapter 9, for example).
- Some of the chapters are written by authors using a formal, academic tone, whereas others embrace a less formal, more reflective approach to express themselves, e.g., asking rhetorical questions (see Chapter 7, for example). This is purposeful as it celebrates the individuality of each author/writing pair, and allows them to be creative with the written word.

SIMON: As the editor, is there anything which you sadly had to 'cut' from the edited book?

Simon: There are two things that come to mind. The first relates to draft two of Chapter 2 where Michelle wrote passionately about *Resilience through Nature*, a funded project by the University of Bristol's Research Culture Fund where 'PhD students from different disciplines were brought together to spend time in nature and have space to discuss and express their feelings about the future in relation to their research and their roles in responding to the climate and ecological crises' (see https://www.bristol.ac.uk/public-engagement/our-engagement-work/projects/). I personally encourage all readers to visit https://www.youtube.com/watch?v=J5q0vi2GtGw and watch the short video which shows how '[t]ogether, researchers develop a sense of purpose and agency to navigate the uncertainty of the environmental crisis, feeling more connected to nature [this being the emphasis of Chapter 2] and each other' (video description).

The second thing is connected to Maria's chapter (Chapter 11) where, as editor, I added some text to the second draft which was eventually removed. I quite like it as it gives readers a wealth of suggestions as to how to deliver feedback to learners. If readers ignore the framing of these ideas around learning styles (which neither of us subscribe to), there is a wealth of 'creative possibilities' for readers to select from and implement:

> Whilst the notion of learning styles, particularly VARK (visual, auditory, reading/writing, kinaesthetic), has been challenged by many (see Newton & Salvi, 2020), Linkedin (2024) argues that instructors should be mindful of the type of learner they are working with so that they can 'choose the best format for delivering … feedback' rather than relying on purely dialogic forms of feedback:
>
> > For visual learners, you can use visual aids, such as screenshots, videos, or slides, to show them what they did well and what they need to improve. For auditory learners, you can use verbal feedback, such as phone calls, voice messages, or face-to-face meetings, to tell them your praise and suggestions. For reading/writing learners, you can use written feedback, such as emails, reports, or comments, to explain your evaluation and recommendations. For kin[a]esthetic learners, you can use practical feedback, such as role-plays, exercises, or scenarios, to let them practice and apply your feedback.

SIMON: Is there anything else that you would like to discuss that you have not had the opportunity to say?

Simon: No, I think it's time for me to shut myself up and let the reader get on with exploring our edited book. Here's hoping that they enjoy it!

References

Abraham, A. (2023, December 4). Why the Standard Definition of Creativity Fails to Capture the Creative Act. *Qeios*. [Online]. https://doi.org/10.32388/LS88G9

Anderson, J. (2023, November 9). Higher Education's Resistance to Change. *Harvard Graduate School of Education*. [Online]. https://www.gse.harvard.edu/ideas/edcast/23/11/higher-educations-resistance-change

Bruner, J. S. (1962). The conditions of creativity. In H. Gruber, G. Terrell, & M. Wertheimer (Eds.), *Contemporary approaches to creative thinking* (pp. 1–30). Atherton.

Cohen-Mansfield, J., Marx, M. S., Freedman, L. S., Murad, H., Regier, N. G., Thein, K., & Dakheel-Ali, M. (2011). The comprehensive process model of engagement. *The American Journal of Geriatric Psychiatry, 19*(10), 859–870. https://doi.org/10.1097/JGP.0b013e318202bf5b

Dow, G. T. (2022). Defining creativity. In J. A. Plucker (Ed.), *Creativity and innovation: Theory, research, and practice* (2nd ed., pp. 5–22). Routledge.

El-Azar, D. (2022, February 7). 4 trends that will shape the future of higher education. *World Economic Forum*. [Online]. https://www.weforum.org/agenda/2022/02/four-trends-that-will-shape-the-future-of-higher-education/

Gouthro, P. A. (2019). Taking time to learn: The importance of theory for adult education. *Adult Education Quarterly, 69*(1), 60–76. https://doi.org/10.1177/0741713618815656

Guàrdia, L., Clougher, D., Anderson, T., & Maina, M. (2021). IDEAS for transforming higher education: An overview of ongoing trends and challenges. *International Review of Research in Open and Distributed Learning, 22*(2), 166–184. https://doi.org/10.19173/irrodl.v22i2.5206

Hansman, C. A., & Mott, V. W. (2010). Adult learners. In C. E. Kasworth, A. D. Rose, & J. M. Ross-Gordon (Eds.), *Handbook of adult and continuing education* (2010 ed., pp. 13–23). Sage Publications, Inc. [Online]. https://www.sagepub.com/sites/default/files/upm-binaries/34503_Chapter1.pdf

Jonasson, J. T. (1999). Traditional university responds to society? *Lifelong Learning in Europe, 4*, 235–243. [Online]. https://uni.hi.is/jtj/files/2020/03/Traditional-University-Responds-to-Society.pdf

Linkedin. (2024). Constructive feedback: How do you give feedback to different types of learners? *Linkedin*. [Online]. https://www.linkedin.com/advice/0/how-do-you-give-feedback-different-types

Newton, P. M., & Salvi, A. (2020). How common is belief in the learning styles neuromyth, and does it matter? A pragmatic systematic review. *Frontiers in Education, 5*(602451), 1–14. https://doi.org/10.3389/feduc.2020.602451

Pham, T. T. K., Vu, D. T., & Dinh, V.-H. (2022). The impact of academic aspect quality on student disengagement in higher education. *Education Sciences, 12*(8), 1–13. https://doi.org/10.3390/educsci12080507

Puryear, J. S., & Lamb, K. N. (2020). Defining creativity: How far have we come since Plucker, Beghetto, and Dow? *Creativity Research Journal, 32*(3), 206–214. https://doi.org/10.1080/10400419.2020.1821552

Rogoff, K. (2018, February 14). Technology in Higher Education – Innovation Policy – Skills – Digital Literacy. *Education Training Society*. [Online]. https://educationtrainingsociety.wordpress.com/2018/02/14/technology-in-higher-education-innovation-policy-skills-digital-literacy/

Runco, M. A., & Jaeger, G. J. (2012). The standard definition of creativity. *Creativity Research Journal, 24*(1), 92–96. https://doi.org/10.1080/10400419.2012.650092

Shuck, B., & Wollard, K. (2010). Employee engagement & HRD: A seminal review of the foundations. *Human Resource Development Review, 9*(1), 89–110. https://doi.org/10.1177/1534484309353560

Walia, C. (2019). A dynamic definition of creativity. *Creativity Research Journal, 31*(3), 237–247. https://doi.org/10.1080/10400419.2019.1641787

Watkins, S. (2018, November 27). Trust in Higher Education Is Collapsing – Here's How to Restore It. *Foundation for Economic Education*. [Online]. https://fee.org/articles/trust-in-higher-education-is-collapsing-heres-how-to-restore-it/

Part I

Engaging experiences

Chapter 1

Large lectures

Active adult instruction and 'creative touches'

Simon Brownhill

Introduction

The academic James L. Bess (1997) made an important assertion: the 'effectiveness of any system of higher education is contingent in some considerable measure on the quality of the teaching enterprise' (p. ix). This has, in part, been corroborated by Coe et al. (2020, p. 6), whose *Evidence Review* found 'giving clear instructions so students understand what they should be doing' to be important in improving student outcomes. Questions have been raised as to how lecturers can assure quality/clear instruction given that there is a continued reliance on the oldest and most widely used teaching method in tertiary educational institutions: the large lecture. Despite these remaining a prominent feature of academic programmes – 'deliver[ing] content information to a large number of students with the least amount of faculty resources' (Russell et al., 2016, p. 37) – its effectiveness has been the subject of much scrutiny (see Schmidt et al., 2015). To positively address issues associated with student attentiveness and their learning, there is a demand for academic staff to 'spice up [their] lectures' (Brigley, 2009, p. 322) through (inter)activity and creativity, engaging 'the lectured' (Trott, 1963, p. 72) in an effort to aid their understanding and to promote learning.

To drive the content of this chapter, two key aims have been formulated:

- To identify activities and resources that can be used in an active way to engage students during large lecture taught input, and
- To introduce readers to the idea of 'creative touches' (Brownhill, 2023a) which can energise large lecture instructional materials and taught delivery through *alterations* and *additions*.

The chapter opens with a short discussion about large lectures at the university level.

DOI: 10.4324/9781032633534-3

Large lectures at the university level

Sloman and Mitchell (2024, p. 2) recognise that large '[l]ectures have been employed for hundreds of years as a platform for disseminating ideas and knowledge'. Described as 'the teaching method most widely used in universities throughout the world' (McKeachie & Svinicki, 2006, p. 57), large lectures are typically categorised as the 'chalk-and-talk' component of a unit or programme where the one-way transmission of course content from lecturer to student occurs. This classic teaching-learning scenario can be readily contextualised with lecturers verbally communicating concepts and facts at the front of a room/hall/theatre, and students passively receiving and encoding this in their memories as they feverishly take or type notes (Hackathorn et al., 2011).

Despite there being a range of styles, approaches, and formats of large lectures (see Center for Educational Innovation, 2019), there are numerous criticisms of the large lecture serving as an effective learning method for students, in part due to the passive method of learning that large lectures characteristically promote (Roberts, 2019):

> The [large] lecture: 'that mysterious process by means of which the contents of the professor's notebooks are transferred by means of the fountain pen to the pages of the student's notebooks without passing through the minds of either'.
>
> (Hamilton Holt, cited in Cooper & Richards, 2017, p. 376)

Whilst Kofinas and Tsay (2021) are in favour of large classes (that partake in large lectures), Cuseo (2007, p. 2) lists a number of 'deleterious outcomes' associated with the lecturing method of instruction, examples of which include:

- 'less *active student involvement* in the learning process',
- 'reduced *depth of student thinking* inside the classroom', and
- 'lower levels of academic *achievement (learning)* and academic *performance (grades)*' (original emphasis).

To positively address the above, Lowman (1987, cited in Kaur, 2011) recognises a range of lecture types which could be used to diversify the lectured experience of students; these include the provocative lecture, lecture-recitation, and lecture laboratory (see p. 11). In more recent years, recommendations from international academic literature, research findings, professional bodies, and the 'student voice' (Kinsella & Kaye, 2022) have collectively advocated a shift in instructional focus to *include* students in the learning process through the promotion of active learning (Wolff et al., 2015). But this raises two important questions: *What is meant by 'active learning'*? and *What is the theoretical basis for this?* The section below initially offers a response to the second question.

Active learning

Advocated by Dewey (1924), Kolb (1984), and Bruner (1990), active learning assumptions are derived from a variety of sources in educational philosophy, cognitive psychology, and learning theory. The Teaching and Learning Team at Cambridge International (Cambridge Assessment International Education [CAIE], 2020) concisely recognise active learning as being based on constructivism, a theory of learning 'which emphasises the fact that learners construct or build their [own] understanding'. With aspects of the nature of active learning being identified in Jean Piaget's processes of adaptation – think assimilation and accommodation which require an active learner (Inhelder & Piaget, 1958) – and Lev Vygotsky's social context and the zone of proximal development (think social constructivism) (cited in Pardjono, 2002), there is strong theoretical evidence to suggest that learning always involves action, be it physical or mental.

A suite of active learning definitions exists in the literature (see Shroff et al., 2021, p. 202). Of interest is the fact that there is no generally accepted definition of active learning, with examples varying in conceptual clarity across different fields. In education, Race (2015, p. 219) simply describes active learning as 'learning by doing', whereas Prince (2004, p. 223) suggests active learning is 'generally defined as any instructional method that engages students in the learning process'. As an academic who is rooted in professional practice, I personally subscribe to the idea of active learning referring to the practical endeavours of lecturers that promote student engagement in the learning context.[1] Glasson and Lalik (1993) validate this, arguing that learning at any level is a constructive process that requires active participation by *both* the teacher (lecturer) and the student. The necessity for this kind of practice cannot be underestimated, especially as Freeman et al. (2014) found that tertiary learners in classes with traditional stand-and-deliver lectures were 1.5 times more likely to fail than students in classes that used more stimulating, active learning methods. Given that students 'can [only] keep tuned into a lecture for no more than 15 to 20 minutes at a time' (Middendorf & Kalish, 1996, p. 2), Bradbury (2016, p. 509) asserts that 'it is the job of the [lecturer] to enhance their

1 It is important to stress that the 'practical endeavours of lecturers' should not be designed with the intent of *entertaining* students. Johnson (2012) asserts that '*Entertainment's* primary purpose is to create an enjoyable experience; *engagement's* primary purpose is to focus attention so learning occurs' (added emphasis). Whilst I am not adverse to students having an enjoyable experience, large lecture-wise (think smiles and laughter), the emphasis should be on student learning.

teaching skills to provide not only rich content but also a satisfying lecture experience for the students'. This can be achieved, in part, by making large lectures as (inter)active as possible with multiple rest periods and engaging activities, improving learning attitudes and assuring higher levels of student attention/retention. Underpinning the above is the need for creativity. Rankin and Brown (2016, p. 94) claim that '[t]he term creativity, although often misunderstood, is recognized as being a central component of active learning'. So, *what is meant by 'creativity'?* and *How does creativity connect to the notion of 'active learning'?*

Creativity and active learning: meaning and connections

For the purpose of this chapter, creativity denotes producing something novel and useful (Williams et al., 2016). In the context of a large lecture, the playing of Rimsky-Korsakov's *Flight of the Bumblebee* (an orchestral interlude) as students engage in what I call 'timed talk' (90 seconds – the duration of the piece of music) is illustrative of these two criteria from an originality and time-management perspective. I believe that creative attributes, such as 'curiosity, imagination, playfulness, creative production, co-creativity [and] innovation' (see Chalkiadaki, 2018, p. 9), are fundamental to the active learning experience for both students and lecturers, especially given that these attributes are also associated with creative teaching, a key element of Rashmi's (2012) *'four elemental model'* of creative pedagogy (p. 194; original emphasis). The model attempts to illustrate the relationship between interrelated elements that yield imaginative, dynamic, and innovative practice; these include teaching for creativity, creative learning, and the psycho-physical environment.

In the report from the National Advisory Committee on Creative and Cultural Education (NACCCE) (1999), teaching creatively is defined as 'using imaginative approaches to make learning more interesting and effective' (p. 102). Rinkevich (2011, p. 219) builds on this, suggesting creative teaching [my preferred term] to be 'a unique, customized, and meaningful exchange of knowledge among all individuals in a learning context'. Grainger et al. (2004, p. 246) talk about creative teaching as a 'creative cocktail' into which are mixed 'areas' that include the following:

- the 'session content' (think knowledge, skills, understanding, and attitudes),
- the 'teaching style' (think taught delivery), and
- the 'learning experience' of students.

This chapter will focus its attention on the latter two areas mentioned above, initially considering how lecturers can activate large lectures to engage students in the learning process.

Activating large lectures

There are numerous ways in which lecturers can make large lectures active for their students (see Ryan, 2021, 2022; Yee, 2021; the supplemental materials of Driessen et al., 2020). Revell and Wainwright (2009, p. 209) suggest that '[a]ctive learning involves discussion, problem solving, presentations, group work such as buzz groups, brainstorming [thought showering], role plays, debates – anything that gets students interacting with each other and engaging with the lecture material'. Tuma (2021) advocates the use of audience response systems – 'a [digital] system of instant feedback … via a student's mobile device or small, dedicated hand-held, remote keypads to respond to questions posed by the educator' (p. 233) – that allow for audience interaction. Table 1.1 summarises a selection of the vast arsenal of strategies available for lecturers to choose from, adapt, and use across the full lecture structure.

Whilst Haxhiymeri and Kristo (2014, p. 456) assert that the use of strategies, such as those in Table 1.1, is 'vital for student learning in higher education', there is a need for 'substantial investment' (Haxhiymeri & Kristo, 2014) to help lecturers energise their transmissive delivery of content and systematic knowledge as part of a large lecture (Russell et al., 2016). At a tactical level, investment could be made in relation to divisional continuing professional development (CPD) opportunities, faculty action research, departmental mentoring, and school-led training events (see Denton & Brownhill, 2018). At an operational level, Aburahma (2015) advocates the use of 'a simple five-step paper based-model' (see Figure 1.1), comprising of 'various student-centred activities presented to initiate students' engagement in large lectures' (p. 91), many of which are likely to be familiar to readers from the field of education.

Of personal concern is the advocation of such an idea as this presents what I call an 'activity procedure' which can quickly become (a) monotonous for students when/if frequently employed, and (b) frustrating for lecturers when it fails to engage learners. There is also a danger that Aburahma's approach above promotes a 'light' or 'surface' level of learning as opposed to one which is 'actively deep'[2] (see Matsushita, 2018). Bereczki and Kárpáti (2021, p. 2) support some of my concerns, arguing that 'no agreed-on formulas or set of instructions … guarantee success'. To counter the above, I encourage readers to embrace the idea of 'creative touches'. Understandably, this is likely to yield questions in the mind of the reader: *What are 'creative touches'?* and *What examples of 'creative touches' exist?* The section overleaf responds fully to these two questions.

---

2 Deep active learning is defined by Matsushita (2018, p. 11) as 'learning that engages students with the world as an object of learning while interacting with others, and helps the students connect what they are learning with their previous knowledge and experiences as well as their future lives'.

Table 1.1 Active learning strategies for use in large lectures

Lecture structure	Strategy	Details
Prior to the start of the lecture	What do you think?	Display a key question relating to the focus of the lecture on your presentation or on a whiteboard for students to discuss as they enter and settle into the lecture space.
	Three guesses	Display an image/picture/object/word/quotation associated with the focus of the lecture – can students guess its significance? Ensure that you refer back to this during the course of the lecture, explaining its importance.
	Break the ice	Engage students in icebreakers/subject-matter mental warm-ups that promote dialogue, build peer relationships, and establish a productive mood for learning in the lecture space (see Chlup & Collins, 2010).
Introduction to the lecture	What do you want to learn?	Get students to talk to their peers about what they want to learn from the lecture. Ask them to make a written/digital note of this. At the end of the lecture ask students to review their learning – did they learn what they wanted to learn, or did they learn something different?
	Commence with a contest	Engage students with a quiz, an exercise, a value line, or a game to survey their initial assumptions and attitudes. Get students to revisit their responses at the end of the lecture to ascertain if/how the lecture has altered their thinking and understanding.
	Trigger some thinking	Open with a 'startling statement, unusual analogy, striking example, personal anecdote, dramatic contrast, powerful quote, short questionnaire ... or mention of a recent news event' (Graduate School of Arts and Sciences Teaching Center [GSASTC], n.d., p. 1) to trigger some student thought, be this internalised or externalised.
Main body of the lecture	Multimedia variety	Offer students a mixture of presentation types, e.g., Prezi, Visme, Keynote, or Canva, along with pictures/images, video clips, music/sounds, and websites/screenshots to vary what they see, hear, and read.
	Real-time use of ICT	Encourage students to use their laptops/tablets or smart phones to communicate with lecturers as part of an online 'chat' or a live discussion board that is visible to all so that they can ask questions, respond to answers, or give feedback (adapted from Morrow & Friel, n.d.).
	Demonstrate	'Arouse student interest and promote memorable learning [by] employing classroom demonstrations' (Eison, 2010, p. 9) – these could be in the form of an experiment, a simulation, or an analysis of secondary data.

(Continued)

Table 1.1 (Continued)

Lecture structure	Strategy	Details
	AI critique	Invite students to compare essay extracts generated by artificial intelligence (AI) with human-written essay extracts that link to the lecture content – *which is factually accurate in comparison to the live taught lecture input?*
	Cast a vote	Canvass student opinions on aspects of the lecture focus through a show of hands, fingers, or large coloured/lettered voting cards, the stamping of their feet, or a collective 'clap' of student hands.
	'Teaching each other' (Healey, 2004)	Working in pairs, get one student to summarise for the other the main points from a short article, extract, case study, scenario, or handout (selected sections/sources) that they have been given time to read either before the lecture (flipped learning) or during the lecture.
Conclusion of the lecture	Written review	Get students to individually write one of the following: 1 A 3-minute micro-essay that summarises the key points of the lecture, 2 A list of key words (between 3 and 5) that encapsulate the subject matter that has been covered, or 3 A review haiku (see Glatch, 2024).
	Ask students to…	1 … select the best response to a relevant problem or situation – A, B, or C? 2 … identify an error in the answer given to a previous examination/essay question. 3 … complete a sentence with a chosen key word/phrase. 4 … support a displayed statement with reference to a relevant academic theory that was discussed in the lecture. 5 … reorder the points in a central argument that relate to the focus of the lecture. 6 … rephrase an idea/concept in plain language (ideas adapted from GSASTC, n.d. p. 3).
	Game play	Engage students with a revision game based on the content of the lecture using well-known TV and radio game show formats such as *Jeopardy, Just a Minute,* and *Who Wants to Be a Millionaire?*

Source: Adapted from the work of Brownhill, 2015, pp. 81–83.

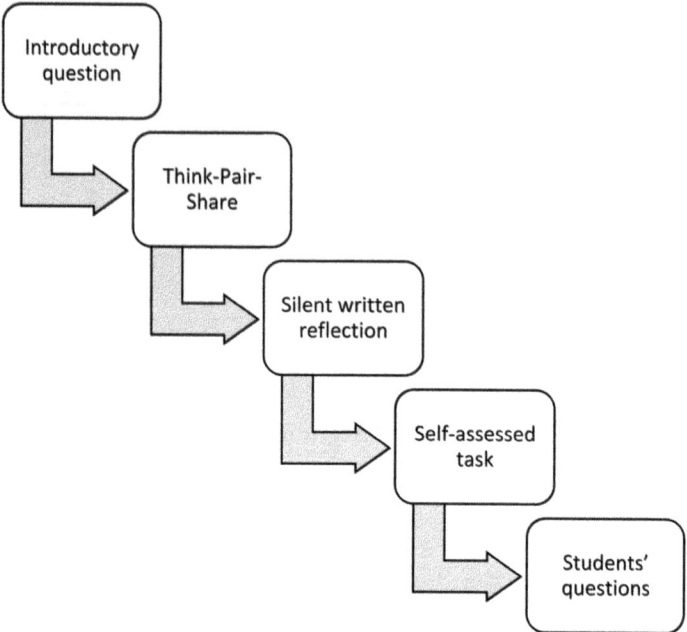

Figure 1.1 The main components of the five-step paper-based approach (adapted from Aburahma, 2015, p. 92).

'Creative touches': an explanation and examples

The origin of 'creative touches' was borne out of a small research study that sought to explore student perceptions of creative ways of demonstrating summative learning at the university level in England (see Brownhill & Godfrey, 2022). As part of an online survey, respondents were asked in what ways their summative unit assessments – think essays, reports, and dissertations – could be made more creative, presentation-wise, through their inclusion/use of what I referred to as 'creative touches', examples of which include infographics, textspeak, comment bubbles, and different languages. Research findings suggested that the use of 'creative touches' could 'provide more information and strengthen the argument [in an assignment] than [just] text, if used properly' (doctoral candidate), opening the assessment up 'to be more representative, personalised and accessible' (master's student). It is personally believed that these findings are true of lecturers who embrace 'creative touches' as part of their large lecture instructional material development/taught delivery.

Put simply, 'creative touches' are defined as *alterations* and *additions* (see Brownhill, 2023a), the former referring to the 'tweaks' [modifications] (p. 69) that are made by lecturers to their instructional materials, with the

Case Study 1.1

In the east of England, a Senior Teaching Associate (STA) was invited to deliver the large (lead) lecture on the development of children's writing (0–11) to the early primary (3–7) and general primary (5–11) students as part of the Postgraduate Certificate in Education (PGCE) English course at a prestigious institution. Being mindful of the fact that the large lecture was to take place on a Friday morning following an intense school placement for all students, the STA set to embrace a select number of 'creative touches' as part of the large lecture content/taught delivery; these included the following:

- Showing students Bason's (2012) 'Dough disco' video (*YouTube*) as an energetic illustration of fine motor exercises to prepare young children for writing (*addition*).
- Getting students to compare their personal writing grip with their peers, attempting to write with their non-dominant hand to practically experience the demands of handwriting (*alteration* – the original plan was to simply discuss select points drawn from the work of Dinehart, 2015).
- Sharing comical, lived experiences of stimulating children's writing in school using unusual surfaces, e.g., the teacher's work shirt (accidental!) and the playground tarmac (*addition*).

Overwhelmingly positive feedback from both the students and the course lead who attended the large lecture resulted in the STA being invited back the following year to deliver the same large lecture, along with a couple of interactive writing workshops.

(Adapted from Brownhill, 2024, p. 4)

latter referring to the inclusion of new and innovative ideas that complement and enhance the taught delivery of the large lecture. Exemplification of the above is offered in Case Study 1.1.

To reinforce the fact that there is no creative practice blueprint available for lecturers, readers are encouraged to *pick-and-mix* [choose] from the selection of 'creative touches' which are offered in Table 1.2, these being drawn from 20 years of personal experience working in academia.

In an effort to illustrate the potential each type of 'creative touches' has, possibilities-wise, Table 1.3 focuses its attention on one select suggestion, offering a suite of strategies that lecturers could use to creatively get students

Table 1.2 'Creative touches' for large lectures – a suite of ideas for lecturers to *pick-and-mix* [choose] from

Type	'Creative touch'	Examples		
Alterations	Presentation slides	Creatively play with the visual aspects of presentation slides that have been developed, e.g., • alter the text size, colour, and font *with a purpose*. • replace dense text with a key word, a phrase, or a quotation. • embrace the use of images – not just those that are literal that 'manifest a visual representation of a subject and furnish a description of the unfamiliar' (Roberts, 2019, p. 66) but also metaphorical and paradoxical ones, as explained below:		
		Image type	*Description*	*Example(s)*
		Metaphorical (also known as figurative)	'...an "image ... used in place of another to suggest an analogy between the two images"' (p. 66).	'...an image of a diamond with blood dripping off it' (p. 66). '...a hand grenade ... situated in proximity to nuclear electricity production to convey a sense of danger' (p. 66).
		Paradoxical	'Paradox images may present as puzzles, creating temporary confusion [and] generating internal attempts at reconciling meaning' (p. 66).	'...a lion looking at itself in a mirror and seeing the reflection of a kitten' (p. 66).
		• use animations to stagger the slide content presented to students. • consider transitions to creatively switch between slides. • mix up the background colour of different presentation slides.		

(Continued)

Table 1.2 (Continued)

Type	'Creative touch'	Examples
	Vehicles for content sharing	Creatively consider different ways students are shown what is known by the lecturer, e.g.,

Dictionary definitions	Song lyrics – chorus	Brochure extracts	Journal abstracts
Script extracts	Short stories	Poems	Report extracts
Advertisements	Extracts from speeches	News bulletins	Timelines
Letter extracts	Instructions	Tweets	Email extracts

(Adapted from For the Teachers, 2024)

Type	'Creative touch'	Examples
Additions	Voice	Add variety to the lecturer's voice during select parts of the large lecture oral input, e.g., • pitch (how high or low their voice sounds). • tone (the emotional sound of their voice). • volume (how loud or quiet their voice is). • pace (the speed at which the lecturer speaks).
	Body positioning	Creatively vary one's own body positioning when giving a large lecture, e.g., • stand behind/in front of/to the side of the lectern/lecturing desk. • sit down on a chair or stool/sit cross-legged on the stage/podium(!). Vary the body positioning of students by getting those who are physically able to stand up in a large lecture during the taught delivery (see Table 1.3).
	Make it tangible	Creatively add in the use of tangible resources to stimulate/sustain student interest, e.g., • worksheets in terms of different designs (see Eambaipreuk et al., 2021). • objects that are passed around, e.g., an artefact or a 'talking stick'. • sensory stimulators, e.g., grated candles in containers (smell), sample trays (of food; taste) or sound buttons (see https://tinyurl.com/3vny3n72).

Table 1.3 Practical strategies to encourage students (who are physically able) to stand up during large lectures

Strategy	Detail
Getting ready to learn	Before the lecture starts, suggest that students stand up and take a few deep breaths, gently shaking out their limbs and tilting their head towards each shoulder in an effort to prepare themselves for lecture learning.
Start with a stand	At the beginning of the lecture, encourage students to stand up and talk to a peer who is in front or behind them, reflecting on what they can remember from the previous lecture.
Diagonal discussion	During the lecture, pause and invite students to stand up and talk to a peer who is stood diagonally to them, discussing the practical application of a taught theory or concept.
Standing vote	During the lecture, ask students to 'ballot with their bodies' [my words], standing up if they are in agreement with a displayed statement or research claim.
Mobile moment	During the lecture, present an image of a smart phone, urging students to stand up and check their device as part of a 2-minute 'brain break'.
Switch seats	During a planned break in the middle of the lecture, suggest that students stand up and move to a different seat in the hall for the second half of the lecture.
Clockwise, anti-clockwise	During the lecture, offer students the opportunity to 'get on your feet' [my words; stand up] and talk to different peers about their professional experiences or personal readings, responding to a timed lecturer request whereby learners are to turn on the spot 90 degrees, clockwise/anti-clockwise.

Source: Adapted from Brownhill, 2023b, p. 2.

(who are physically able to) to stand up during large lectures (see Brownhill, 2023b).

There are, of course, many other 'creative touches' that lecturers could embrace as part of their large lecture material development/taught delivery, some of which are clearly fuelled by creative 'outside the box' thinking (see Ali et al., 2022 and Figure 1.2)!

Concluding comments

This chapter has set out to identify activities and resources that can be used in an active way to engage students during large lecture taught input, introducing readers to the idea of 'creative touches' (Brownhill, 2023a) which can energise large lecture instructional materials and taught delivery through *alterations* and *additions*. There is a wealth of additional practical ideas which could have been advocated in this chapter, examples of which include the use of podcasts, Reduced Shakespeare-style [condensed] topic input, and preparing slides that encourage students to raed wrods with jubmled lettres

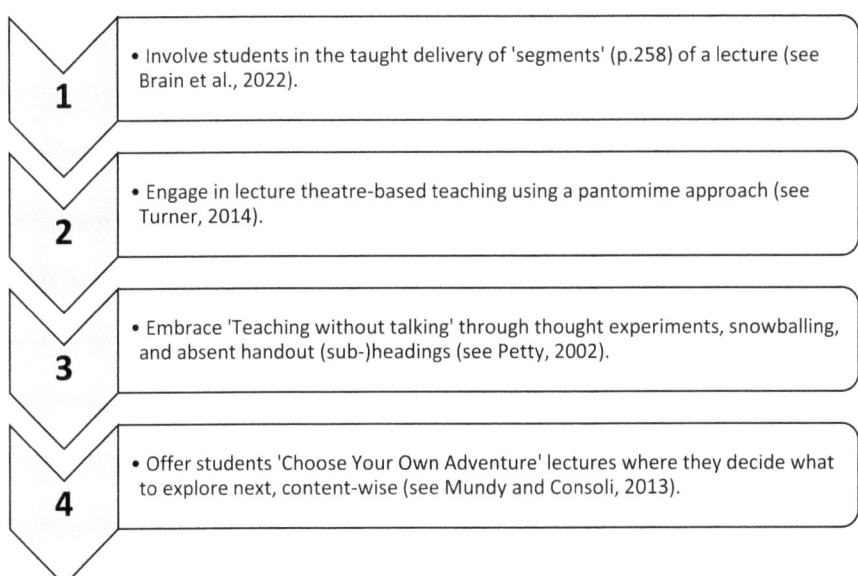

1
• Involve students in the taught delivery of 'segments' (p.258) of a lecture (see Brain et al., 2022).

2
• Engage in lecture theatre-based teaching using a pantomime approach (see Turner, 2014).

3
• Embrace 'Teaching without talking' through thought experiments, snowballing, and absent handout (sub-)headings (see Petty, 2002).

4
• Offer students 'Choose Your Own Adventure' lectures where they decide what to explore next, content-wise (see Mundy and Consoli, 2013).

Figure 1.2 'Creative touches' that are fuelled by creative 'outside the box' thinking.

(see Rayner et al., 2006)! This highlights an important point: readers should not rely on this chapter for 'all of the answers' [my words]. I encourage other suggestions to be sought by engaging with professional contacts and organisations, online publications, and ideas that are generated within the reader's own head.

A second point of importance recognises the issue of reader resistance. Despite the abundance of practical strategies offered in this chapter, there are likely to be numerous readers who are reticent to embrace these ideas as part of their professional practice. This is completely understandable. Putri et al. (2023, p. 1) assert that 'there are several issues that can hamper academics' engagement with creativity including demands of performance indicators and limited freedom to experiment with teaching'. To be actively creative in the large lecture space requires lecturers who are brave enough to 'have a go' and fail. Sadly, there is no guaranteed way of integrating active learning and 'creative touches' into practice at the tertiary level – what works for one lecturer with a group of students may not work with another. The only way to embrace these ideas as part of quality lecturing is to select just one idea and try it out. Without 'creative experimentation' [my words; trial and error], lecturers who choose to *play it safe* are unlikely to ever know the positive impact active learning and 'creative touches' can have on re-energising professional practice and motivating the student body, with the intent of improving student learning.

Acknowledgements

Miguel García López for his constructive feedback on an earlier draft of this chapter.

Suggested further reading

Ashton, S., & Stone, R. (2021). *An a-z of creative teaching in higher education* (2nd ed.). Sage Publications.

Betts, T., & Oprandi, P. (Eds.). (2022). *100 ideas for active learning*. University of Sussex Library. [Online]. https://doi.org/10.20919/OPXR1032

Lloyd-Strovas, J. (2015). *Tips for teaching large classes*. The University of Texas at Austin. [Online]. https://ctl.utexas.edu/sites/default/files/TipsForTeachingLarge Classes.pdf

References

Aburahma, M. H. (2015). Do not lose your students in large lectures: A five-step paper-based model to foster students' participation. *Pharmacy (Basel, Switzerland), 3*(3), 89–100. https://doi.org/10.3390/pharmacy3030089

Ali, E. A. W., Fares, A., Maher, H. M., & Saad, M. G. (2022). Thinking out of the box: Educational applications. *Journal of Research in Education and Psychology, 37*(1), 783–800. [Online]. https://mathj.journals.ekb.eg/article_216941.html?lang=en

Bason, S. (2012, March 26). Dough Disco. *shonettebason*. [Video]. YouTube. https://www.youtube.com/watch?v=i-IfzeG1aC4

Bereczki, E. O., & Kárpáti, A. (2021). Technology-enhanced creativity: A multiple case study of digital technology-integration expert teachers' beliefs and practices. *Thinking Skills and Creativity, 39*, 100791, 1–27. https://doi.org/10.1016/j.tsc.2021.100791

Bess, J. L. (Ed.). (1997). *Teaching well and liking it: Motivating faculty to teach effectively*. John Hopkins University Press.

Bradbury, N. A. (2016). Attention span during lectures: 8 seconds, 10 minutes, or more? *Advances in Physiology Education, 40*(4), 509–513. https://doi.org/10.1152/advan.00109.2016

Brain, R., Ezekiel, L., Mansur, A., Marshall, N., Mulwanda, N., Okafor, D., & Tyrrell, H. (2022). The student as lecturer: Building confidence, collaboration, and community in first year undergraduate law lectures. *The Law Teacher, 56*(2), 257–270. https://doi.org/10.1080/03069400.2021.1973276

Brigley, S. (2009). How to … Spice up your lectures. *Education for Primary Care, 20*(4), 322–323. https://doi.org/10.1080/14739879.2009.11493805

Brownhill, S. (2015). "Engaging and educating, not entertaining": Planning for active large lectures. *Pedagogical Dialogue, 1*(11), 80–90.

Brownhill, S. (2023a). 'Creative touches': Enhancing children's digital writing. *Pedagogical Dialogue, 2*(44), 66–75.

Brownhill, S. (2023b). *Making a stand!* Getting students to physically stand up in the large lecture hall. *College Teaching*, 1–4. https://doi.org/10.1080/87567555.2023.2269457

Brownhill, S. (2024). *Surprise, surprise!* (Re-)grabbing the attention of students in the university classroom through creative touches. *Journal of Education & Language Studies (OAJELS), 1*(4), 555568. (1–7). https://doi.org/10.19080/OAJELS.2024.01.555568

Brownhill, S., & Godfrey, J. (2022, February 15). Show me what you know! An exploration of student perceptions of creative ways of demonstrating summative learning at university. *Bristol Conversations in Education*. [Video]. YouTube. https://www.youtube.com/watch?v=G9qtbJF8RuU&list=PL8VOXK6Ou24pEGvky7txolIpF0H mQ93_Z&index=11

Bruner, J. S. (1990). *Acts of meaning*. Harvard University Press.

Cambridge Assessment International Education (CAIE). (2020). *Active learning*. April. [Online]. https://www.cambridgeinternational.org/Images/271174-active-learning.pdf

Center for Educational Innovation. (2019). *Types of lectures – Planning for interactive teaching and learning*. University of Minnesota. [Online]. https://oaa.osu.edu/sites/default/files/uploads/nfo/2019/Types-of-Lectures.pdf

Chalkiadaki, A. (2018). A systematic literature review of 21st century skills and competencies in primary education. *International Journal of Instruction*, *11*(3), 1–16. [Online]. https://www.e-iji.net/dosyalar/iji_2018_3_1.pdf

Chlup, D. T., & Collins, T. E. (2010). Breaking the ice: Using ice-breakers and re-energizers with adult learners. *Adult Learning*, *21*(3–4), 34–39. https://doi.org/10.1177/104515951002100305

Coe, R., Rauch, C. J., Kime, S., & Singleton, D. (2020). *Great teaching toolkit: Evidence review*. June. Evidence Based Education in partnership with CIAE. [Online]. https://evidencebased.education/great-teaching-toolkit-evidence-review/

Cooper, A. Z., & Richards, J. B. (2017). Lectures for adult learners: Breaking old habits in graduate medical education. *The American Journal of Medicine*, *130*(3), 376–381. https://doi.org/10.1016/j.amjmed.2016.11.009

Cuseo, J. (2007). The empirical case against large class size: Adverse effects on the teaching, learning, and retention of first-year students. *The Journal of Faculty Development*, *21*(1), 5–21. [Online]. https://www.classsizematters.org/wp-content/uploads/2012/11/Week-13-Cuseo-1.pdf

Denton, A., & Brownhill, S. (2018). *Becoming a brilliant trainer: A teacher's guide to running sessions and engaging learners*. Routledge.

Dewey, J. (1924). *The school and society*. University of Chicago Press.

Dinehart, L. H. (2015). Handwriting in early childhood education: Current research and future implications. *Journal of Early Childhood Literacy*, *15*(1), 97–118. https://doi.org/10.1177/1468798414522825

Driessen, E. P., Knight, J. K., Smith, M. K., & Ballen, C. J. (2020). Demystifying the meaning of active learning in postsecondary biology education. *CBE Life Sciences Education*, *19*(4), ar52 (1–9). https://doi.org/10.1187/cbe.20-04-0068

Eambaipreuk, A., Arayathanitkul, K., Emarat, N., & Sharma, M. D. (2021). Ways of incorporating active learning experiences: An exploration of worksheets over five years in a first year Thai physics courses. *European Journal of Physics*, *42*(3), 035703 (1–17). [Online]. https://iopscience.iop.org/article/10.1088/1361-6404/abcdde

Eison, J. (2010). *Using active learning instructional strategies to create excitement and enhance learning*. [Online]. https://www.amherst.edu/system/files/media/Active%2520Learning%2520-%2520Creating%2520Excitement%2520in%2520the%2520Classroom%2520-%2520Handout.pdf

For the Teachers. (2024). 101 ways to show what you know. *For the Teachers*. [Online]. https://www.fortheteachers.org/friday-five-ways-to-show-what-you-know/

Freeman, S., Eddy, S. L., McDonough, M., Smith, M. K., Okoroafor, N., Jordt, H., & Wenderoth, M. P. (2014). Active learning increases student performance in science, engineering, and mathematics. *PNAS*, *111*(23), 8410–8415. https://doi.org/10.1073/pnas.1319030111

Glasson, G., & Lalik, R. (1993). Reinterpreting the learning cycle from a social constructivist perspective: A qualitative study of teachers' beliefs and practices. *Journal of Research in Science Teaching, 30*(2), 187–207. https://doi.org/10.1002/tea.3660300206

Glatch, S. (2024, January 18). Haiku poems: How to write a haiku. *Writers.com.* [Online]. https://writers.com/how-to-write-a-haiku-poem

Graduate School of Arts and Sciences Teaching Center (GSASTC). (n.d.). The do's and don't's of effective lectures. *Scribd.* [Online]. https://www.scribd.com/document/260649611/Lectures

Grainger, T., Barnes, J., & Scoffham, S. (2004). A creative cocktail: creative teaching in initial teacher education. *Journal of Education for Teaching, 30*(3), 243–253. https://doi-org.bris.idm.oclc.org/10.1080/0260747042000309475

Hackathorn, J., Solomon, E. D., Blankmeyer, K. L., Tennial, R. E., & Garczynski, A. E. (2011). Learning by doing: An empirical study of active teaching techniques. *The Journal of Effective Teaching, 11*(2), 40–54. [Online]. https://eric.ed.gov/?id=EJ1092139

Haxhiymeri, V., & Kristo, F. (2014). Teaching through lectures and achieve active learning in higher education. *Mediterranean Journal of Social Science, 5*(19), 456–467. [Online]. https://www.richtmann.org/journal/index.php/mjss/article/view/4277

Healey, M. (2004). 'Teaching each other': An example of active learning in a lecture, tutorial, or workshop. In M. Healey & J. Roberts (Eds.), *Engaging students in active learning: Case studies in geography, environment, and related disciplines* (pp. 42–44). University of Gloucestershire, Geography Discipline Network and School of Environment.

Inhelder, B., & Piaget, J. (1958). *The growth of logical thinking from childhood to adolescence.* Basic Books.

Johnson, D. (2012, April 16). Doug Johnson's tech proof: Engage or entertain? *Education World.* [Online]. https://www.educationworld.com/a_tech/columnists/johnson/johnson026.shtml#:~:text=Entertainment's%20primary%20purpose%20is%20to,and%20deals%20with%20important%20issues

Kaur, G. (2011). Study and analysis of lecture model of teaching. *International Journal of Educational Planning & Administration, 1*(1), 9–13. [Online]. http://www.ripublication.com/Volume/ijepav1n1.htm

Kinsella, C., & Kaye, L. (2022, August 30). You said, we did – Now what? Why student voice initiatives need a rethink. *Times Higher Education.* [Online]. https://www.timeshighereducation.com/campus/you-said-we-did-now-what-why-student-voice-initiatives-need-rethink

Kofinas, A. K., & Tsay, C. H.-H. (2021). In favor of large classes: A social networks perspective on experiential learning. *Journal of Management Education, 45*(5), 760–785. https://doi.org/10.1177/10525629211022819

Kolb, D. (1984). *Experiential learning: Experience as the source of learning and development.* Prentice-Hall.

Matsushita, K. (2018). Introduction. In *Deep active learning: Toward greater depth in university education* (pp. 1–12). Springer. [Online]. https://link.springer.com/chapter/10.1007/978-981-10-5660-4_1

McKeachie, W. J., & Svinicki, M. (2006). *McKeachie's teaching tips: Strategies, research, and theory for college and university teachers* (12th ed.). Houghton Mifflin.

Middendorf, J., & Kalish, A. (1996). The "change-up" in lectures. *The National Teaching & Learning Forum, 5*(2), 1–5. [Online]. https://www.learningenvironments.unsw.edu.au/sites/default/files/documents/2.%20The%20Change%20up%20in%20Lectures.pdf

Morrow, L. I., & Friel, N. (n.d.). *Making lectures more interactive – A student's informed view and an academic's implementation*. Poster. [Online]. http://www.gla. ac.uk/media/media_148140_en.pdf

Mundy, D. P., & Consoli, R. (2013). Here be dragons: Experiments with the concept of 'choose your own adventure' in the lecture room. *Innovations in Education and Teaching International, 50*(2), 214–223. https://doi.org/10.1080/14703297.20 12.760869

National Advisory Committee on Creative and Cultural Education (NACCCE). (1999). *All our futures: Creativity, culture and education*. DfEE. [Online]. https:// sirkenrobinson.com/pdf/allourfutures.pdf

Pardjono, P. (2002). Active learning: The Dewey, Piaget, Vygotsky, and constructivist theory perspectives. *Journal ILMU Pendidkan, 9*(3), 163–178. [Online]. https:// journal.um.ac.id/index.php/jip/article/view/487

Petty, G. (2002). 25 ways for teaching without talking: Presenting students with new material in theory lessons. *Geoffpetty.com*. [Online]. https://geoffpetty.com/ for-teachers/active-learning/

Prince, M. (2004). Does active learning work? A review of the research. *Journal of Engineering Education, 93*(3), 223–231. https://doi.org/10.1002/j.2168-9830.2004. tb00809.x

Putri, I. G. A. P. E., Widdop Quinton, H., & Selkrig, M. (2023). Reshaping teaching in higher education through a mandala of creative pedagogies. *Teaching in Higher Education*, 1–20. https://doi.org/10.1080/13562517.2023.2193665

Race, P. (2015). *The lecturer's toolkit: A practical guide to learning, teaching and assessment* (4th ed.). Routledge.

Rankin, J., & Brown, V. (2016). Creative teaching method as a learning strategy for student midwives: A qualitative study. *Nurse Education Today, 38*, 93–100.https:// doi.org/10.1016/j.nedt.2015.12.009

Rashmi, R. (2012). Fostering creativity: A four elemental model of creative pedagogy. *Journal of Education and Practice, 3*(12), 190–201. [Online]. https://www.iiste. org/Journals/index.php/JEP/article/viewFile/2898/2924

Rayner, K., White, S. J., Johnson, R. L., & Liversedge, S. P. (2006). Raeding wrods with jubmled lettres: There is a cost. *Psychological Science, 17*(3), 192–193. https:// doi.org/10.1111/j.1467-9280.2006.01684.x

Revell, A., & Wainwright, E. (2009). What makes lectures 'unmissable'? Insights into teaching excellence and active learning. *Journal of Geography in Higher Education, 33*(2), 209–223. https://doi.org/10.1080/03098260802276771

Rinkevich, J. L. (2011). Creative teaching: Why it matters and where to begin. *The Clearing House, 84*(5), 219–223. https://doi-org.bris.idm.oclc.org/10.1080/000 98655.2011.575416

Roberts, D. (2019). Higher education lectures: From passive to active learning via imagery? *Active Learning in Higher Education, 20*(1), 63–77. https://doi.org/ 10.1177/1469787417731198

Russell, J., Horne, S. V., Ward, A. S., Bettis, E. A., III, Sipola, M., Colombo, M., & Rocheford, M. K. (2016). Large lecture transformation: Adopting evidence-based practices to increase student engagement and performance in an introductory science course. *Journal of Geoscience Education, 64*(1), 37–51. https://doi. org/10.5408/15-084.1

Ryan, M. F. (2021). *Compendium of active learning: Strategies for student engagement*. LIT Quality, Teaching & Learning. [Online]. https://hub.teachingandlearning.ie/ wp-content/uploads/2021/06/26.-Compendium-of-Active-Learning-2021-2.pdf

Ryan, M. F. (2022). *Compendium of active learning assessment for student engagement: Vol. 2*. TUS-MMW. [Online]. https://research.thea.ie/handle/20.500.12065/4042

Schmidt, H. G., Wagener, S. L., Smeets, G. A. C. M., Keemink, L. M., & van der Molen, H. T. (2015). On the use and misuse of lectures in higher education. *Health Professions Education*, *1*(1), 12–18. https://doi.org/10.1016/j.hpe.2015.11.010

Shroff, R. H., Ting, F. S. T., Lam, W. H., Cecot, T., Yang, J., & Chan, L. K. (2021). Conceptualization, development, and validation of an instrument to measure learners' perceptions of their active learning strategies within an active learning context. *International Journal of Educational Methodology*, *7*(1), 201–223. https://doi.org/10.12973/ijem.7.1.201

Sloman, J., & Mitchell, C. (2024). *Lectures in economics* (Updated: January). The Economics Network. [Online]. https://economicsnetwork.ac.uk/handbook/lectures2024

Trott, J. R. (1963). Lectures, lecturers, and the lectured. *Improving College and University Teaching*, *11*(2), 72–75. https://doi.org/10.1080/00193089.1963.10532218

Tuma, F. (2021). The use of educational technology for interactive teaching in lectures. *Annals of Medicine and Surgery*, *62*, 231–235.https://doi.org/10.1016/j.amsu.2021.01.051

Turner, I. (2014). Lecture theatre pantomime: A creative delivery approach for teaching undergraduates. *Innovative Practice in Higher Education*, *2*(1), 1–13. https://journals.staffs.ac.uk/index.php/ipihe/article/view/139

Williams, R., Runco, M. A., & Berlow, E. (2016). Mapping the themes, impact, and cohesion of creativity research over the last 25 years. *Creativity Research Journal*, *28*(4), 385–394. https://doi.org/10.1080/10400419.2016.1230358

Wolff, M., Wagner, M. J., Poznanski, S., Schiller, J., & Santen, S. (2015). Not another boring lecture: Engaging learners with active learning techniques. *The Journal of Emergency Medicine*, *48*(1), 85–93. https://doi.org/10.1016/j.jemermed.2014.09.010

Yee, K. (2021). *Interactive teaching techniques*. Teaching and Learning Center. [Online]. https://tlc-uva.github.io/Interactive_Teaching_Techniques/

Chapter 2

Environment

Learning creatively beyond the Higher Education classroom

Michelle Graffagnino

Introduction

Transmissive lectures, those in which students primarily listen to the lecturer and take notes, remain commonplace in Higher Education (HE) (Gynnild et al., 2021). This suggests that a typical student at the tertiary level spends hours, week after week, in a sitting position, listening to academics, often not knowing the people they are sitting next to. At the postgraduate (taught) level (PGT), students can spend a substantial amount of time alone every day, this being within the four walls of a study space or a laboratory, with little access to nature and/or creative engagement with their peers. Virtually all students leave university with the qualification they set out to acquire, but an important question needs to be asked: *at what cost does this have on their social, emotional, and spiritual development?* This chapter aims to encourage HE educators to include outdoor learning as part of the taught curriculum. Through a critical exploration of practice, the chapter will reflect on the benefits that outdoor learning has for adult learners, e.g., developing class cohesion and stimulating aspects of creativity (Eraut, 2000). The discussion will emphasise the value of our senses in these outdoor environments, recognising that outdoor indulgence can fuel learner inspiration (Stanton, 2019). The chapter will also argue that the environment, which serves as 'the third teacher' in early childhood literature (Blaustein, 2005), needs to become more of an influence in HE, particularly given the deficit of outdoor learning that many students are likely to have experienced in their 'learning journey' to date. The chapter will conclude with a passionate plea to make more use of the local outdoor environment when teaching adult learners, thus encouraging creativity and social interactions outside of the traditional HE classroom.

Two key aims have been formulated to drive the content of this chapter:

- To explore the current profile of HE students in England and the need for learning creatively beyond the classroom walls, and
- To identify select activities and resources that can be used to engage students during outdoor learning, reflecting on the benefits of learning outdoors.

DOI: 10.4324/9781032633534-4

The chapter opens with an exploration of why students should engage with, and educators should encourage, learning beyond the HE classroom walls.

Engaging with and encouraging learning beyond the HE classroom walls

Learning outside is defined by the Council for Learning Outside the Classroom (2021) as 'the use of places other than the classroom for teaching and learning'. Outdoor learning is not a new concept; indeed, from an educational perspective, writers such as Rousseau (1783) recognised the benefits of the natural environment as a setting for learning. Frampton et al. (2015) argue that it is intuitively compelling that the natural environment should confer significant benefits for human health and well-being. Despite the above, research has only recently begun to *systematically* explore the value of outdoor learning for students, this being focused on school-aged pupils (the Kindergarten to Year 12 age range; see Mann et al., 2022). Sadly, little has been written about the benefits of learning outside in the HE sector, despite researchers acknowledging that learning outside is linked to increased learner benefits in terms of cognitive performance, well-being, and creativity (Besser, 2021; Mason et al., 2022; McMahan & Estes, 2015).

I firmly believe, more than ever before, that adult learners need frequent exposure to learning beyond the classroom. Various reasons underpin this viewpoint, several of which are recognised here. The world is in permacrisis given that, in the last two decades, it has been bombarded with health and ecological disasters, wars and violence, and the displacement of many people (Giroux, 2021). Coupled with this is the thinking of Kohls et al. (2023, p. 2) who note that 'even before the onset of the COVID-19 pandemic, young adults and especially university students were considered to be a vulnerable group for mental disorders, with reports of one in five students suffering from mental health issues'. Adult learners are now having to leave the safety of their homes/computer screens and physically step back into HE classrooms/seminar spaces. For some, this return is overwhelming to the senses. However, it is important to remember that the ability to feel, see, hear, smell, and taste[1] helps us to interact with the world, although people rarely seize the opportunity to give these respect and disciplined space in their busy lives despite the widely known benefits (Parsons, 1991; Stanton, 2019; Ulrich, 1979).

As recognised in the chapter introduction, there is much evidence to suggest that the natural environment is an essential space for learning. This is often referred to as the 'third teacher' (Reggio Emilia; Strong-Wilson & Ellis,

---

1 Unless individuals have a sensory impairment or sensory disability.

2007), with Frampton, Jenkins, and Waters (2015, p. 122) recognising numerous benefits of this in relation to the development of young children:

> Freedom to move through space enables children to discover spatial relationships, which in turn are fundamental building blocks of higher-level thinking skills. Exploring and developing physical skills such as balance and movement has a direct positive effect on well-being and self-esteem. The outdoor environment can also be a powerful place for children to explore their creativity.

Of concern is the evidence which suggests that learners in England, not just young children, are spending less and less time outdoors (White et al., 2019). For starters, the perceived risks of the outdoors and adult over-estimation of harm have seriously curtailed the freedom of children and young people to explore their outdoor world (Gill, 2010). Secondly, educational settings are faced with continued constraints on both time and resources, along with the pressures of standardised testing (Chang & Kidman, 2020), contributing to less 'availability' [my words] for outdoor exposure. As such, Louv (2005) claims that there is a need to save children from what he calls *nature-deficit disorder*[2] as this could be contributing to a wide range of behavioural problems.

Whilst interesting, readers are likely to question how the discussion above connects to adult learners in HE. In the words of Warber et al. (2015, p. 1), Louv 'proposes that direct exposure to nature is essential for the physical and emotional health of both children *and adults*' (added emphasis), a notion advocated by the British fitness coach, television presenter/personality, and best-selling author Joe Wicks (itvX, 2024). Penazzi et al. (2022) extend these benefits, acknowledging how a three-day residential course involving outdoor learning for students transitioning to university yielded a positive impact on attainment, together with increased student participation and engagement. There is evidence to suggest that green spaces such as community woodlands, urban parks, and gardens can help adult learners to regulate their nervous system, with Garden's (2023) observations of HE students, when learning outdoors, to be more alert and engaged, them using a more relaxed and interactive tone when contributing to discussions; this being attributed, in part, to the outdoor surroundings, the presence of fresh air, and exposure to nature.

Of interest to this chapter is the connection between nature and creativity. Research has consistently demonstrated the enhanced creativity of humans after their immersion in natural environments (see Plambech & van den Bosch, 2015). Atchley et al. (2012), for example, found that a four-day (technology-free) hike increased participants' creativity by 50%, this being measured by the

---

2 Renata (n.d.) states that 'this refers to the detrimental consequences of a modern lifestyle characterised by reduced exposure to the natural world'.

Remote Associates Test to ascertain levels of creative thinking, insight, and problem-solving. Shuda et al. (2020) argue that humans function better in natural environments because historically their brains and bodies evolved *in* and *with* nature; because of this exposure, it helps to instil feelings of calm and well-being in adult learners, allowing their thinking to be clearer and more positive. I argue that the association with nature being a 'safe place' for learners can encourage creativity. Grahn et al. (2021) support my assertion, proposing that oxytocin (the 'bonding' hormone) may be behind this phenomenon, exerting its powerful antistress and restorative effects when individuals are in natural settings. It is important to remember that outdoor learning experiences are often multi-sensory, which awaken the senses, and involve whole brain learning which leads to improved cognitive function, problem-solving abilities, and creativity (Berman et al., 2012). The benefits of outdoor spaces on creativity can also be seen through the work of Lefebvre (1991) and Massey (2005), who argue that outdoor spaces provide opportunities for exploration, discovery, and new ways of thinking, all of which are of benefit to adult learners.

Outdoor environments that benefit learning and teaching

Being outdoors itself has numerous benefits, but if learners choose an outdoor concrete space, e.g., the quad or a Wi-Fi-equipped tent on a cordoned off university carpark, this is likely to be of less benefit than the restorative nature of a forested area (for example). Clear connections exist between nature and brain function, with Wolf et al. (2017) recognising the superiority of 'higher-quality environments' [my words], these being places with a rich biodiversity (think both plant and animal species) that yield less anxiety and better mood. This finding is of personal concern for adult learners who live in one of the world's most nature-deprived nations: Great Britain. It would appear that they are 'missing out'; adult learners who are located where there is an abundance of 'real-world nature' (think New Zealand, Norway, Australia, Austria, and Iceland) are likely to demonstrate improvements in mood and aspects of cognitive performance such as perception, memory, reasoning, judgement, imagination, and problem-solving (Ohly et al., 2016).

Sadly, few of these benefits are likely to be experienced by those adult learners who spend little/limited time in nature. A government survey (Natural England, 2022) found that a quarter of adults (aged 16+) had not once visited a green or natural space in the 14 days previous to the undertaking of the survey – these could be 'everything from parks and open countryside to gardens and other greenspaces' (Sustainable Development Commission, 2008, p. 8). Beyer et al. (2018) suggest that there is a toxic trend towards increasingly sedentary lifestyles which increases the risk of obesity, chronic disease incidences, and mortality. With this in mind, I strongly advocate that students are encouraged to both learn in HE outdoor settings – think in agoras with stone benches, on uncovered grassed areas, and under gazebos on the sports field (adapted from

Ayotte-Beaudet et al., 2020, p. 9) – and take regular 'green walks' [my words] to stimulate movement and creative growth in terms of improved visual attention, fluency, intelligence, and intellectual development (Besser, 2021).

Physical activity has been proven to unlock the creativity of individuals due to the fact that exercise can improve both mental health and cognitive function; indeed, aerobic activity, particularly that which is undertaken outdoors, can increase brain volume which benefits many aspects of cognition, such as working memory, attentional control, and information-processing, giving the brain more potential to be creative (Kekäläinen et al., 2023). As educators, it is our responsibility to encourage and facilitate regular movement breaks in our learners as this acute exercise improves blood circulation, brings fresh oxygen to the brain, and increases the production of proteins that promote the growth and survival of brain cells to improve memory (Stimpson et al., 2018). It is important to remember that this physical activity should not be mentally demanding; an easy walk or a short run outside can be undertaken to 'free up' the minds of learners, which can allow them to hit on a great idea or solution even though they may not be consciously thinking about it. As personal tutors, teaching tutors, and supervisors at the university level, I advocate that we should all be encouraging students to move more outdoors as part of the process of 'taking themselves away' [my words] from computer/television/phone screens, facilitating a 'state transition' (Rominger et al., 2023) which allows the mind to wander from current tasks to unrelated thoughts and feelings which can often draw connections between diverse ideas, encouraging novel thoughts and boosting creativity (Macaulay et al., 2024).

Sadly, there appears to be an increasingly high number of students who are disengaged with the natural world. Many of those who sit before us in lecture theatres at the HE level have an inherited fear of green spaces. As a result, they have no frame of reference from their childhood to learn or recall traditions, e.g., *Poohsticks* (the dropping of sticks in a river to race in the flow of the water, as described in the books by A. A. Milne and animated in Disney films). It could be argued that since the introduction of the National Curriculum in England in 1988, learners have experienced a more structured education (Aldrich, 2003); this, along with a heightened concern for outdoor dangers, has resulted in university students having had a reduced experience of outdoor learning when at primary and secondary school (Prince & Diggory, 2023).

Question to self: Is this why some *adult learners are afraid of wild spaces?*
Answer to self: Possibly.
Question to self: *If our students do not feel connected with the outdoors, how can we expect them to know how to interact with it?*
Answer to self: It is a morbid thought that some HE students may be scared of the environment, simply because they are not familiar with it.

In the context of children, Moss (2012, p. 9) states that those 'who learn outdoors know more, understand more, feel better, behave better, work more cooperatively and are physically healthier'. I assert that this is not a bad result from simply changing the location as to where they are being taught!

Simon (editor): So does this mean that educators at the university level should be 'simply changing the location'?

Michelle (author): My response, Simon, to your question is a simple **YES!**

A growing body of research demonstrates the importance of being outside (Mental Health Foundation, 2021), and, as educators, we should be modelling best practice and encouraging our students to go outside, not just in their own free time but also in relation to a class in terms of learning in the outdoors. For years to come, educators will be teaching and supporting university students who have lived through the COVID-19 pandemic lockdowns and many of whom have a nature deficit (see Louv, 2005). Case Study 2.1 offers an interesting example for how students at the university level were encouraged outside with sticks (not in a harmful way, mind!).

As educators, it is important that opportunities for outdoor learning, such as that which is described in Case Study 2.1, are built into the curriculum to help overcome perceived/actual barriers to the outdoors. Other opportunities include 'outdoor adventure education, [university] gardens, field trips, and … subjects taught in natural environments' (Mann et al., 2022, p. 1). If the next generation are to learn to love and respect the natural world, and better yet, to

---

Case Study 2.1

As a geographer teacher, a Duke of Edinburgh co-ordinator, and an outdoor enthusiast, I was perplexed when I felt a resistance amongst trainee teachers who were studying for their primary Postgraduate Certificate of Education (PGCE) qualification. We had been exploring the importance of outdoor learning, and the students knew that as part of the sequence of learning we were going to the local woods to create journey sticks. Journey sticks serve as a tactile way of recording a journey, their creation helping to develop spatial thinking through visualising, interpreting, and reasoning by using place, location, distance, direction, relationships, movement, and the dynamic use of space (Dolan & Liston, 2020).

By way of an explanation, the idea is to find natural items such as leaves, feathers, small stones, seeds, moss, and fallen petals, attaching these items (in chronological order) to the stick using glue, tape, and/or string. The items on the journey sticks are individual to each student, each one creating a 'personal experience' (Whittle, 2006). Students can then use their journey stick as a prompt in their storytelling. However, it has far more significance than just recalling a journey; it encourages students to be observant in nature, inspiring creativity in the retelling of the journey. It is argued that creating a journey stick is one way to poetically or artistically strengthen our connection to the natural world given that they intertwine person, place, and time. They can be adapted to many different disciplines, but their importance remains the same: bringing the person to the present, awakening one's senses, helping to alleviate anxiety, and allowing individuals to re-connect with nature. Journey sticks also provide an opportunity for learners to reflect and share their experiences as a group.

Of personal interest are Aboriginal Australians who, when returning home after a long absence, used their journey sticks to remember and recount their stories, forming a verbal map which facilitated a communal sharing of the journey (Dolan & Liston, 2020). People from numerous countries have created journey sticks to help recount the story of their journey, tying to stick objects and colours that represent their experiences and feelings or parts of their journey – it develops mapping skills, engages students with a traditional method of mapping journeys, and provides them with an opportunity to connect with nature (see Dolan & Liston, 2020).

However, I was faced with a group of 30 reluctant trainee teachers, many of whom were moaning that their new white trainers were going to get 'trashed' by going into the dirty woods! I eventually persuaded them to venture out with me that day, and they all collected journey sticks and quite enjoyed the process. Their *moans and groans* turned to laughter as they relaxed in the presence of the woods. We returned as a group to the classroom fresh-faced, re-energised, and ready to embrace the next part of our learning, working in small groups to re-tell our story through the journey stick, developing oracy skills, and making connections between the group as an 'ice breaker' activity.

understand their part in it, I strongly believe that this needs to be an integral part of their education. It is possible that educators are likely to find themselves with students who emulate the thinking of Woody Allen who amusingly said: 'I love nature; I just don't want to get any of it on me' (Quotefancy, 2024). Yet, readers should not be discouraged by this. Indeed, Berman et al. (2012) reported that participants in their research walked at different times of the year, even in the depths of winter when it was zero degrees outside – despite people stating that they did not enjoy the nature walk, they still experienced performance improvements in tests they undertook, showing that participants did not have to 'like' the nature exposure to reap the cognitive benefits (Stenfors et al., 2019).

When reflecting on my own professional experience, students seem to find a way of connecting with each other when in nature – it helps to bring a group *together*. This is of importance because, in tandem with the notion of creativity being a sociocultural phenomenon, there is evidence to suggest that creativity happens when humans are in dialogue with each other, communicate with one another, and work together (Smith, 2023). This collectively helps to promote a sense of inclusion in education which is important as it ensures that every learner feels valued and respected and can enjoy a clear sense of belonging (UNESCO, 2020). By coming together, this can nurture new understandings and meanings through the development of individuals (think personal growth) rather than simply recycling already existing knowledge (Osberg & Biesta, 2008). The students in Case Study 2.1 clearly felt uneasy at the thought of going outside to collect items for a journey stick to begin with, yet I believe that this experience served as an opportunity to nurture select creative capacities, as recognised in Table 2.1.

In light of the discussion above, I assert that creativity is as much a result of nurture (environmental factors) as it is of nature (genetics), and that nurturing creativity can be hard work (Smith, 2023). To alleviate some of the difficulties associated with this, John-Steiner (1997, 2006) states that sociocultural connections are necessary to inspire creativity, highlighting the importance of partnerships (think in science or with artists), communities (across generations or of women), and friendship groups, the latter of which was partially utilised within Case Study 2.1. This is of importance to educators (Smith, 2023) when considering the best pedagogical approach to embrace when learning outdoors.

Table 2.1 Examples of creative capabilities, as recognised in the work of Barron et al. (1997) and Haste (2008)

Barron et al. (1997, p. 12)	Originality	Adaptive flexibility
	Fluency and volume of ideas	Sensitivity to problems
	Spontaneous flexibility	Expressional fluency
Haste (2008, p. 96)	Exploring non-obvious connections	Critical evaluation
	Flexibility	Taking multiple perspectives

Learning outdoors by embracing a different pedagogical approach

In HE, the distinction between macro and micro contexts of learning spaces is valuable, given that this allows educators to consider not only the physical layout of classrooms (*macro*) but also the intricacies of spatial physical arrangements (e.g., pathways for movement, and the ability to engage in smaller group discussion or one-to-one questioning) and environmental factors (e.g., background noise) that influence learning experiences (*micro*; Peacock, 2011). These combined can encourage collaboration and facilitate a more active, personal learning experience for students. By way of illustration, the use of a public outdoor space (think community centre, college, or the local park) can stimulate student collaboration, idea sharing, and collective action. Embracing these spaces helps to stress the value of *nature-relatedness* in outdoor learning programmes, as highlighted by Barrable and Arventis (2019) and Garden (2022), the concept informing the development of curricula and learning environments that encourage students to forge a deeper connection with the natural world, fostering a sense of responsibility and environmental stewardship, whilst developing their own collaborative and creative growth (Garden, 2023).

When we get students working outdoors, educators are able to stimulate increased levels of participation and collaboration given that research suggests that outdoor learning environments offer more physical mobility and less structure than classroom environments, typically increasing the physical space around students (Harris, 2021). In comparison to indoor classrooms which are typically 'controlled', outdoor learning environments offer more freedom for students to interact with a wider range of peers and engage more effectively in collaborative work (Waite, 2019).

Learning in the outdoors: formally, informally, and non-formally

One thing I am keen to emphasise in this chapter is that there are multiple benefits of embracing a hybrid approach to learning in the outdoor environment, this being facilitated via a combination of formal, informal, and non-formal learning opportunities. By way of a definition, the thinking of Johnson and Majewska (2022, p. 4; added emphasis) is subscribed to the following:

- '**Formal learning** broadly aligns with organised, institutionalised learning models (such as learning seen in schools)' [think a lead lecture delivered on a sports field],
- '[I]**nformal learning** describes the everyday learning that people experience throughout their lives, and which can go easily unrecognised' [think a gentle stroll outside],

- 'Non-formal learning is a hybrid of the other forms of learning, meaning that it is in the interaction of formal and informal elements that non-formality attains its special character' [think the delivery of adult literacy programmes in an outside tent or gazebo].

Educators are encouraged to consider how they can incorporate these different learning opportunities in the curricula they offer students, ensuring that they [students] are offered a suite of opportunities across the full unit/term/year rather than just being a summer 'one-off' when the weather is fine (remember Wainwright's (1973) famous quote: 'There's no such thing as bad weather, only unsuitable clothing'). Every year, some of the students who enter or return to HE are overwhelmed or intimidated by the buildings which make up the institution. I assert that there is a need for students to be exposed to more dynamic and socially responsive environments that consider the diverse experiences and needs of those we teach (see Garden, 2023). Indeed, teacher education can benefit from this by recognising that the spaces where educators are trained, particularly outdoor learning environments, provide greater opportunities for social interaction and student autonomy, the outdoor setting allowing HE students to experience a different way of learning and teaching, with less structure and more engagement with peers being facilitated (Garden, 2023). A pedagogical shift in 'cultural borders' can also occur as relationships between tutors and students can be re-defined within the outdoor space, breaking down power dynamics and creating a communal feel that allows for more interactive and learner-oriented approaches to teaching (Garden, 2023; Harris, 2021). For teaching tutors and lecturers, relationships with colleagues and expectations of student behaviour can be adapted, with skills and approaches to teaching being subtly altered in the outdoor environment, individuals thus operating at multiple trajectories through the same space (Garden, 2023; Harris, 2021), these collectively encouraging creative growth.

At a time when people feel more and more disconnected from the natural world, the relationship between humans and their environment needs support (Schultz, 2000). It is personally hoped that embedding outdoor learning into the HE curricula can promote a healthy relationship with nature, engaging students with creating more preferable futures that enable them to solve problems, find alternative ways to do things, and contribute to a full life (Seltzer & Bentley, 1999). A significant benefit will be for students to develop critical thinking, creativity, communication, and collaboration, which have been identified as essential competencies and skills vital for success in 21st-century work and life (Kotsiou et al., 2022), these being of particular importance for those students who may decide to dedicate part/all of their working career to one or more green jobs.[3]

---

3 'Green jobs are jobs that have a focus on either reducing carbon emissions, restoring nature or making similar environmental improvements' (Friends of the Earth, 2024) – think sustainability managers in businesses, green transport officers, and thermal heating specialists.

Concluding comments

This chapter has set out to encourage educators to use the outdoors as a learning environment, be it formally, informally, or non-formally. Efforts have been made to emphasise the 'background' of students we currently work with, many of who arrive at HE with a *nature deficit*, and are often sat inside, rarely knowing those around them in a lecture theatre. Select research has been shared in an effort to recognise the benefits of outdoor learning in relation to the mental health and well-being of students. In alignment with the overarching theme of this edited book, the chapter has highlighted how outdoor learning can increase cognition, collaboration, and, most importantly, aspects of student creativity. Outdoor learning has the potential to support educators in creating an inclusive pedagogy, thus helping all learners to thrive in HE. As educators, we need to make planned and spontaneous efforts to encourage students across our programmes to embrace nature and to see time in the outdoors as a valuable opportunity to re-awaken the senses and 'let their thoughts drift' [my words] to encourage creative growth.

As educators, we have an individual and collective responsibility to ensure our students are prepared for life beyond the classroom (Biesta, 2006). I passionately encourage the use of outdoor learning in HE to equip the next generation with the mental tools they need to create and advocate for a sustainable future. In doing so we can turn their 'nature deficit' into gain by nurturing students' connection to nature, metaphorically planting a seed that will grow throughout their lives. The importance of inspiring their passion at the tertiary level and subsequent career choices cannot be underestimated, especially if this ultimately helps the environment to thrive for generations to come.

Acknowledgements

I would like to thank Simon (editor) for his supportive editing of this chapter when the OFSTED call came.

Suggested further reading

Department for Education. (2023). *Sustainability and climate change: a strategy for the education and children's services systems*. A policy paper. DfE. [Online]. https://tinyurl.com/6k527zwa

Wall Kimmerer, R. (2020). *Braiding sweetgrass: Indigenous wisdom, scientific knowledge and the teachings of plants*. Penguin Books.

References

Aldrich, R. (Ed.) (2003). *A century of education*. Routledge.

Atchley, R. A., Strayer, D. L., & Atchley, P. (2012). Creativity in the wild: Improving creative reasoning through immersion in natural settings. *PLoS ONE, 7*(12), e51474 (1–3). https://doi.org/10.1371/journal.pone.0051474

Ayotte-Beaudet, J.-P., Beaudry, M.-C., Bisaillon, V., & Dubé, M. (2020). *Outdoor education in higher education during the context of Covid-19 in Canada: Pedagogical guide to support teachers.* Université de Sherbrooke. [Online]. http://hdl.handle.net/11143/17295

Barrable, A., & Arventis, A. (2019). Flourishing in the forest: Looking at forest school through a self-determination theory lens. *Journal of Outdoor and Environmental Education, 22*(1), 39–55. https://doi.org/10.1007/s42322-018-0018-5

Barron, F., Montuori, A., & Barron, A. (1997). *Creators on creating: Awakening and cultivating the imaginative mind.* Penguin.

Berman, M. G., Kross, E., Krpan, K. M., Askren, M. K., Burson, A., Deldin, P. J., Kaplan, S., Sherdell, L., Gotlib, I. H., & Jonides, J. (2012). Interacting with nature improves cognition and affect for individuals with depression. *Journal of Affective Disorders, 140*(3), 300–305. https://doi.org/10.1016/j.jad.2012.03.012

Besser, L. (2021). Outdoor green space exposure and brain health measures related to Alzheimer's disease: A rapid review. *BMJ Open, 11*(e043456), 1–13. https://doi.org/10.1136/bmjopen-2020-043456

Beyer, K. M. M., Szabo, A., Hoormann, K., & Stolley, M. (2018). Time spent outdoors, activity levels, and chronic disease among American adults. *Journal of Behavioural Medicine, 41*(4), 494–503. https://doi.org/10.1007/s10865-018-9911-1

Biesta, G. (2006). *Beyond learning: Democratic education for a human future.* Paradigm Publishers.

Blaustein, M. (2005). See, hear, touch! The basics of learning readiness. *Journal of the National Association for the Education of Young Children, 41*(1), 45–47.

Chang, C. H., & Kidman, G. (2020). Dawn of a new decade – What can geographical and environmental education offer for the 2020s. *International Research in Geographical and Environmental Education, 29*(1), 1–6. https://doi.org/10.1080/10382046.2020.1691334

Council for Learning Outside the Classroom. (2021). LOtC – What and Why? *Council for Learning Outside the Classroom.* [Online]. https://www.lotc.org.uk/educators/i-work-in-education/lotc-what-and-why/

Dolan, A., & Liston, J. (2020). Developing spatial thinking with journey sticks. *Teaching Geography, 45*(3), 94–96.

Eraut, M. (2000). Non-formal learning and tacit knowledge in professional work. *British Journal of Educational Psychology, 70*(1), 113–136. https://doi.org/10.1348/000709900158001

Frampton, I., Jenkin, R., & Waters, P. (2015). Researching the benefits of the outdoor environment for children. In S. Hay (Ed.), *Early years education and care: New issues for practice from research* (Chapter 7; pages unknown). Routledge.

Friends of the Earth. (2024). What's a green job and how can we create more of them? *Friends of the Earth.* [Online]. https://friendsoftheearth.uk/climate/whats-green-job-and-how-can-we-create-more-them

Garden, A. (2022). An exploration of children's experiences of the use of digital technology in forest schools. *Journal of Adventure Education and Outdoor Learning, 24*(1), 93–107. https://doi.org/10.1080/14729679.2022.2111693

Garden, A. (2023). The university forest school space in England: Taking seminars outdoors for early years undergraduates. *Education 3-13,* 1–16. https://doi.org/10.1080/03004279.2023.2280720

Gill, T. (2010). *Nothing ventured. Balancing risk and benefits in the outdoors.* English Outdoor Council.

Giroux, H. A. (2021). *Race, politics, and pandemic pedagogy: Education in a time of crisis.* Bloomsbury Publishing.

Grahn, P., Ottosson, J., & Uvnäs-Moberg, K. (2021). The oxytocinergic system as a mediator of anti-stress and instorative effects induced by nature: The calm and connection theory. *Frontiers in Psychology, 12*(617814), 1–23. https://doi.org/10.3389/fpsyg.2021.617814

Gynnild, V., Leira, B. J., Holmedal, L. E., Mossige, J. C., & Myrhaug, D. (2021). From teaching as transmission to constructive alignment: A case study of learning design. *Nordic Journal of STEM Education, 4*(2), 1–11. https://doi.org/10.5324/njsteme.v4i1.3402

Harris, F. (2021). Developing a relationship with nature and place: The potential role of forest school. *Environmental Education Research, 27*(8), 1214–1228. https://doi.org/10.1080/13504622.2021.1896679

Haste, H. (2008). Good thinking: The creative and competent mind. In A. Craft, H. Gardner, & G. Claxton (Eds.), *Creativity, wisdom and trusteeship: Exploring the role of education* (pp. 96–104). Corwin Press.

itvX (2024). Joe Wicks and Dr Julie on the health benefits of the great outdoors. *itvX*, 11 June. [Online]. https://www.itv.com/thismorning/articles/joe-wicks-and-dr-julie-on-the-health-benefits-of-the-great-outdoors

Johnson, M., & Majewska, D. (2022). *Formal, non-formal, and informal learning: What are they, and how can we research them?* Cambridge University Press & Assessment Research Report. [Online]. https://www.cambridgeassessment.org.uk/Images/665425-formal-non-formal-and-informal-learning-what-are-they-and-how-can-we-research-them-.pdf

John-Steiner, V. (1997). *Notebooks of the mind: Explorations of thinking* (Revised ed.). Oxford University Press.

John-Steiner, V. (2006). *Creative collaboration.* Oxford University Press.

Kekäläinen, T., Luchetti, M., Terracciano, A., Gamaldo, A. A., Mogle, J., Lovett, H. H., Brown, J., Rantalainen, T., Sliwinski, M. J., & Sutin, A. R. (2023). Physical activity and cognitive function: Moment-to-moment and day-to-day associations. *International Journal of Behavioral Nutrition and Physical Activity, 20*(1), 137 (1–12). https://doi.org/10.1186/s12966-023-01536-9

Kohls, E., Guenthner, L., Baldofski, S., Brock, T., Schuhr, J., & Rummel-Kluge, C. (2023). Two years COVID-19 pandemic: Development of university students' mental health 2020-2022. *Frontiers in Psychiatry, 14,* 1122256 (1–15). https://doi.org/10.3389/fpsyt.2023.1122256

Kotsiou, A., Fajardo-Tovar, D. D., Cowhitt, T., Major, L., & Wegerif, R. (2022). A scoping review of future skills frameworks. *Irish Educational Studies, 41*(1), 171–186. https://doi.org/10.1080/03323315.2021.2022522

Lefebvre, H. (1991). *The production of space.* Blackwell Publishers.

Louv, R. (2005). *Last child in the woods: Saving our children from nature-deficit disorder.* Atlantic Books.

Macaulay, R., Johnson, K., Lee, K., & Williams, K. (2024). Examining the facets of mindful engagement and mind wandering in nature. *Journal of Environmental Psychology, 94,* 1–13. https://doi.org/10.1016/j.jenvp.2024.102253

Mann, J., Gray, T., Truong, S., Brymer, E., Passy, R., Ho, S., Sahlberg, P., Ward, K., Bentsen, P., Curry, C., & Cowper, R. (2022). Getting out of the classroom and into nature: A systematic review of nature-specific outdoor learning on school Children's learning and development. *Frontiers in Public Health, 10*(877058), 1–12. https://www.frontiersin.org/journals/public-health/articles/10.3389/fpubh.2022.877058

Mason, L., Ronconi, A., Scrimin, S., & Pazzaglia, F. (2022). Short-term exposure to nature and benefits for students' cognitive performance: A review. *Educational Psychology Review, 34*(2), 609–647. https://link.springer.com/article/10.1007%2Fs10648-021-09631-8

Massey, D. (2005). *For space*. Sage.

McMahan, E. A., & Estes, D. (2015). The effect of contact with natural environments on positive and negative affect: A meta-analysis. *The Journal of Positive Psychology*, *10*(6), 507–519. https://doi.org/10.1080/17439760.2014.994224

Mental Health Foundation. (2021). *Nature: How connecting with nature benefits our mental health*. Mental Health Foundation. [Online]. https://www.mentalhealth.org.uk/our-work/research/nature-how-connecting-nature-benefits-our-mental-health

Moss, S. (2012). *Natural childhood*. National Trust. [Online]. https://bio-diverse.org/wp-content/uploads/2013/02/natural-childhood-report.pdf

Natural England. (2022). The People and Nature Surveys for England: Monthly indicators for March 2022 (Official Statistics). *Gov.uk*, May 18. [Online]. https://www.gov.uk/government/statistics/the-people-and-nature-survey-for-england-monthly-indicators-for-march-2022-official-statistics

Ohly, H., White, M. P., Wheeler, B. W., Bethel, A., Ukoumunne, O. C., Nikolaou, V., & Garside, R. (2016). Attention restoration theory: A systematic review of the attention restoration potential of exposure to natural environments. *Journal of Toxicology and Environmental Health, Part B*, *19*(7), 305–343. https://doi.org/10.1080/10937404.2016.1196155

Osberg, D., & Biesta, G. (2008). The emergent curriculum: Navigating a complex course between unguided learning and planned enculturation. *Journal of Curriculum Studies*, *40*(3), 313–328. https://doi.org/10.1080/00220270701610746

Parsons, T. (1991). *The social system* (2nd ed.). Routledge.

Peacock, A. (2011). Managed learning spaces and new forms of learning outside the classroom. In S. Waite (Ed.), *Children learning outside the classroom. From birth to eleven* (pp. 188–200). Sage.

Penazzi, D., McCready-Fallon, J., & Rosser, S. (2022). Experiential and outdoor learning in the transition to university courses – The mathematics case. *PRIMUS*, *33*(2), 123–136. https://doi.org/10.1080/10511970.2022.2040665

Plambech, T., & van den Bosch, C. C. K. (2015). The impact of nature on creativity – A study among Danish creative professionals. *Urban Forestry & Urban Greening*, *14*(2), 255–263. https://doi.org/10.1016/j.ufug.2015.02.006

Prince, H. E., & Diggory, O. (2023). Recognition and reporting of outdoor learning in primary schools in England. *Journal of Adventure Education and Outdoor Learning*, 1–13. https://doi.org/10.1080/14729679.2023.2166544

Quotefancy. (2024). "I love nature, I just don't want to get any of it on me." — Woody Allen. *Quotefancy*. [Online]. https://quotefancy.com/quote/949483/Woody-Allen-I-love-nature-I-just-don-t-want-to-get-any-of-it-on-me

Renata. (n.d.). Nature Deficit Disorder: The Importance of Outdoors for Mental Well-being. *Leaf Complex Care*. [Online]. https://leafcare.co.uk/blog/nature-deficit-disorder-the-importance-of-outdoors-for-mental-well-being/

Rominger, C., Fink, A., Weber, B., Benedek, M., Perchtold-Stefan, C. M., & Schwerdtfeger, A. R. (2023). Step-by-step to more creativity: The number of steps in everyday life is related to creative ideation performance. *The American Psychologist*. Advance online publication. https://doi.org/10.1037/amp0001232

Rousseau, J. J. (1783). *Émile, ou De l'éducation*. H. Baldwin.

Schultz, P. W. (2000). Empathizing with nature: The effects of perspective taking on concern for environmental issues. *Journal of Social Issues*, *56*(3), 391–406. https://doi.org/10.1111/0022-4537.00174

Seltzer, K., & Bentley, T. (1999). *The creative age: Knowledge and skills for the new economy*. Demos.

Shuda, Q., Bougoulias, M. E., & Kass, R. (2020). Effect of nature exposure on perceived and physiologic stress: A systematic review. *Complementary Therapies in Medicine*, *53*, 102514., 1-8. https://doi.org/10.1016/j.ctim.2020.102514

Smith, L. (2023). *Creativity in the English curriculum: Historical perspectives and future directions.* Routledge.

Stanton, P. (2019). *Conscious creativity: look, connect, create.* Leaping Hare Press.

Stenfors, C. U. D., Van Hedger, S. C., Schertz, K. E., Meyer, F. A. C., Smith, K. E. L., Norman, G. J., Bourrier, S. C., Enns, J. T., Kardan, O., Jonides, J., & Berman, M. G. (2019). Positive effects of nature on cognitive performance across multiple experiments: Test order but not affect modulates the cognitive effects. *Frontiers in Psychology, 10*, 1413, 1–21. https://doi.org/10.3389/fpsyg.2019.01413

Stimpson, N. J., Davison, G., & Javadi, A. H. (2018). Joggin' the Noggin: Towards a physiological understanding of exercise-induced cognitive benefits. *Neuroscience and Biobehavioral Reviews, 88*, 177–186.https://doi.org/10.1016/j.neubiorev.2018.03.018

Strong-Wilson, T., & Ellis, J. (2007). Children and place: Reggio Emilia's environment as third teacher. *Theory Into Practice, 46*(1), 40–47. https://doi.org/10.1080/00405840709336547

Sustainable Development Commission. (2008). *Health, place and nature how outdoor environments influence health and well-being: A knowledge base.* Sustainable Development Commission. [Online]. https://www.sd-commission.org.uk/data/files/publications/Outdoor_environments_and_health.pdf

Ulrich, R. S. (1979). Visual landscapes and psychological well-being. *Landscape Research, 4*(1), 17–23. https://doi.org/10.1080/01426397908705892

UNESCO (2020). *Global education monitoring report 2020: Inclusion and education – All means all* (3rd ed.). UNESCO. [Online]. https://www.unesco.org/gem-report/en/inclusion

Wainwright, A. (1973). *A coast to coast walk: a pictorial guide.* Westmorland, England: Westmorland Gazette. In: Snowdon (Yr Wyddfa) Info (2024). There's no such thing as bad weather. *Snowdoninfo.com.* [Online]. https://tinyurl.com/yc5h6mvs

Waite, S. (2019). *Teaching and learning outside the classroom: Personal values, alternative pedagogies and standards.* Routledge.

Warber, S. L., DeHudy, A. A., Bialko, M. F., Marselle, M. R., & Irvine, K. N. (2015). Addressing "Nature-deficit disorder": A mixed methods pilot study of young adults attending a wilderness Camp. *Evidence-Based Complementary and Alternative Medicine, 2015*(1), 651827 (1–13). https://doi.org/10.1155/2015/651827

White, M. P., Alcock, I., Grellier, J., Wheeler, B. W., Hartig, T., Warber, S. L., Bone, A., Depledge, M. H., & Fleming, L. E. (2019). Spending at least 120 minutes a week in nature is associated with good health and wellbeing. *Scientific Reports, 9*(1), 7730. https://doi.org/10.1038/s41598-019-44097-3

Whittle, J. (2006). Journey sticks and affective mapping. *Primary Geographer, 59*, 11–13.

Wolf, L. J., zu Ermgassen, S., Balmford, A., White, M., & Weinstein, N. (2017). Is variety the spice of life? An experimental investigation into the effects of species richness on self-reported mental well-being. *PLoS ONE, 12*(1), e0170225. https://doi.org/10.1371/journal.pone.0170225

Chapter 3

Technology

Its creative role in personalising adult education

Ibrahim Berksoy and Nurul Nakiah Abdullah

Introduction

The 21st century has seen a rapid technological evolution that has profoundly reshaped adult education (AE). The era of passive lectures and static textbooks has shifted, with technology now infusing adult learning (AL) with interactivity, engagement, and personalised approaches (Timotheou et al., 2023). Virtual reality (VR) simulations (Lampropoulos et al., 2022) and gamified platforms (Browne et al., 2014; Landers et al., 2019) are just two examples of the myriad of possibilities technology can offer to enhance AL experiences. However, transforming traditional learning into autodidactic learning remains a challenge given the complexity of AL theory (see Firat, 2023, p. 1). Educators are currently grappling with deploying technology as a dynamic force, in an effort to innovatively shift the traditional learning paradigm. Moreover, creating avenues for adult learners to integrate their lived experiences into conventional classrooms poses challenges, especially amidst traditional instructional requirements. Bridging this gap between conventional teaching strategies and the unique traits of adult learners is vital, particularly in navigating this digital era (Knowles, 1980).

To steer the direction of this chapter, two aims are outlined below:

- To explore practical ways in which technology can serve as a creative tool to actively engage adult learners in the co-construction of knowledge for personalised learning, and
- To offer readers, through practical examples, how technology can serve as a link to revitalise AL for adults facing accessibility challenges as conduit to inclusive and personalised AL.

The chapter commences with a brief discussion about andragogy in terms of what it means and how it links to AL in Higher Education (HE).

Understanding how adults learn: andragogy

In the 1970s, when the notion of adults and children having distinct learning styles (Knowles, 1980) gradually became a revolutionary concept, the birth

DOI: 10.4324/9781032633534-5

of andragogy ignited extensive research and debate (McCarthy & Anderson, 2000). By definition, Knowles (1980, p. 43) regarded andragogy as 'the art and science of helping adults to learn'. Andragogy, in his proposals, comprised a set of core AL principles that apply to all AL situations (Knowles, 1980, p. 43). Knowles' work outlined key characteristics of adult learners, including self-directedness, experience, readiness to learn, and orientation to learning. These ideas were built upon some essential assumptions regarding the traits of ma-ture learners, contrary to the assumptions of how children learn that underlie traditional pedagogy. These assumptions propose that as individuals mature:

1 their self-perception evolves from dependence to becoming a self-directed individual,
2 they amass an expanding reservoir of experiences, transforming these into an increasingly valuable learning resource,
3 their readiness to learn becomes progressively aligned with the develop-mental tasks associated with their social roles, and
4 their time perspective shifts from deferring the application of knowledge to an immediate application, leading to a 'change in their learning orientation from subject-centeredness to performance-centeredness' (Knowles, 1980, pp. 44–45).

Subsequently, Knowles (1985) introduced a fifth assumption, stating that as individuals mature, their motivation to learn becomes internal.

Assumptions about adult learners profoundly impact instructional design at the HE level. Adults value autonomy in their learning journey (Knowles, 1980), unlike traditional instructor-led approaches that may hinder it. It is argued that overlooking the rich life experiences adults bring to the class-room can disconnect them from deployed educational methods (Merriam & Bierema, 2014; Wang, 2019). This dimension of experience is a key character-istic of an adult learner that sets adults 'off from the world of children' (Kidd, 1973, p. 46). Lindeman (1961, p. 6) equates this as 'the resource of highest value', serving as a 'living textbook' (Lindeman, 1961, p. 7) for adult learners and providing them with 'prolonged motivation [as an] independent explorer in [their] education' (Arnett & Tanner, 2006, p. 469). Put simply, AL moti-vation and approaches differ significantly from those of children due to their life experiences. Therefore, there is a strong claim that AE should shift from knowledge transmission to knowledge discovery, recognising and utilising this diversity to enhance engagement and relevance for adult learners (Knowles, 1985).

Reflections on the discussion above raise an important question in our minds which we are keen to answer in the following section: *how can digital technology creatively promote such access to meaningful AL, reconciling the gap of the traditional approach to learning and teaching (L&T) to support adult learners and foster their active role in learning?*

Bridging AL and andragogy: technology as a creative link

In this chapter, creativity refers to novelty and usefulness (Williams et al., 2016), as previously conceptualised in Chapter 1. The past few decades have seen a surge in creativity and innovation driven by digital technologies (Selwyn et al., 2006), profoundly shaping how adults learn, work, and communicate (Selwyn, 2019). Therefore, new technologies have reshaped learning landscapes in AE (Parker, 2013).

In HE, digital tools extend beyond information repositories to become catalysts for engagement and collaboration (Jewitt, 2012). They offer flexibility, convenience, and interactive learning experiences, as well as reduce costs and facilitate effective knowledge accumulation (Lin et al., 2017). For instance, during the COVID-19 pandemic, Divjak et al. (2022) observed that the flipped classroom emerged as a dynamic solution, creatively leveraging technology to adapt traditional learning methods in many countries, examples of which include China, the USA, Spain, Germany, Portugal, the Netherlands, Peru, UAE, Korea, and Australia. While challenges persisted, including initial dissatisfaction and increased workload for teachers, innovative combinations like problem-based learning and game-based learning demonstrated promising results (Divjak et al., 2022). As the educational landscape evolves, these findings emphasise the ongoing need for creativity and innovation in AE, these advocating a forward-thinking approach to AL.

In addition, multimedia and hybrid courses provide a great alternative to traditional teaching methods by enabling learners to investigate and acquire knowledge at individualised speeds, ensuring that each adult can reach their maximum learning potential (Garnham & Kaleta, 2002; Tway, 1995, cited in Teoh & Neo, 2006). For instance, in 2012, the Massachusetts Institute of Technology (MIT) and Harvard University launched *edX*, a non-profit, massive open online course (MOOC) platform for adult learners. It is one of the most successful online learning spaces, passing 110 million global enrolments (edX Press, 2020). Indeed, the evolution of technological advancement in recent years has the ability to reconcile the lack of personalisation to AL brought upon by traditional methods of L&T. When purposely designed and curated within the principles and adapted practices of andragogy (Knowles, 1980), it is likely that the creative technology integration of MOOCs can result in a more learner-centric and interactive approach, allowing for personalised AL experiences (Shah et al., 2022).

Put simply, our exploration of technology as a creative link between traditional methods and the needs of adult learners reveals a multitude of opportunities. This perspective positions technology not only as a resource but as a dynamic force driving transformative educational approaches. Moreover, while discussing the potential of technology in education, it is crucial to illustrate its inclusive and adaptive nature with concrete examples. By way of illustration, access to learning materials via various devices like laptops, tablets, and smartphones, combined with students' active contributions via voice, chat, or video facilities during online sessions, exemplifies how technology can foster inclusivity and adaptability. Additionally, providing 24-hour access to session recordings further enhances accessibility and flexibility, ensuring that learners can engage with the material at their own pace and convenience. These practical illustrations not only articulate the theoretical benefits of technology but also demonstrate its tangible impact in creating a more inclusive, novel, and useful learning environment for adult learners.

As leveraging technology for adult learners hinges on the concept of personalised learning (Wanner & Palmer, 2015), our chapter delves further into framing personalised AL through technology integration. This exploration aims to elucidate how educators and instructional designers can creatively employ digital tools to tailor learning experiences and accommodate the diverse backgrounds, preferences, and paces of adult learners.

Personalised AL

Personalised (adult) learning is a pedagogical approach that recognises the unique needs of individual learners (Campbell et al., 2007). Indeed, Bartle (2015) defines personalised learning as a method that enables students to actively shape their learning journey, allowing them to customise learning activities to align with their unique needs, capabilities, and interests. At its core, personalised learning aims to inspire learners, irrespective of their backgrounds, to take an active role in determining both what they wish to learn and how they wish to learn it (Campbell et al., 2007). These points align closely with Knowles' (1980) assumptions of andragogy by recognising and catering to the self-directed, experiential, and internally motivated nature of adult learners. Merriam and Bierema (2014, p. 55) build on this, recognising that adult learners approach learning differently with a 'rich reservoir of life experiences and knowledge' drawn from previous social roles that offer them 'teachable moments' (p. 55). Thus, in the context of AE, where learners often come with varied experiences, educational backgrounds, and time constraints, the importance of personalised learning is significant. In this regard, the creative application of emerging technologies might facilitate the adoption of cost-effective, sustainable, and scalable methods for L&T, emphasising personalised and active approaches (Bartle, 2015).

Technology-enhanced approaches and digital tools for personalised learning

There are numerous ways educators and instructional designers can transform L&T through the creative use of technology-enhanced approaches for adult learners (see Dabbagh & Kitsantas, 2012; Hemmi et al., 2009; Sarrion, 2023).

Specifically, we explore how these assumptions can be brought to fruition through the creative incorporation of artificial intelligence (AI) and interactive multimedia.

Artificial Intelligence (AI)

Although AI is not a new technology, its development and integration into different sectors, especially generative AI (GenAI), have gained huge momentum in recent years (Michel-Villarreal et al., 2023). However, there is a lack of consensus, with some calling for a ban due to concerns about it undermining the goal of fostering independent and critical thinking, while others see GenAI as a highly transformative technology (Robert & Muscanell, 2023). Regardless of this uncertainty, GenAI can creatively revolutionise personalised learning by analysing individual learner data (Pratama et al., 2023). Through its abilities to track learners' individual progress and identify learning patterns, GenAI tools can tailor AL content by recommending learning materials that fit individual's learning needs, approaches to learning, and differentiated L&T goals. More significantly, GenAI tools can be creatively used to relieve lecturers of labour-intensive tasks such as creating assessments, providing formative feedback to students, and addressing grammatical errors (Educause, 2023). Therefore, lecturers can have more time to interact with students and address more complex responsibilities that include supporting them to synthesise and analyse information, and generating new knowledge. Case Study 3.1 offers a creative example of the use of AI (ChatGPT) in HE.

Case Study 3.1 aligns with Knowles' (1985) andragogy principles, emphasising self-directed learning and the need for feedback tailored to individual learners. The study shows that the integration of ChatGPT might foster creativity in assessment methods and accessibility by offering feedback independent of teacher availability. This provides adult learners with greater accessibility and autonomy, enabling them to embark on meaningful self-directed learning journeys. Furthermore, as an additional appendage to the chapter, we actively sought insights from the ChatGPT (version 3.5) itself on five creative ways to utilise ChatGPT in HE. These were generated in response to the following prompt: 'List five creative uses of ChatGPT in higher education'. The answer that was offered by the AI chatbot is presented in Figure 3.1.

We assert that these applications demonstrate how AI tools like ChatGPT can creatively contribute to various aspects of L&T, fostering a more interactive and supportive educational environment.

Interactive multimedia

Personalised (adult) learning gains a dynamic dimension through the creative integration of interactive multimedia such as VR simulations and videos. Praheto et al. (2020) assert that interactive multimedia can accommodate

Case Study 3.1

Lu et al. (2024) conducted a study with 46 undergraduate students in China, in which they aimed to evaluate the effectiveness of GenAI tools, specifically ChatGPT, in terms of marking assessments and providing feedback to students. The students were asked to compose an abstract for a specified article. Then, the abstracts were assessed based on five criteria by their tutors and ChatGPT:

1 The research objective,
2 Methodology,
3 Results,
4 Implications, and
5 Language conventions.

Drawing from both the interview data and quantitative findings, the study uncovered three ways in which ChatGPT complements teacher assessment, benefiting students with various writing proficiency levels:

1 Fostering deeper comprehension of teacher assessments among students,
2 Encouraging students to make judgements regarding feedback, and
3 Promoting independent thinking about revisions.

individual needs, provide rich learning opportunities, increase classroom engagement, and enhance motivation through its interactive and diverse elements. For example, Case Study 3.2 is a creative example of using augmented reality (AR) in medical education.

Case Study 3.2 highlights the role of AR in actively engaging students and providing experiential learning opportunities. Such a creative application of AR technology aligns well with Knowles' (1985) principles of andragogy, which emphasise the value of experiential, hands-on learning tailored to adult learners. The immersion and interaction provided by AR can also promote inclusivity and cater to diverse learning preferences within the adult learner population. Therefore, utilising interactive media might serve as a basis for transforming the learning process into a creative, innovative, collaborative, accessible, and more dynamic environment for students (Syahputra & Maksum, 2020).

In conclusion, the integration of technology and personalised learning is reshaping the landscape of AE. Instructional designers have a wealth of digital tools at their disposal. However, the potential for further customisation and

ChatGPT can be a versatile tool in HE, enhancing both learning and teaching experiences. Here are five creative uses:

1 **Virtual Teaching Assistant:** ChatGPT can be used as a virtual teaching assistant in online courses. It can answer students' frequently asked questions about course content, assignments, deadlines, and more. This frees up time for instructors to focus on more complex pedagogical tasks and provides students with instant support whenever they need it.
2 **Customised Learning Experiences:** ChatGPT can help create personalised learning journeys for students by adapting content and resources to meet individual learning styles and paces. For example, it can suggest additional reading materials, videos, and practice problems based on the student's performance in quizzes and assignments.
3 **Enhancing Research Skills:** ChatGPT can assist students in developing their research skills by helping them refine their research questions, suggesting databases and resources, and providing tips on evaluating these. This can be particularly useful in introductory research courses or for students unfamiliar with academic research methodologies.
4 **Interactive Simulations and Role-Play:** ChatGPT can drive interactive scenarios such as simulations and role-play, where students can engage in virtual dialogues to explore different perspectives in case studies or historical events. This can enhance understanding in subjects like ethics, history, and law by allowing students to 'speak' with historical figures or fictional characters.
5 **Feedback and Revision Tool:** ChatGPT can offer preliminary feedback on student essays and reports by identifying areas that might need more clarity, suggesting improvements in structure, and pointing out grammatical errors. This can accelerate the revision process and help students learn to critique their own work before submitting it for formal evaluation.

Figure 3.1 Five creative ways to utilise ChatGPT in HE (generated on 17 April 2024 via ChatGPT version 3.5).

refinement of these tools may be limited by some considerations such as budgetary constraints and technological accessibility. Thus, while the technology has the potential to enhance learning experiences, educators must carefully weigh the costs and challenges associated with their implementation to ensure they truly meet the diverse needs of adult learners in the modern educational landscape. In tandem with personalisation, accessibility is a cornerstone of effective AE which needs to be considered (Papastamatis & Panitsidou, 2009).

Accessibility in the digital environment

Accessibility is key when designing adaptive learning platforms for inclusive AE. The European Agency for Development in Special Needs Education (2012) describes inclusive education as a human right since education needs to be based upon equity. Therefore, in practice, to ensure the success of all students, HE institutions should prioritise creative and inclusive policies, strategies, and

Case Study 3.2

Christopoulos et al. (2022) undertook an innovative exploration into the integration of AR technology in medical education in Greece, focusing on the dual metrics of learning effectiveness (academic performance) and training satisfaction. Their findings revealed that AR not only significantly enhances knowledge acquisition and retention compared to traditional learning methods but also increases student satisfaction, making a compelling case for incorporating AR into online medical education strategies. This approach is seen as a particularly effective solution to the challenges posed by remote teaching environments. The researchers advocated the adaptation of learning materials to be platform-independent and suggested the restructuring of traditional lectures to better integrate AR technology. This would allow for the use of AR in various learning contexts, enhancing student engagement through interactive and supplementary methods. Furthermore, they recommended that AR-based materials be used alongside collaborative activities to facilitate deeper exploration and discussion among students.

actions. This might include creating fully accessible physical spaces based on universal design principles, facilitating smooth transitions for students with disabilities, and providing faculty training in inclusive pedagogy and universal designs for learning (Moriña, 2017). A small selection of practical suggestions is offered below for reader reflection and implementation:

- Employing VR simulations to provide immersive experiences that simulate various physical environments, allowing students to navigate and familiarise themselves with spaces before encountering them in-person (Lampropoulos et al., 2022).
- Utilising AR applications to overlay digital information onto physical environments, offering real-time guidance and support for students with diverse needs as they navigate campus facilities (Christopoulos et al., 2022).
- Developing interactive online modules that incorporate gamification elements, such as challenges and rewards, engaging students in learning about inclusive practices and universal design principles (Oliver, 2017).
- Hosting inclusive design 'hackathons' or workshops where students, faculty, and community members can co-create innovative solutions to address accessibility challenges on campus and beyond (Moys et al., 2023).

By incorporating these creative approaches, HE institutions can proactively foster inclusive environments that cater to the diverse needs of all students.

1. Speech-to-text tools	2. Text-to-speech tools	3. Screen readers	4. Gesture-to-speech tools	5. Communication Software
• Google docs voice typing (free) • Google live transcribe (free) • Apple dictation (Integrated into Apple devices) • Microsoft voice typing (Integrated into MS Windows devices)	• naturalreaders. com (free) • Tobii Dynavox TD Talk • Tobii Dynavox Communicator 5	• Apple VoiceOver (Integrated into Apple devices) • VoX (free Chrome extension) • JAWS (for MS Windows devices)	• Apple VoiceOver gestures (Integrated into Apple devices) • SIGNS (1) • Integrated speech and gesture tools: Tacotron2-ISG and GlowTTS-ISG (2)	• Tobii Dynavox Grid 3 • Tobii Dynavox Sono Flex

Figure 3.2 Examples of assistive tools that can be used to enhance accessibility in HE.

Source: **(1)** Please visit https://www.mrm.com/en/work-case-studies/frankfurt-amazon-signs.html **(2)** Wang, S., Alexanderson, S., Gustafson, J., Beskow, J., Henter, G. E., & Székely, É. (2021). Integrated speech and gesture synthesis. In: *Proceedings of the 2021 International Conference on Multimodal Interaction* (pp. 177–185), October. [Online]. https://www.speech.kth.se/tts-demos/wang2021integrated-final.pdf

Furthermore, inclusive design principles might go beyond mere accessibility, emphasising the creation of digital interfaces and content that are usable by individuals with a wide range of abilities and disabilities (Fornauf & Erickson, 2020). In the context of AL, this means that digital resources should be designed with consideration for users with varying levels of technological proficiency, ensuring that the learning experience is seamless and intuitive for all.

In addition, assistive technologies can make digital content more accessible to learners with disabilities (Chambers, 2021). The World Health Organisation (WHO) (2022) defines assistive technology as a comprehensive term encompassing assistive products, related systems, and services that facilitate the inclusion, participation, and engagement of individuals with disabilities. A suite of assistive tools is offered for reader consumption in Figure 3.2.

By way of an example, we have converted the abstract for this chapter from text-to-speech (TTS) via *naturalreaders.com* (see Box 2, Figure 3.2) to illustrate how these assistive tools can be implemented in lesson designs. Readers are invited to scan the QR code (Figure 3.3) to access the speech file.

We see the above as a fundamental technology, without which individuals may not be able to 'achieve greater independence and [a] better quality of life' (Dawson et al., 2019, p. 226). At least from the AE standpoint, it is essential to incorporate AE to support adults with disabilities by creating a space where they can participate fully and independently in the learning process. However, a successful integration of these tools relies on practical considerations such as securing adequate funding, providing comprehensive training, and developing technology integration plans (McNicholl et al., 2021).

Figure 3.3 The speech file of the abstract for this chapter as an illustration of how TTS can be used in learning and teaching.

Note: At the time of writing, the QR code offered in Figure 3.3 was working/active. As material on the internet is regularly changed, updated, or removed, it is anticipated that this may eventually not work for readers. We apologise in advance for this, but it is hoped that readers will appreciate that this is out of our control.

Indeed, Ameen et al. (2019) encountered several challenges when integrating e-learning systems into universities in Iraq; these included the following:

- Limited internet connectivity and costly access to reliable connections,
- Bureaucratic barriers hindering stakeholder collaboration,
- Difficulty in delivering tailored training sessions, and
- A lack of technical support.

Overcoming these challenges is important, not least to aid adult learners with additional needs who may struggle with their reading – in terms of decoding fluency and comprehension – which can lead to reading anxiety (Bone & Bouck, 2017). TTS features can help alleviate these issues by providing auditory support, allowing learners to access written material through listening. Chambers (2021, p. 100) describes TTS as a 'powerful assistive technology [that] empowers learners to overcome [learning] challenges'. As a special needs educator himself, Chambers stresses that TTS affordability in leveraging accessibility to democratise learning for adult learners should be capitalised as one of L&T's 'must-try' practices. Therefore, such a creative use of technology can offer an alternative mode of accessing information that may be more comfortable or effective for some individuals in HE.

Understandably, several factors affect technology integration. Bekele et al. (2023), in their study in Africa, highlight the necessity for universities to reconsider their approach to humanity and knowledge, emphasising values like inclusivity and engagement for successful technology integration. However, challenges such as institutional resistance to innovation, outdated curricula, and the 'digital divide' must also be addressed to effectively implement these philosophical perspectives in learning and teaching practices. In particular, the digital divide significantly impacts accessibility, defined here as the gap between those who have access to and can use digital media and those who lack such access and usage (Van Dijk, 2019).

In the pursuit of an inclusive digital environment, addressing affordability and connectivity is paramount. While technology offers immense potential, it is essential to address the digital divide to ensure that all adult learners have equal access to educational resources (Mason et al., 2023). Initiatives aimed at providing affordable devices and software, internet connectivity, and digital literacy training might contribute to bridging this gap, ensuring that socio-economic factors do not hinder individuals from benefiting from the trans-formative power of technology in HE. For instance, during the COVID-19 pandemic, both private and public universities in Ghana, with government support, provided free internet connections to students and lecturers (Kumi-Yeboah et al., 2023), as did other countries such as Italy, China, UAE, the USA, and Portugal (ITU, 2020).

In summary, creativity and technology intersect to enrich accessibility in the digital realm for adult learners. Beyond the mere application of adaptive learning platforms and inclusive design principles lies an opportunity to in-novate and reimagine the educational landscape. By infusing creativity into the technology integration, we can transcend traditional boundaries and forge new pathways for AL. As we navigate the ever-evolving landscape of AE, it becomes imperative to not only embrace technological advancements but also explore creative approaches to foster inclusivity. This dynamic synergy between creativity and technology can ensure that education becomes a truly transformative force, empowering individuals from all walks of life and 'opening doors' to boundless opportunities.

Concluding comments

This chapter has explored different ways in which technology can serve as a creative tool to actively engage adult learners in the co-construction of knowl-edge for personalised learning. We have informed readers, through practical examples, how technology can serve as a link to revitalise AL for adults facing accessibility challenges as conduit to inclusive and personalised AL. In our at-tempt to reposition AL, we situate andragogy as a framework to redefine AE in HE, both in the present and in the future. Specifically, through the lens of andragogy, as proposed by Knowles (1980), we have drawn connections between the characteristics of adult learners and how technology could be tai-lored to actualise personalised learning experiences and accessibility for adults.

As we conclude this chapter, we reflect on the symbiotic relationship between technology and andragogy. Given the fast-growing evolution to digital applications in the 21st century in AE, we are hopeful that technology – when purposively and creatively designed within the principles of andragogy – can act as a catalyst to foster personalised and accessible learning. With this in mind, the chapter recognises how instructional designers and educators can embrace the transformative potential of technology to unlock creative and accessible learning experiences for adult learners in the 21st century.

Suggested further reading

Rogers, D. L. (2000). A paradigm shift: Technology integration for higher education in the new millennium. *AACE Review (Formerly AACE Journal)*, *1*(13), 19–33. [Online]. https://www.learntechlib.org/primary/p/8058/

Nerantzi, C., Abegglen, S., Karatsiori, M., & Martinez-Arboleda, A. (Eds.). (2023). *101 Creative ideas to use AI in education. A collection curated by #creativeHE*. CC-BY-NC-SA 4.0. [Online]. https://doi.org/10.5281/zenodo.8355454

Marquis, E., Jung, B., Fudge Schormans, A., Lukmanji, S., Wilton, R., & Baptiste, S. (2016). Developing inclusive educators: Enhancing the accessibility of teaching and learning in higher education. *International Journal for Academic Development*, *21*(4), 337–349. https://doi.org/10.1080/1360144X.2016.1181071

References

Ameen, N., Willis, R., Abdullah, M. N., & Shah, M. (2019). Towards the successful integration of e-learning systems in higher education in Iraq: A student perspective. *British Journal of Educational Technology*, *50*(3), 1434–1446. https://doi.org/10.1111/bjet.12651

Arnett, J. J., & Tanner, J. L. (Eds.). (2006). *Emerging adulthood in America: Coming of age in the 21st century*. American Psychological Association.

Bartle, E. (2015). *Personalised learning: An overview*. The Institute for Teaching and Learning Innovation, The University of Queensland. [Online]. https://itali.uq.edu.au/files/1264/Discussion-paper-Experiential_learning_an_overview.pdf

Bekele, T. A., Amponsah, S., & Karkouti, I. M. (2023). African philosophy for successful integration of technology in higher education. *British Journal of Educational Technology*, *54*(6), 1520–1538. https://doi.org/10.1111/bjet.13364

Bone, E. K., & Bouck, E. C. (2017). Accessible text-to-speech options for students who struggle with reading. *Preventing School Failure: Alternative Education for Children and Youth*, *61*(1), 48–55. https://doi.org/10.1080/1045988X.2016.1188366

Browne, K., Anand, C., & Gosse, E. (2014). Gamification and serious game approaches for adult literacy tablet software. *Entertainment Computing*, *5*(3), 135–146. https://doi.org/10.1016/j.entcom.2014.04.003

Campbell, R. J., Robinson, W., Neelands, J., Hewston, R., & Mazzoli, L. (2007). Personalised learning: Ambiguities in theory and practice. *British Journal of Educational Studies*, *55*(2), 135–154. http://www.jstor.org/stable/4620550

Chambers, M. (2021). Assistive technology critique: Don't forget about text-to-speech. *Adult Learning*, *32*(2), 99–100. https://doi.org/10.1177/1045159520969853

Christopoulos, A., Pellas, N., Kurczaba, J., & Macredie, R. (2022). The effects of augmented reality – Supported instruction in tertiary-level medical education. *British Journal of Educational Technology*, *53*(2), 307–325. https://doi.org/10.1111/bjet.13167

Dabbagh, N., & Kitsantas, A. (2012). Personal learning environments, social media, and self-regulated learning: A natural formula for connecting formal and informal learning. *The Internet and Higher Education*, *15*(1), 3–8. https://doi.org/10.1016/j.iheduc.2011.06.002

Dawson, K., Antonenko, P., Lane, H., & Zhu, J. (2019). Assistive technologies to support students with dyslexia. *Teaching Exceptional Children*, *51*(3), 226–239. https://doi.org/10.1177/0040059918794027

Divjak, B., Rienties, B., Iniesto, F., Vondra, P., & Žižak, M. (2022). Flipped classrooms in higher education during the COVID-19 pandemic: Findings and future research recommendations. *International Journal of Educational Technology in Higher Education*, *19*(9), 2–24. https://doi.org/10.1186/s41239-021-00316-4

Educause. (2023). *2023 Educause horizon report: Teaching and learning edition*. Educause. [Online]. https://library.educause.edu/resources/2021/2/horizon-reports

edX Press. (2020, December 15). edX passes 110 million total global enrollments, up 29 million year over-year test text. *edX*. [Online]. https://press.edx.org/edx-passes-110-million-total-global-enrollments-up-29-million-year-over-year

European Agency for Development in Special Needs Education. (2012). *Teacher education for inclusion: Profile of inclusive teachers*. European Agency for Development in Special Needs Education. [Online]. https://www.european-agency.org/sites/default/files/Profile-of-Inclusive-Teachers.pdf

Firat, M. (2023, January 12). How ChatGPT can transform autodidactic experiences and open education? *OSF PrePrints*. [Online]. https://doi.org/10.31219/osf.io/9ge8m

Fornauf, B. S., & Erickson, J. D. (2020). Towards an inclusive pedagogy through universal design for learning in higher education: A review of the literature. *Journal of Postsecondary Education and Disability*, *33*(2), 183–199. https://files.eric.ed.gov/fulltext/EJ1273677.pdf

Garnham, C., & Kaleta, R. (2002). *Introduction to hybrid courses* (pp. 1–4). [Online]. https://hccelearning.files.wordpress.com/2010/09/introduction-to-hybrid-course1.pdf

Hemmi, A., Bayne, S., & Land, R. (2009). The appropriation and repurposing of social technologies in higher education. *Journal of Computer Assisted Learning*, *25*(1), 19–30. https://doi.org/10.1111/j.1365-2729.2008.00306.x

International Telecommunication Union (ITU). (2020, May 6). COVID-19: Here's how some countries are addressing the digital education divide. *ITU*. [Online]. https://www.itu.int/hub/2020/05/covid-19-heres-how-some-countries-are-addressing-the-digital-education-divide/

Jewitt, C. (2012). *Technology, literacy, learning: A multimodal approach*. Routledge.

Kidd, J. R. (1973). *How adults learn* (Revised ed.). Association Press.

Knowles, M. S. (1980). *The modern practice of adult education: From pedagogy to andragogy*. Cambridge - The Adult Education Company.

Knowles, M. S. (1985). *Andragogy in action: Applying modern principles of adult education*. Jossey Bass.

Kumi-Yeboah, A., Kim, Y., & Armah, Y. E. (2023). Strategies for overcoming the digital divide during the COVID-19 pandemic in higher education institutions in Ghana. *British Journal of Educational Technology*, *54*(6), 1441–1462. https://doi.org/10.1111/bjet.13356

Lampropoulos, G., Keramopoulos, E., Diamantaras, K., & Evangelidis, G. (2022). Augmented reality and virtual reality in education: Public perspectives, sentiments, attitudes, and discourses. *Education Sciences*, *12*(11), Art. 798 (1–23). [Online]. https://doi.org/10.3390/educsci12110798

Landers, R. N., Auer, E. M., Helms, A. B., Marin, S., & Armstrong, M. B. (2019). Gamification of adult learning: Gamifying employee training and development. In R. N. Landers (Ed.), *Cambridge handbook of technology and employee behavior* (pp. 271–295). Cambridge University Press.

Lin, M. H., Chen, H. C., & Liu, K. S. (2017). A study of the effects of digital learning on learning motivation and learning outcome. *Eurasia Journal of Mathematics, Science and Technology Education*, *13*(7), 3553–3564. https://doi.org/10.12973/eurasia.2017.00744a

Lindeman, E. C. (1961). *The meaning of adult education in the United States*. Harvest House.

Lu, Q., Yao, Y., Xiao, L., Yuan, M., Wang, J., & Zhu, X. (2024). Can ChatGPT effectively complement teacher assessment of undergraduate students' academic writing? *Assessment & Evaluation in Higher Education*, 1–18. https://doi.org/10.1080/02602938.2024.2301722

Mason, A. M., Spencer, E. A., Westhoff, M. C., Livingston, K. M., & Compton, J. (2023). Surveilling the web, mobile, and language accessibility of communication's digital presence within institutions of higher education globally. *Journal of Communication Pedagogy*, *7*(1), 130–147. https://doi.org/10.31446/JCP.2023.1.09

McCarthy, J. P., & Anderson, L. (2000). Active learning techniques versus traditional teaching styles: Two experiments from history and political science. *Innovative Higher Education*, *24*, 279–294. https://doi.org/10.1023/B:IHIE.0000047415.48495.05

McNicholl, A., Casey, H., Desmond, D., & Gallagher, P. (2021). The impact of assistive technology use for students with disabilities in higher education: A systematic review. *Disability and Rehabilitation: Assistive Technology*, *16*(2), 130–143. https://doi.org/10.1080/17483107.2019.1642395

Merriam, S. B., & Bierema, L. L. (2014). *Adult learning: Linking theory and practice*. John Wiley & Sons.

Michel-Villarreal, R., Vilalta-Perdomo, E., Salinas-Navarro, D. E., Thierry-Aguilera, R., & Gerardou, F. S. (2023). Challenges and opportunities of generative AI for higher education as explained by ChatGPT. *Education Sciences*, *13*(9), Art.856 (1–18). https://doi.org/10.3390/educsci13090856

Moriña, A. (2017). Inclusive education in higher education: Challenges and opportunities. *European Journal of Special Needs Education*, *32*(1), 3–17. https://doi.org/10.1080/08856257.2016.1254964

Moys, J.-L., Hwang, F., Marsili, U., Nunes, R., Tagg, A., & Vasilikou, C. (2023). 'The inclusive way' hackathon – Inclusive wayfinding and pedagogy. *InfoDesign – Revista Brasileira De Design Da Informação*, *20*(2), 1–14. https://doi.org/10.51358/id.v20i2.1091

Oliver, E. (2017). Gamification as transformative assessment in higher education. *HTS Theological Studies*, *73*(3), 1–15. https://doi.org/10.4102/hts.v73i3.4527

Papastamatis, A., & Panitsidou, E. (2009). The aspect of 'accessibility' in the light of European lifelong learning strategies: Adult education centres – A case study. *International Journal of Lifelong Education*, *28*(3), 335–351. https://doi.org/10.1080/02601370902799143

Parker, J. (2013). Examining adult learning assumptions and theories in technology-infused communities and professions. In V. Bryan & V. Wang (Eds.), *Technology use and research approaches for community education and professional development* (pp. 53–65). IGI Global. https://doi.org/10.4018/978-1-4666-2955-4.ch004

Praheto, B. E., Andayani., Rohmadi, M., & Wardani, N. E. (2020). The effectiveness of interactive multimedia in learning Indonesian language skills in higher education. *Rupkatha Journal on Interdisciplinary Studies in Humanities, 12*(1), 1–11. https://dx.doi.org/10.21659/rupkatha.v12n1.34

Pratama, M. P., Sampelolo, R., & Lura, H. (2023). Revolutionizing education: Harnessing the power of artificial intelligence for personalized learning. *Klasikal: Journal of Education, Language Teaching and Science, 5*(2), 350–357. https://doi.org/10.52208/klasikal.v5i2.877

Robert, J., & Muscanell, N. (2023). *2023 Educause horizon action plan: Generative AI.* Educause. [Online]. https://library.educause.edu/resources/2023/9/2023-educause-horizon-action-plan-generative-ai

Sarrion, E. (2023). *Exploring the power of ChatGPT.* Apress.

Selwyn, N. (2019). *What is digital sociology?* Polity Press.

Selwyn, N., Gorard, S., & Furlong, J. (2006). *Adult learning in the digital age: Information technology and the learning society.* Routledge.

Shah, V., Murthy, S., Warriem, J., Sahasrabudhe, S., Banerjee, G., & Iyer, S. (2022). Learner-centric MOOC model: A pedagogical design model towards active learner participation and higher completion rates. *Educational Technology Research and Development, 70*(1), 263–288. https://doi.org/10.1007/s11423-022-10081-4

Syahputra, F., & Maksum, H. (2020). The development of interactive multimedia learning in information and communication technology subjects. *Journal of Education Research and Evaluation, 4*(4), 428–434. https://doi.org/10.23887/jere.v4i4.29931

Teoh, B. S. P., & Neo, T.-K. (2006). Innovative teaching: Using multimedia to engage students in interactive learning in higher education. Paper presented at the *2006 7th International Conference on Information Technology Based Higher Education and Training* (pp. 329–337), Ultimo, Australia. https://doi.org/10.1109/ITHET.2006.339782

Timotheou, S., Miliou, O., Dimitriadis, Y., Sobrino, S. V., Giannoutsou, N., Cachia, R., Monés, A. R., & Ioannou, A. (2023). Impacts of digital technologies on education and factors influencing schools' digital capacity and transformation: A literature review. *Education and Information Technologies, 28*(6), 6695–6726. https://doi.org/10.1007%2Fs10639-022-11431-8

Tway, L. (1995). Multimedia in action. In B. S. P. Wang & T.-K. Neo (2006). Innovative teaching: Using multimedia to engage students in interactive learning in higher education. Paper presented at the *2006 7th International Conference on Information Technology Based Higher Education and Training* (pp. 329–337), Ultimo, Australia. https://doi.org/10.1109/ITHET.2006.339782

Van Dijk, J. (2019). *The digital divide.* John Wiley & Sons.

Wang, Q. (2019). Modern education technology changed traditional adult teaching mode. *Frontier of Higher Education, 1*(1), 22–26. https://doi.org/10.36012/fhe.v1i1.572

Wanner, T., & Palmer, E. (2015). Personalising learning: Exploring student and teacher perceptions about flexible learning and assessment in a flipped university course. *Computers & Education, 88,* 354–369.https://doi.org/10.1016/j.compedu.2015.07.008

Williams, R., Runco, M. A., & Berlow, E. (2016). Mapping the themes, impact, and cohesion of creativity research over the last 25 years. *Creativity Research Journal, 28*(4), 385–394. https://doi.org/10.1080/10400419.2016.1230358

World Health Organization (WHO). (2022). *Global report on assistive technology.* WHO and UNICEF. [Online]. https://www.who.int/publications/i/item/9789240049451

Chapter 4

Self-reflective journals

Creative approaches to re-creating reflection

Lucy Kelly

Introduction

This chapter explores creative approaches to self-reflection, focusing specifically on self-reflective journals. I argue that, if lecturers want to use self-
reflective journals to develop the metacognitive skills of undergraduate and
postgraduate students (including those engaged in Initial Teacher Training
[ITT]), along with their creative mindsets and their views around success,
then lecturers must expand journalling as a concept so that it becomes a multimodal, creative canvas for students to use in a personalised way.

It is important to state from the outset that, whilst I will draw attention to
digital journals, this chapter is predominantly about physical journals. Indeed,
I want to emphasise the importance of 'creativity through the fingertips', and
how embodied and affective learning can take place through self-reflective
journalling. Essentially, a creative, embodied, multimodal approach enables
students to expand the 'meaning-making' process (Cooper & Stevens, 2006,
p. 350) and to construct meaning in new and exciting ways, which can resonate with the student on a personal and academic level, leading to improved
wellbeing. Taking a creative, personalised approach to self-reflection – one
that is grounded in the physical artefact of the journal – helps students to
step away from technology and, through this, promotes student engagement,
which is key to improving the retention and success of those in Higher Education (HE) (Thomas et al., 2021).

By revisiting the research of Cooper and Stevens (2006) through the use
of a multimodal and creative lens, this chapter energises their work with new
ideas, thinking, and practice, including the impact journalling can have on
wellbeing (Kelly, 2023). The chapter also moves their work from HE professionals in the United States (US) to HE students within the United Kingdom (UK). Specifically, I use Cooper and Stevens' focus on *Conversation,
Organisation, Individualised strategies*, and *Review* to offer a range of practical
ideas and suggestions on how students can use self-reflection through journal-
keeping so that it becomes a more 'naturalistic' and 'self-created' experience
(Cooper & Stevens, 2006, p. 350), which can positively impact students' lives

DOI: 10.4324/9781032633534-6

inside and outside the classroom. Whilst these ideas and activities are aimed at lecturers to use with their students, lecturers could also use them as part of their own reflective practice and professional development.

The aims of the chapter are as follows:

- To consider how self-reflective journals enable students to develop their metacognitive strategies, creative skillset, and personalised versions of success, which can improve their wellbeing, engagement, and academic/personal outcomes.
- To explore the self-reflective journal as a multimodal and creative space by revisiting and re-energising the work of Cooper and Stevens (2006) in order to offer a range of practical tips and strategies for lecturers to try out with their students.

This chapter begins with a short discussion on the benefits of self-reflective journals for students in HE.

Self-reflection, creative mindsets, and metacognition

According to Cooper and Stevens (2006, p. 350), self-reflection is a 'process of meaning-making'. Through the act of self-reflection (which, for the purposes of this chapter, focuses on self-reflective journals), students get to know the various facets of themselves at a deeper level and what they need to flourish, both short-term and long-term (Kelly, 2023), this being an opportunity to gather personal and professional 'data' (Cooper & Stevens, 2006, p. 358). This awareness or 'data' (Cooper & Stevens, 2006, p. 358) allows students to 'develop new insights and understandings that help us to improve our actions' (Ghaye, 2011, p. 1). Indeed, self-reflection, as Ghaye (2011, p. 1) acknowledges, 'help[s] us to understand the links between feeling, thinking, and doing'. It is this understanding – an ability to 'join the dots' and 'see the links' [my words] – that enables students to develop their creative skillset and take a more creative approach when it comes to their personal and professional growth. For Smith (2023, p. 3), '[t]he term "creative" is associated with making, developing, inspiration, artistry, originality, the imagination, and working things out', all of which can be linked to self-reflective journals.

In the context of undergraduate and postgraduate students, self-reflection via journalling empowers them to expand their creative adeptness and thinking through developing their metacognitive skills which, as McCrindle and Christensen (1995, p. 167) identify, is having the 'knowledge and awareness of one's own cognitive processes and the ability to actively control and manage those processes'. Alt and Raichel (2020, p. 146) support this viewpoint, suggesting that '[k]nowledge of cognition is a state in which we are aware of what is known (tasks, specific knowledge). It includes the ability to identify what we do and do not know and our awareness of our thought processes'. Indeed, for Alt and Raichel (2020, p. 147), 'reflection and metacognition are pillars for a richer learning experience' because students have a greater awareness of the learning process, which deepens it. According to Lew and Schmidt (2011, p. 520), this deeper learning comes from articulating the 'connections between new information, ideas, [and] prior or existing knowledge [...]. This in turn enhances the learner's cognition and metacognition'. Taken together, what is fundamental within the quotations above is the focus on 'awareness'. Being aware of the 'learning process' and how students, as individuals, learn enables 'deeper learning' because they [students] can make (and articulate) connections in new and creative ways. Through self-reflective journals, students can imagine and 'test out' a range of ideas within a safe environment (Kelly, 2023, p. 10). This enables students to solve problems in new and innovative ways, resulting in better student outcomes (McCrindle & Christensen, 1995).

Much of the literature on this topic area supports the view that self-reflection through journalling leads to better academic performance of HE students (Draissi et al., 2021; McCrindle & Christensen, 1995; Or, 2018). As Lew and Schmidt (2011) note, the reason for these improved outcomes is because journalling gives students a place to consider how course material and/or information is learned; it is an opportunity for students to develop their metacognitive skillset and experience different perspectives on their learning. This process then allows students to approach their learning in creative and transformative ways. For example, in their study focusing on 40 first-year undergraduate Biology students, McCrindle and Christensen (1995) found that those students who were assigned to a group using learning journals did better than those assigned the task of completing a scientific report at the end of the unit. Emphasising the interplay between self-reflection, a creative mindset, and metacognition, McCrindle and Christensen (1995, p. 181) suggest that students using the learning journal 'saw learning less as a process of [the] acquisition of knowledge and facts and more as a process of comprehension, analysis and interpretation'. The reference to 'interpretation' (McCrindle & Christensen, 1995, p. 181) is important here and reminds us of Smith's (2023) definition of the word 'creative' presented earlier in the chapter. A recent study carried out by Draissi et al. (2021) supports the importance of 'interpretation' (McCrindle & Christensen, 1995, p. 181), suggesting that journalling encourages students to see themselves – and external events/situations – from multiple perspectives. They propose that writing in reflective journals enables students to 'overcome challenges' (Draissi et al., 2021, p. 395) within their own learning, due to improving 'motivation, self-confidence, [and] metacognition' (Draissi et al., 2021, p. 395). These findings correlate with Or's (2018) study that focused on the use of reflective journals with a group of undergraduate students studying sexual health and human sexuality in Hong Kong. For Or (2018, p. 605), '[t]he reflective journals recorded the process of students coming to terms with their own learning. Writing journals forced learners to filter, reconstruct, and organize the knowledge and experience they encountered'.

It is this enhanced creative learning and thinking, stimulated by approaches such as reflective journaling, which, according to Ghanizadeh (2017, p. 102), is

> the core objective of the agenda of Higher Education. Scholars in the field of Higher Education contend that rational and deep thought is a standard of intellectual excellence required for full and constructive participation in [the] academic, individual, and social lives of students.

This cultivation of 'thinking skills and self-regulatory abilities' (Ghanizadeh, 2017, p. 102) is what leads to '[a]cademic success' (Ghanizadeh, 2017, p. 109) because self-reflection fosters critical thinking. However, success in HE goes beyond academic success. As Thomas et al. (2021, p. 17) recognise, '[s]uccess traditionally includes persisting with and completing academic programmes on time, but it can also be understood more broadly, encompassing personalised notions of success and outcomes both before and beyond graduation'. Indeed, this is where creative approaches to self-reflection can help because they allow students to use their creative mindsets to personally explore what success means to them, and to bring these definitions to their HE experience. Using self-reflective journals to explore academic performance and 'personalised notions of success' (Thomas et al., 2021, p. 17) might help to increase engagement, retention, and academic success across a variety of demographic groups, specifically 'socio-economic status, race and ethnicity, sex, and geographical location', within the HE sector (Eather et al., 2022, p. 224).

One way of using the self-reflective journal to incorporate personalised approaches to success is through growth goals. These could focus on academic success/outcomes or personal ones; essentially though, they enable students to develop their creative mindset – and improve their wellbeing – through imagining their future and the different ways they would like to grow. As Cooper and Stevens (2006, p. 361) note, the journal is not just an opportunity for participants to '*organize* [sic] their multifaceted lives', it is also a chance for them to explore and consider their lives. Travers et al. (2015) support this viewpoint, stating that there are many benefits to using growth goals:

> The setting of growth goals and making progress towards them (e.g., better academic performance) increased [students'] self-esteem (p. 236) [...], (positive self-evaluation) and self-efficacy (task-specific confidence). For many, a growth goal increased the efficiency of their time and improved stress management. Success encouraged many students to set higher growth goals for the future and energized those who were less motivated academically. Students made substantial gains in self-insight and became more skilled in monitoring their own thoughts and habits, including study habits. Many supported others in their growth-goal striving and provided

feedback and accountability. They acquired key transferable skills and developed growth goal-setting mindsets, such that many experienced transcendence in academic growth.

(p. 238)

Despite the above, I would argue that, in order for students to get to know themselves better and determine what their growth goals might be, as well as what a personalised version of success looks like to them, students – encouraged by their lecturers – must take a more creative, multimodal approach to self-reflective journals. As Brownhill (2022, p. 60) recognises, '[s]timulating self-reflection requires the use of different strategies and ideas'. It is to this stimulation through 'different strategies and ideas' (Brownhill, 2022, p. 60) that the chapter will now focus its attention on.

Creative approaches to self-reflective journals

As previously highlighted, self-reflective journals offer students a place to develop their creative mindset and metacognitive skills, as well as an opportunity to take a more creative, expansive view of success and growth. However, to fully reap these benefits, the self-reflective journal itself needs to be viewed as a creative canvas for students to use in a way that resonates with them. The journal must be seen as multifaceted and multidimensional: an 'on-going, evolving, unfolding space' (Kelly, 2023, p. 7). Indeed, this is where taking a multimodal approach to the self-reflective journal is important. Moffatt et al. (2016, p. 765) define multimodality as 'the variety of mediums and modes available and utilised for communication. These may be written, oral, aural, visual, or performative tools that can be used to create meaning'.

However, as shown in the studies described in the preceding section, self-reflective journals within the HE sector tend to consist of written entries. In order to 'create meaning' (Moffatt et al., 2016, p. 765) in the deepest, most powerful way, I argue that students' entries should use more than writing (Kelly, 2023). Kress (1997) explores this idea in his influential book, *Before Writing*, suggesting that '[d]ifferent modes give rise to different types of thinking' (p. xv). Thus, if lecturers want undergraduate and postgraduate students to be successful within the HE space (and I am using the word 'successful' here in a broad sense), then, as advocated by Kress, 'we must use multiple approaches when communicating with ourselves and our environments' (Kelly, 2023, p. 36) in order to fully 'develop our understanding of the internal and external worlds we inhabit' (Kelly, 2023, p. 36). To restrict self-reflective journals to one mode (such as writing) means limiting the 'transformative process' (Barton & Ryan, 2014, p. 410) that occurs when journalling and what students can harness from this tool. This includes an opportunity to explore 'multiple meanings' (Moffatt et al., 2016, p. 766), which is key to fostering a creative mindset and improving student wellbeing.

I would argue that part of the 'transformative process' (Barton & Ryan, 2014, p. 410) the student undergoes when journalling is linked to the physicality of the journal itself and the materials students choose to use. Creating a multimodal, physical journal allows students to bring their 'embodied experience[s]' (Botelho, 2021, p. 156) and the 'different worlds' (Botelho, 2021, p. 152) they inhabit onto the page. The process of physically crafting a journal allows students to step away from the busyness of the world around them – including the *pings and dings* of technology (Kelly, 2023) – and to see 'reflection as occurring within the constant movement of experience and perception' (Botelho, 2021, p. 156). This ongoing, ever-evolving narrative of the self will, in turn, support student wellbeing because it is a space where students can 'make sense' of themselves, their worlds, and their experiences (Kelly, 2023, p. 20).

To help students achieve this deeper insight, their journals could incorporate multicoloured paper and card, different types of pens (including scented ones), paint, chalk, photographs, clippings from newspapers and magazines, and links to music and online material. Whilst notebooks are typically used as journals, the notebook itself could be hardback or soft-bound, lined, plain or dotted, paper-wise, and A4, A5, or A3 in size. The journal does not have to be a physical item – it could be digital (Kelly, 2023) or a combination of both. The limitless options the journal as a form provides are important to be aware of because they allow lecturers and their students to expand the self-reflective journal to encompass the person using it; for it to be a space where, through the creative act itself, students can – as one of the participants from Cooper and Stevens' study (2006, p. 359) acknowledged – 'recreate [their] life'. However, compiling a creative, multimodal self-reflective journal does not need to be expensive, and it is important to share this message with students from the outset. Indeed, students should be encouraged to use and/or recycle existing materials, as well as utilising personal items, such as photographs or maps of favourite places. The more personal the journal is to the user, the greater the benefits (Kelly, 2023).

Nevertheless, whilst lecturers might recognise these benefits of taking a multimodal and creative approach to self-reflective journalling, putting this into practice can be difficult. As Barton and Ryan (2014, p. 412) recognise, there needs to be

> a common understanding of the context in which it [reflection] takes place. Whether it is the teacher demonstrating reflective practice or a student reflecting on practice, this may be evidenced through a combination of modes or singular approaches. Acknowledging that time, space and place can also impact on the ways that reflective action takes place is also significant. This is particularly evident through the teaching and learning of specific-academic disciplines.

I now wish to delve deeper into the work of Cooper and Stevens (2006) in order to explore a range of creative approaches that expand the self-reflective journal into a multimodal and creative space. I will then share further practical strategies with the use of a scenario, taking into account Barton and Ryan's (2014) concerns above, particularly around space and place. In their study, Cooper and Stevens (2006) explored the naturalistic journalling practices of four professionals in HE. Drawing on the findings from semi-structured interviews and excerpts from the participants' journals, Cooper and Stevens (2006) suggested that these participants used their journals in four ways (these are recognised in detail at the bottom of this page and at the top of p. 72). As mentioned earlier, whilst I am mindful that Cooper and Stevens' (2006) study focused on professionals within the HE sector, I believe their findings are applicable to students studying within this space, as well as lecturers wishing to take a more creative approach to the use of self-reflective journals within their units/teaching, either as self-development tools or as part of formative/ summative assessment. Indeed, Cooper and Stevens (2006, p. 364) actively encourage their work to be built on and revisited, stating that:

> These findings may also have important implications for educators who re- quire reflective journals in the classroom. Classroom practices should mimic the methods these naturalistic journal keepers have found to be most use- ful, in order to mitigate the danger that students will see their assigned journals as meaningless busy work.

Drawing on the points above, it is my intention to use Table 4.1 to show that a range of creative, 'naturalistic' (Cooper & Stevens, 2006, p. 364) strategies (which consider students' whole lives and resemble activities they might do outside of their academic studies) can be easily implemented into the HE class- room so that self-reflective journals become enjoyable and meaningful for stu- dents, rather than 'meaningless busy work' (Cooper & Stevens, 2006, p. 364).

Cooper and Stevens (2006, p. 350) found that participants used their jour- nals in four ways to support 'the process of meaning-making':

1 *'Conversation.* These academic professionals are holding conversations with themselves about their work and their lives.
2 *Organization.* By being organized and having many things in this one place, they are coping with the complex external demands of their jobs, the "plates in the air" that must all be kept from falling.
3 *Individualized strategies.* By developing a set of journal-keeping strategies that fit their own needs and expectations, journal-keepers are coping with the complex mental demands of their work in uniquely individual ways, which vary according to their personality and experience[,] and which fur- ther affirm their work and perspective.

Table 4.1 Creative approaches to self-reflective journals (using activities and adapted examples from Kelly, 2023)

Focus area	Creative approaches	Purpose
Conversation	*Storyboarding:* Students could script a conversation between themselves and somebody else using visuals (including photographs or magazine cuttings) and writing. This conversation could be on a particular event, situation, and/ or learning opportunity. For digital journals, students could use a programme such as Microsoft PowerPoint to create their storyboard.	This task allows students to explore different perspectives, which promote deeper insights into their own learning.
	Audio-recording: Using a phone or another recording device, students could record a conversation with themselves and then play it back. This conversation could be on a particular topic, seminar, lecture, or it might be a general reflection on the student's day and/or week. This activity would be the same for those completing a physical or digital journal.	Through conversing with themselves verbally, students might reveal something that would not come through via the written word. Students can then consider the key insights from their conversation and explore how they might use them to move forward, personally and academically.
	Letter from/to your future self: Students could write a letter from/ to their future self and use it to help their learning in the present. This might be linked to the concept of success and what success means to them, individually. A macro-approach to success could be taken, e.g., the entirety of their university degree, or a micro one, e.g., a particular module/unit. For digital journals, this letter could be typed and sent to themselves via email.	This activity helps students to consider where they want their academic journey to go. Focusing on the destination first helps students to reflect on the journey in more detail and the various steps they need to take; this links to the idea of growth goals, as detailed earlier.

(Continued)

Table 4.1 (Continued)

Focus area	Creative approaches	Purpose
Organisation	*'Ta-Dah' list*: Encourage students to create a daily and/or weekly 'Ta-Dah' list where they celebrate managing the multiple demands on their time. A 'Ta-Dah' list could also focus on learning within a particular unit/module of study. These lists could be handwritten or typed, or they could use drawings (one per 'Ta-Dah'), or an audio-recording. For digital journals, students might like to use a programme where they can use text, drawings and images; it might also include hyperlinks.	Students could build up their 'Ta-Dah' lists across their university degree in order to see just how well they are doing and how they are meeting their growth goals. This will help with engagement and motivation because students can visibly see the incremental steps they are taking.
	Daily or weekly review: Ask students to reflect on a WWW (What Went Well) and EBI (Even Better If) from their lecture, seminar, and/or week. Students could capture these WWWs and EBIs in a variety of different ways by using a range of materials. For example, they might use a series of drawings or they might choose to use photographs. One colour could be used for the WWWs and another colour could be used for the EBIs. For digital journals, students might have an ongoing document – such as in a word processing package – where they can simply add their weekly/daily reviews; this would also enable the student to clearly see their entries and to reflect on them.	The purpose of this activity is for students to continue with the WWWs and make changes around the EBIs in order to support them moving forward. This might be a springboard into a conversation around upcoming assessments and how to prepare for them. For example, a student might take a WWW around meeting a friend for coffee into the following week because they noticed the positive impact this connection had on their mood, motivation, and engagement.
	24-hour check-in: Ask students to give a breakdown of the past 24 hours. A student might choose to list this information or they could draw a clock and divide it up into 24 segments; each segment could then be populated using different colours, symbols, words, and/or images. Students might consider how many hours they have spent on their academic studies (including attending lectures and seminars), socialising with friends/family, paid work, sleep, rest, and movement. For digital journals, students might like to use a programme such as Microsoft Excel, which would enable them to easily divide up their day; one cell could equate to one hour and they could be colour-coded accordingly.	The purpose of this activity is for students to reflect on how they are spending their time and where changes need to be made so they can flourish, both academically and personally. For example, a student might notice that movement is missing from their day, so they plan and factor this in, which will make them more productive and have a positive impact on their wellbeing. This activity can also be used to reflect on whether or not students are 'spending' their time in a way that aligns with their personalised version of success and helps them to fulfil their growth goals.

(Continued)

Table 4.1 (Continued)

Focus area	Creative approaches	Purpose
Individualised strategies	*Scrapbooking:* Students could be invited to use a range of physical and/or digital materials to represent themselves and the various segments of their lives. This could be taken further by inviting students to create an entry representing their approach to learning and what they hope to get from the course/unit, as well as previous experiences of academic study. For digital journals, students might also include hyperlinks and citations.	This can be a useful way for lecturers to get to know their students and their needs, as well as an opportunity for students to get to know each other. Furthermore, it offers students the chance to harness what they know about themselves, including their interests and approaches to learning, which can then inform their future studies so that they get the most out of their HE experience.
	Goal for the day/seminar/lecture: At the start of a session, ask students to use their self-reflective journals to set a goal for the day, seminar, and/ or lecture – students can then reflect on whether they met this goal at the end. This goal could be written down, typed, or represented visually, including the use of photographs. For digital journals, students might like to type their goal, use a photograph, or audio-record it.	This approach enables students to go into the seminar/lecture/day intentionally and to take ownership of it. For example, if a goal for the day is to contribute to a whole-class discussion, then this can be at the forefront of their mind when they enter the session. This experience can then become one of their WWWs or an item on their 'Ta-Dah' list.
	Vision board: Ask students to use a range of images and words to create a vision board of the person they would like to be in the future; this might include their career aspirations, as well as personal targets, such as running a marathon. Vision boards can be for short-, medium-, and long-term goals, so an alternative might be to create a vision board for a unit of study or the first year of their degree. For digital journals, students might like to use a visual discovery engine such as *Pinterest* to create their vision board. This could include text, photographs, audio-recordings, hyperlinks, and citations.	This activity offers students a chance to see the bigger picture and reflect on where they want to be in the future; for example, in a particular career. Having this knowledge boosts engagement and motivation because students have a visual representation of what they want to achieve (in its broadest sense). This insight offers students an internal 'compass' for some of the other activities listed in Table 4.1, which they can draw upon in their entries.

(Continued)

Table 4.1 (Continued)

Focus area	Creative approaches	Purpose
Review and reflection	*Summarise a lecture/seminar in one line: What is the student's 'key takeaway'?* This could be recorded using writing, a photograph, a drawing, or an audio-recording. These suggestions would also work for those students keeping a digital journal.	This activity gives students a chance to capture their learning and use it to move forward, perhaps as a revision tool.
	Sketch-noting: Review learning across a week and/or unit using a range of images, words, and materials (including recycled paper, different coloured pens, and magazine cuttings). For digital journals, students could combine photographs and images with text.	This suggestion gives students a chance to step-back and consider different aspects of their learning and to make connections between them. Using this approach might result in new and transformative connections, which can then lead to further insight when completing some of the other activities described in Table 4.1.
	Emoji tracker: Encourage students to use/draw an emoji to represent every session of a module/unit and/or their day. If students find it difficult to choose an emoji that resonates with how they are feeling, then encourage them to create their own. It might be that they choose a palette of 5–10 emojis across the emotion range. For digital journals, students could choose 5–10 emojis online and then, on a private social media account, copy and paste the appropriate emoji for the session.	This activity allows students to get a bigger picture of their learning: *are particular emojis being repeated? If so, why? If this is an emoji with negative connotations, then what might they do to change it? If there are emojis with positive associations, then what can they do to keep this going?*

4 *Review and reflection*. By reviewing and rereading what they have written, these professionals are coping with multiple roles, that of teaching, research and administration, often switching between these with little time or preparation. This function is metacognitive in nature, providing time to see the larger picture, and to reflect on overall career or organizational direction' (p. 360, original emphasis).

It is my intention to consider each one of the four ways in turn, as shown in Table 4.1. It is crucial to reiterate that, rather than adapting or analysing Cooper and Stevens' (2006) findings, I will, instead, be using them to show how HE lecturers might support their students to develop their self-reflective journalling practice so that it not only becomes a piece of 'art' (p. 359), but also one that 'allow[s] for a more metacognitive view of their lives' (Cooper & Stevens, 2006, p. 362). One significant addition to Cooper and Stevens' (2006) argument is that whilst their study focused on the benefits of professional/work-related journals, I will show that their findings can also be applied to journals drawing on the personal aspects of life.

Now that readers have a suite of creative approaches to expand self-reflective journals as a format, I would like to share a scenario on how an HE lecturer might implement some of the above suggestions into a taught session.

Scenario 4.1

A lecturer teaching students on an ITT course decides to incorporate some of the ideas shared in Table 4.1 into a taught session welcoming student teachers back to university. This is the first university session following their initial school placement and is two hours in length. The purpose of the session is to encourage student teachers to reflect on their first placement, and to consider how they will use this experience to inform the next one. With the busyness of school life, this might be the first chance student teachers have to reflect on their experiences and development as teachers. The two-hour session is structured in the following way:

- *30 minutes:* As student teachers enter the room, they are invited to use the storyboarding activity to capture their placement in six images and captions. The lecturer will live-model this activity and will reassure student teachers that they are not being 'judged' on their artwork. The storyboarding template will be distributed as a physical resource to save time, but student teachers could complete the activity digitally, perhaps using a programme such as Microsoft PowerPoint.

- *15 minutes:* At the end of the task, student teachers will be encouraged to walk around the room and look at/learn from each other's storyboards as part of a 'gallery' activity.
- *45 minutes:* The main task of the session is to create a vision board in response to the question '*What do you want your next placement to consist of?*' Student teachers can use their self-reflective journals from the course, as well as their storyboards from the first activity, as starting points, but additional prompt questions will be shared by the lecturer; these include the following:

a *What do you want to take forward from your first placement?* and
b *What do you want to do differently?*

   The lecturer will encourage student teachers to consider all aspects of their placement, including teaching, pastoral support, getting involved in the wider life of the school, as well as life outside of school. The latter will encourage student teachers to use their self-reflective journal as a wellbeing tool. The vision boards can be created physically or digitally. A variety of materials will be available for students to use – including different types of paper and pens – but student teachers might prefer to use materials they have brought in from home.

- *10 minutes:* Student teachers will be encouraged to share their vision board with another person, talking through each aspect.
- *5 minutes:* Student teachers will be asked to summarise the session in one line, focusing, in particular, on their 'key takeaway'. This might be something connected to their vision board that they want to take into the future, or it might be a reflection from their first placement that came to light in the storyboard activity. This summary could be written by hand in a physical journal or typed for those student teachers keeping a digital journal.

Concluding comments

This chapter has set out to consider how self-reflective journals enable students to develop their metacognitive strategies, creative skillset, and personalised version of success, as well as exploring the self-reflective journal as a multimodal and creative space. By drawing on the work of Cooper and Stevens (2006), and exploring it through a creative and multimodal lens, I hope this chapter has shown the value of revisiting earlier studies and their findings, and the importance of sharing them with a new audience. Indeed, by paying close attention to Cooper and Stevens' (2006) study, this chapter has highlighted some of the many benefits of students keeping a self-reflective journal, including its use as a wellbeing tool. My intention with writing this chapter was to share a range of practical, creative, and multimodal strategies in order to encourage lecturers – and students – to continue reimagining the self-reflective journal within the context of HE.

Suggested further reading

CASEL (2020). *SEL Reflection Prompts*. CASEL. [Online]. https://casel.s3.us-east-2. amazonaws.com/SEL-Reflection-Prompts.pdf

Kelly, L. (2021). Playing with the diary: How crafting a multimodal and sensory diary can have a positive impact on teacher wellbeing. *Reflective Practice*, 23(1), 1–16. https://doi.org/10.1080/14623943.2021.1973986

Kirkman, P., & Brownhill, S. (2020). Refining professional knowledge as a creative practice: Towards a framework for self-reflective shapes and a novel approach to reflection. *Reflective Practice*, 20(1), 94–109. https://doi.org/10.1080/14623943. 2020.1712195

References

Alt, D., & Raichel, N. (2020). Reflective journaling and metacognitive awareness: Insights from a longitudinal study in higher education. *Reflective Practice*, 21(2), 145–158. https://doi.org/10.1080/14623943.2020.1716708

Barton, G., & Ryan, M. (2014). Multimodal approaches to reflective teaching and assessment in higher education. *Higher Education Research & Development*, 33(3), 409–424. https://doi.org/10.1080/07294360.2013.841650

Botelho, N. (2021). Reflection in motion: An embodied approach to reflection on practice. *Reflective Practice*, 22(2), 147–158. https://doi.org/10.1080/14623943. 2020.1860926

Brownhill, S. (2022). Asking key questions of self-reflection. *Reflective Practice*, 23(1), 57–67. https://doi.org/10.1080/14623943.2021.1976628

Cooper, J. E., & Stevens, D. D. (2006). Journal-keeping and academic work: Four cases of higher education professionals. *Reflective Practice*, 7(3), 349–366. https:// doi.org/10.1080/14623940600837566

Draissi, Z., Zhang, B., & Zhan Yong, Q. (2021). Reflective journals: Enhancing doctoral students' engagement. *Reflective Practice*, 22(3), 381–399. https://doi.org/10. 1080/14623943.2021.1893166

Eather, N., Myrto, M. F., Sharp, H., & Parkes, R. (2022). Programmes targeting student retention/success and satisfaction/experience in higher education: A systematic review. *Journal of Higher Education Policy and Management*, 44(3), 223–239. https://doi.org/10.1080/1360080X.2021.2021600

Ghanizadeh, A. (2017). The interplay between reflective thinking, critical thinking, self-monitoring, and academic achievement in higher education. *Higher Education*, 74(1), 101–114. https://doi.org/10.1007/s10734-016-0031-y

Ghaye, T. (2011). *Teaching and learning through reflective practice: A practical guide for positive action* (2nd ed.). Routledge.

Kelly, L. (2023). *Reimagining the diary: Reflective practice as a positive tool for educator wellbeing*. John Catt Educational Ltd.

Kress, G. (1997). *Before Writing: Rethinking the paths to literacy*. Taylor & Francis.

Lew, D. N. M., & Schmidt, H. G. (2011). Writing to learn: Can reflection journals be used to promote self-reflection and learning? *Higher Education Research & Development*, 30(4), 519–532. https://doi.org/10.1080/07294360.2010.512627

McCrindle, A. R., & Christensen, C. A. (1995). The impact of learning journals on metacognitive and cognitive processes and learning performance. *Learning and Instruction*, 5(2), 167–185. https://doi.org/10.1016/0959-4752(95)00010-Z

Moffatt, A., Barton, G., & Ryan, M. (2016). Multimodal reflection for creative facilitators: An approach to improving self-care. *Reflective Practice*, 17(6), 762–778. https://doi.org/10.1080/14623943.2016.1220935

Or, P. (2018). Reflective journal writing of undergraduate students enrolled in sex education in Hong Kong. *Reflective Practice*, 19(5), 599–608. https://doi.org/10.1080/14623943.2018.1538950

Smith, L. (2023). *Creativity in the English curriculum: Historical perspectives and future directions*. Routledge.

Thomas, L., Kift, S., & Shah, M. (2021). Student retention and success in higher education. In M. Shah (Ed.), *Student retention and success in higher education: Institutional change for the 21st century* (pp. 1–16). Palgrave Macmillan.

Travers, C. J., Morisano, D., & Locke, E. A. (2015). Self-reflection, growth goals, and academic outcomes: A qualitative study. *British Journal of Educational Psychology*, 85(2), 224–241. https://doi.org/10.1111/bjep.12059

Part II

Engaging groups

Chapter 5

Student teachers

Creativity in initial teacher education

Nicola Warren-Lee

Introduction

Over the last ten years, there have been significant changes in university-led secondary teacher education in England in relation to what student teachers are expected to learn and how they are expected to learn it. These changes are linked to school-based curriculum changes for 11–18 year olds who have been tasked with learning knowledge deemed to be 'the best that has been thought and said' (Arnold, 1869, p. 56), a phrase revived by various ministers at the Department for Education (DfE) in England since the early 2010s. This focus on knowledge has continued, and in the words of the Minister of State for School Standards, Nick Gibb (DfE and Gibb, 2021), 'teachers must mak[e] sure that every child is taught the same knowledge' and 'transmission of rich subject knowledge should be the priority for schools'. Of interest to this chapter is the choice of the word 'transmission'. This is a word which conjures up a traditional teaching style of pupils sat in rows, listening intently, writing furiously and copiously – a style which positions pupils as absorbing the 'facts' through memorisation and recall. Student teachers and the training courses they follow have been affected by the 'knowledge turn' (Lambert, 2011, p. 245) and the associated pedagogies of instruction that have followed, leading Initial Teacher Education (ITE) to become diminished, partial, and technicist (Hordern & Brooks, 2023). Indeed, it has been stated recently that 'England now has the most tightly regulated and centrally controlled system of ITE anywhere in the world' (Childs & Ellis, 2023, p. 2). This tight control has led teacher educators to question the purpose of their work and the methods by which their students (student teachers) learn (Steadman, 2024; Warren-Lee et al., 2024).

This chapter initially aims to:

- Consider how university-led ITE can respond to a prescription of rote learning and memorisation (for student teachers as well as school pupils), with a focus on why creativity in learning is important for adult learners (who are training to teach) and, as a result, the pupils they teach.

DOI: 10.4324/9781032633534-8

The chapter opens with a recognition of the importance of beliefs about the nature of learning in influencing teaching methods, followed by an outline of recent changes to the curriculum for student teachers. It then critiques these changes for the pedagogical approaches they engender, reliant as they are on a linear, often didactic, teacher-as-expert style. The chapter also aims to:

- Offer a visionary outline (in the sense of being ambitious rather than grandiose) of how creativity can support learning and teaching as a student teacher, culminating in illustrated descriptions of two approaches to learning and teaching on a Post Graduate Certificate in Education (PGCE) Secondary course.

Importantly, there are three levels of educator/learner being referred to throughout this chapter:

1 University-based teacher educators who are responsible for designing and enacting ITE curricula,
2 Student teachers involved in both learning and teaching in university and school settings, and
3 School pupils aged 11–18.

All people involved throughout the levels are connected in different ways, each working together in their respective learning environments. Importantly, what happens at any one level (from levels 1 to 3) will influence what happens across the other two.

The chapter begins with an exploratory understanding of how learning happens as being pivotal in teaching design.

Understanding how learning happens as being pivotal in teaching design

The importance of understanding how learners learn cannot be understated (Muijs, 2012). Research and associated publications exist on a wide variety of interpretations and understandings about learning; these include:

- the importance of the social element to learning (Vygotsky, 1978),
- the relevance of the age of the learner, the stages of cognitive growth, and prior learning (Piaget, 1978),
- the need for experiential investigation (Dewey, 1919),
- individuals' self-regulation and needs (Zimmerman, 2008), and
- the need for engagement and motivation (Deci & Ryan, 2000; Kenrick et al., 2010).

In seeking the best ways of engendering learning in any setting, be they Higher Education institutions (HEIs) or schools, knowing how to create the conditions for learning relies upon at least two things:

1 A clear vision or understanding of what is to be learned, and
2 Appropriate methods to facilitate new thinking.

The latter of the two points above opens a vast array of educational debates. Bruner (1996), e.g., wrote about folk pedagogies, which, crudely defined, are the personal beliefs educators have about how others' minds work, which lead to the ways in which teaching is enacted. As originally described:

Teaching, in a word, is inevitably based on notions about the nature of the learner's mind. Beliefs and assumptions about teaching, whether in a school or in any other context, are a direct reflection of the beliefs and assumptions the teacher holds about the learner.

(Bruner, 1996, pp. 5–6)

Relating Bruner's folk pedagogies to teacher education accounts for how teacher educators hold their own ideas about the ways student teachers will engage in the learning opportunities offered. These ideas (on how learning will take place) influence the nature of the learning opportunities offered. Elucidating this, Bruner (1996, p. 8) suggests that '[d]ifferent approaches to learning and different forms of instruction – from imitation, to instruction, to discovery, to collaboration – reflect differing beliefs and assumptions about the learner – from actor, to knower, to private experiencer, to collaborative thinker'.

Building on the importance of teachers' beliefs and assumptions about how learners learn, it becomes apparent that in any attempt to include creative pedagogies in teacher education courses (with the aim of engendering similar creativity in schools), teacher educators must look at their own existing beliefs and assumptions about student teacher learning.

Transmission teaching and learning (T&L)

In addition to teacher educators' personal pedagogical beliefs about how student teachers learn, there are (at any given time) ideologies on teaching and learning (T&L) as part of a hegemonic philosophy of education. As such, there are prevalent ideas from which will influence T&L experiences – certain educational ideas and approaches become popular and are given credence according to current thinking on 'what works'. Whatever contemporary educational thinking includes will directly influence the T&L experiences student teachers will become familiar with. Expressed more simply, whatever the general and most popular ideas on 'best practice' in T&L are at the time, these will have an impact on the day-to-day activities student teachers are involved in, both as learners and teachers.

Contemporary educational thinking changes over time, and in the 18th-century Rousseau (2015, p. 73) wrote, 'Let [a child] know nothing because you have told him (sic), but because he has learnt it for himself. If ever you substitute authority for reason [they] will cease to reason, [becoming] a mere plaything of other people's thoughts'. One might think that this is uncontroversial as an approach to education today; however, reflecting upon Gibb's (DfE and Gibb, 2021) words on transmission (see p. 79), teaching children the same knowledge – including the dominance of references to recall, memorisation, transmission, and experts (see chapter introduction) – one could be forgiven for asking if we need to reassert Rousseau's calls for developing enquiring young minds.

Shifting forwards, over two centuries later, there has been a return to knowledge in the English education system, leading to 'knowledge-rich' curricula often dependent upon school students listening to expert teachers who are encouraged to use a more 'traditional' pedagogy, such as memory retrieval tasks, exposition, and deliberative practice. This 'knowledge turn' (Lambert, 2011, p. 245) has impacted upon how student teachers are experiencing the practicum of their ITE courses and, subsequently, poses challenges for teacher education partnerships in Higher Education (Warren-Lee et al., 2024). Through the movement towards more didactic, expert-novice styles in secondary education, the place of learning through exploration and creativity has suffered. This is exemplified in a 40% decline in pupil uptake for creative subjects at secondary GCSE level between 2010 and 2022 (Joint Council for Qualifications, 2024).

Since the introduction of 'knowledge-rich' curricula and associated pedagogies of instruction, student teachers are increasingly likely to observe colleagues in school settings who are using teaching methods of direct instruction, veering away from enquiry-based, exploratory, and creative learning. This is despite school teachers advocating for creative, active, and enquiry-rich T&L (Perryman & Calvert, 2020). School curricula sit within an education system which has a clear accountability agenda: an agenda which 'stifles creativity' (Perryman & Calvert, 2020, p. 16), and this is particularly concerning when 35% of teachers in a survey of over 1000 said they went in to teaching 'to be creative' (Perryman & Calvert, 2020, p. 11). Accountable as they are, headteachers are influenced by government notions of high-quality teaching. These notions are currently promoted by certain 'traditionalist educators who oppose anything that they regard as progressive education', thus headteachers 'may feel under considerable pressure to steer their staff in the direction of traditional' approaches to teaching (Davis, 2018, p. 135). Indeed, a House of Lords' Education Committee (House of Lords, 2023) which gathered information from pupils, teachers, and academics, reported on the burdensome exam system, an over reliance on rote learning, and stated an urgent need for creativity, including a richer, more varied school experience for school pupils.

Creativity in the ITE curriculum

University-based ITE courses (being as they are situated within a different governance and accountability system) are arguably less reactive to government notions of quality teaching and have greater ability to withstand the 'faddish' fluctuations facing schooling (Sodha, 2023). However, for student teachers moving between the learning sites of university and school, divergent accounts of how T&L can be enacted can result in conflicting situations where theoretical guidance does not appear to align with school priorities and practices. Conflicts between theoretical understandings of how young people learn (e.g., those discussed at the university level) and the teachers' experiences (e.g., at school) can negatively affect student teacher progress (Alverman & Hayes, 1989) unless they are carefully supported, e.g., through practical theorising (see Firth & Warren-Lee, 2022). On a challenging full-time master's level course, sources of dissonance and confusion are not helpful, and, whilst university-led ITE courses do not always seek to reflect and legitimise the pedagogical beliefs and practices of partnered schools, there is a logical need for teacher preparation programmes to train teachers for the profession they are entering into. This creates difficult decision-making for teacher educators in Higher Education as they negotiate both secondary school curricula and their own ITE curricula (which must work in some alignment with each other). In addition to this tension, many teacher educators – those who would like to offer ITE courses which develop creative, agentic, intellectual, and progressive secondary school teachers – are also obliged to follow a government-prescribed ITE curriculum [the *ITT Core Content Framework*; DfE, 2019], which does not outwardly promote these ideals (Hordern & Brooks, 2023; Turvey, 2024).

A creative ITE curriculum can mean different things to different people (Kind & Kind, 2007), and creativity itself has been acknowledged as having a vast number of interpretations (Lucas, 2016), often being seen as complex and multi-faceted (Treffinger et al., 2002). These factors make the task of implementing creative T&L approaches in teacher education variable or even idiosyncratic. Nevertheless, the importance of student teachers learning about creativity *through* creative approaches has been highlighted by Swanzy-Impraim et al. (2022), so that they [student teachers] are ready to teach school pupils in similarly creative ways. Creative teacher education can challenge a narrowing of school pedagogy, which closes out opportunities for expressive, social, and inspirational forms of learning (Ball et al., 2011; Patston et al., 2018). An example of foregrounding creativity in teacher education can be seen in the work of Vally et al. (2019), where a course on creativity during an ITE programme enhanced student teacher understanding and efficacy in creativity, along with its application in school settings. This draws us to the importance of the role of teacher educators (e.g., those based in a university setting) in developing a programme of T&L which develops student teachers' creative thinking and skills and, at the same time, their capacity to do the same for the school pupils they are learning to teach (Lorencová et al., 2019).

Teacher educators can develop ambitiously creative opportunities for student teacher learning. Just as Smith (2023, p. 26) uncovered secondary school English teachers who 'manage to be creative in spite of the [c]urriculum', teacher educators can develop inspiring and imaginative conditions for learning even though the prescribed ITE curriculum does not explicitly advocate for this. In Smith's (2023) school example, one teacher expressed their vision of the classroom as 'an organic thing, like [...] a greenhouse or orangery in which the climatic conditions are such that things can spring to life and grow' (p. 111); this aligns with Hjorth et al.'s (2008) work on the importance of developing a playful, encouraging environment for inspiration to occur. Such a vision is illustrative of the pivotal role teachers and teacher educators have in the development of pupil and student teacher creativity, especially during periods which promote top-down, knowledge reproduction.

Creative teacher learning

Despite what the current teacher education curriculum in England offers, learning to teach does not happen through simplistic rehearsal and application of generalised ideas on 'best evidence' (Lofthouse, 2024). University-based teacher education can offer student teachers a space to critically examine dynamic, contested, and intellectually challenging ideas, especially those which are said to be essential for teaching (UCET, 2020). If school education is valued for nurturing ingenuity and innovation, then engagement in dynamic, innovative, and intellectual challenge for student teachers is crucial; if this is not embraced, then 'we accept and recreate rather than transform and renew current schooling' (Vanassche et al., 2019, p. 485), stifling both critical and creative thinking.

Generating creative learning experiences, which can result in 'flow' states of mind (Csikszentmihalyi, 1997), encourage connections and new solutions, and can be a valuable addition to pedagogical variety in teacher education, creative pedagogical approaches have been shown to increase engagement in (and out of) classrooms (Davies et al., 2013), offering student teachers in university settings a chance to engage in and explore the methods and value of creative approaches to T&L. An ITE curriculum that includes opportunities to experiment with ideas, which can offer an engaging and creative experience, is more likely to result in school classrooms where pupils will be taught in creative and engaging ways (Nygaard et al., 2010).

The Organisation for Economic Co-operation and Development (OECD) agrees on the value of developing creativity within education internationally,

Table 5.1 The OECD rubric on creativity and critical thinking (Vincent-Lancrin et al., 2019)

	Creativity *Coming up with new ideas and solutions*	Critical thinking *Questioning and evaluating ideas and solutions*
Inquiring	Make connections to other concepts and knowledge from the same or from other disciplines.	Identify and question assumptions and generally accepted ideas or practices.
Imagining	Generate and play with unusual and radical ideas.	Consider several perspectives on a problem based on different assumptions.
Doing	Produce, perform, or envision a meaningful output that is personally novel.	Explain both strengths and limitations of a product, a solution, or a theory justified on logical, ethical, or aesthetic criteria.
Reflecting	Reflect on the novelty of the solution and of its possible consequences.	Reflect on the chosen solution/ position relative to possible alternatives.

producing a series of resources communicating the importance of developing teachers' understanding and skills in this area (readers are encouraged to visit https://tinyurl.com/y5py66da). The OECD has also developed a rubric to support the teaching, learning, and assessment of creativity (Vincent-Lancrin et al., 2019), which can offer teacher educators a way to think about designing creative T&L approaches across four domains: *Inquiring, Imagining, Doing*, and *Reflecting*. Table 5.1 shows a simplified version of the rubric for developing students' creativity and critical thinking (viewed by the OECD as interlinking and complimentary). This rubric is not exhaustive, but it can offer ideas to support teacher educators in planning for learning about teaching.

In the next couple of sections, two T&L examples build upon several aspects of the creativity and critical thinking rubric presented above.

Example 1: Split-Screen Dramatisation

For student teachers, being seen as the 'real thing' (van Velzen et al., 2010) is a major concern in the early stages of assimilating into a school environment. This includes working out how to develop knowledge of teaching into the skills of enactment (Janssen et al., 2015). Student teachers need access to pedagogical reasoning from the very start of their teacher education (Loughran et al., 2016) in order to develop the sophisticated process of decision-making, which will tie together T&L in productive ways.

Teacher education courses have developed ways to unveil the pedagogical reasoning of experienced teachers, which has been recognised as notoriously difficult to achieve (Eraut, 2000). Using a stimulated recall method, Ethel and McMeniman (2000) worked with student teachers to unpack the thinking of experienced teachers in action. The method aimed to allow access to the minds of experienced teachers, not just the observable behaviours; this resulted in one student teacher commenting:

> *I have seen heaps of teachers teach, but I don't think I've seen anyone reflect on their own teaching like you. This is the first time I have been able to sort of get inside a teacher's head and get a glimpse of all the things [they] thought about which influenced what we were seeing as [their] teaching.*

(p. 93)

Drawing on the idea of enabling access to pedagogical reasoning, the method of split-screen dramatisation can offer student teachers an opportunity to practice their ideas for teaching whilst also sharing their intentions for learning, illuminating the concept that T&L are in close relationship with one another.

Split-screen dramatisation draws upon Claxton's (2007) description of school teachers' work as having one 'screen' inside their heads where they think about how to help pupils learn the content; on the other 'screen' (at the same time), they think about how to help pupils develop their learning capacities, e.g., creative thinking. This approach evidently works towards multiple goals at the same time, something which has been attributed to the work of teachers on a number of occasions (Hammerness et al., 2005; Kennedy, 2010; Kriewaldt & Turnidge, 2013). The example offered below is different to Claxton's (2007) in the following ways:

- Firstly, the student teachers' learning is the main goal within the split-screen dramatisation (not school pupils).
- Secondly, the two 'screens' referred to are not exactly as Claxton (2007) describes. The first 'screen' is the thinking that takes place to describe, explain, order, and elicit the content of the lesson (here, on Russia); the second 'screen' is the thinking that takes place to explain and justify the decisions informing the enactment of the dramatised 'lesson'.

Geography student teachers initially take part in a simulated school lesson where the teacher educator takes on the part of the 'teacher' and the student teachers are the 'pupils'. During the 'lesson', the intended learning outcomes are shared (these are related to life and overcoming challenges in Oymyakon, Russia); a starter episode, including the use of photos (e.g., a man with frozen eyelashes, a snowy landscape, and noodles/a cracked egg, each of which is frozen in mid-air) to stimulate partner talk via what, where, when, who, and why question stems, is followed by an activity to establish how to describe the location of Oymyakon using the acronym CLOCC (continent, lines of latitude, oceans and seas, country, compass rose).

After this, a climate graph is introduced to form an understanding of fluctuations in temperature and precipitation over time with the use of the acronym TEA (trend, example, anomaly). Finally, a video excerpt showing how inhabitants in Oymyakon live in extreme conditions facilitates an extended written/verbal activity where 'pupils' pull together the different sources of information and imagine they are either an inhabitant talking to a journalist on what life is like in Oymyakon, or they are the journalist asking questions and leading an interview.

As the student teachers participate in the 'lesson', the facilitating teacher educator shows, as transparently as possible, the nature of split-screen thinking – the pedagogical reasoning for the decisions, choices, and actions taken, including resources, questions, and words chosen. For example:

- *Why would it be useful to show interesting imagery at the start of a lesson?*
  To establish what pupils already think and know, to gather the pupils' questions, and to stimulate a sense of intrigue.
- *Why would it be useful to share an acronym for describing location?*
  To give younger/less abled pupils an idea of expected items to be included and to offer an organised approach.
- *Why would it be useful to give a choice of extended tasks to describe and explain what life is like in Oymyakon?*
  To allow pupils to have some ownership over their work, to adapt to the strengths and needs within the class, and to promote a variety of outputs for sharing across the classroom.

Fundamentally, the aim of split-screen dramatisation is for student teachers to see beyond the activity of words and tasks, focussing more on the intended learning outcomes desired through the activity.

Having participated in the Oymyakon 'lesson', the student teachers are then encouraged to develop their own version of a split-screen lesson in pairs, based on a chosen geographical theme which can be used as the basis for a lesson episode. The student teachers are encouraged to make their pedagogical choices explicit and to teach their peers: one teaches (showing the first thinking 'screen') and the other narrates (showing the second 'screen' of pedagogical reasoning). A suggested sequence for a split-screen dramatisation is shown below, the sequence resonating somewhat with that which was experienced by the geography student teachers (as per page 86):

1 Teacher educator models the practice by delivering an episode of teaching to student teachers (who take part as school pupils) and, at the same time,

talks through the pedagogical reasoning for the chosen content/activity/procedure. This can be supported, e.g., through slides that offer pedagogical annotations in different colours.

2   Student teachers work in pairs to develop a lesson sequence on their chosen subject theme/concept. As part of the planning (e.g., what intended learning objectives, what ideas to include, what to present, which resources/activities to include, what order to do things in), student teachers consider and write down the reasons for why they have made the choices they have, indicating how their teaching is aimed at building learning.

3   Student teachers teach some/all of their planned lesson sequence to their peer group, sharing at strategic moments their reasoning. Strategic moments can include transition points, particular instructions or language used, key resources, and questions asked. These moments can offer good examples for sharing pedagogical reasoning. There should be a balance between how much of 'screen one' and 'screen two' are presented and discussed to avoid overloading the rest of the peer group.

Example 2: Craftivism

Using expressive forms of creation and crafting as tools for forms of activism – often known as *craftivism* – has a long history and connection with a range of social issues. Craftivism can take many forms and include digital multimedia, mixed media, textiles, or other arts and crafts materials. Coined by Betsy Greer in 2003, craftivism encourages gentle protest and positive change and has been used in educational settings to alter conventional stand-and-deliver methods. Previous research has shown how craftivist activities have supported students' presence, voice, and agency in educational environments, offering ways to build creative spaces for important conversations regarding many complex and potentially frightening issues, such as conflict and climate change (Rowsell & Shillitoe, 2019).

Student teachers across all subject areas are becoming more involved in the teaching of climate change education (CCE), whether in their own subject disciplines, through Personal Social Health Education (PSHE) or interdisciplinary work across subjects, such as Geography and English departments working together on climate crisis poetry.[1] The development of a shared responsibility for CCE in schools has led to an increasing need for student teachers to learn not only what the issues surrounding climate change are, but also how the issues relate to their own subject discipline.

---

1   For an international example of interdisciplinary CCE work, see *We Are The Ocean*, an anthology of poems created by school children in the UK and the United Arab Emirates (Emirates Literature Foundation and University of Exeter, 2023).

Figure 5.1 A giant sea creature made from recycled materials during a climate craftivism workshop.

As both student teachers and pupils can find talking about climate change-related issues difficult and emotional (Ojala, 2015), using creative ways of building a safe and supportive space can help. One such way is craftivism. In the example below, student teachers from Geography, Music, and English were involved in workshops with pupils from local schools, building sea creatures from reclaimed and recycled waste (see Figures 5.1 and 5.2; both copyright of the author and are included in the chapter with their permission).

The sea creatures were then 'brought to life' and were interviewed about the changes to their environments brought on by the changing climate. These activities allowed the student teachers to engage with pupils on the concepts of and anxieties connected to climate change, including ocean acidification (caused by increased CO_2), habitat destruction, questions of blame, and ideas of local action. Whilst making the sea creatures, the student teachers were able to spend time talking with pupils at their crafting tables, developing an informal, conversational atmosphere. Student teachers (often new to the position of responsibility and authority) can struggle to build relationships and initiate positive conversations whilst keeping a focus on learning (Lindqvist et al., 2023). The craftivism approach reduced the intensity associated with more conventional teaching methods of exposition and requesting answers, which can place pressure on teacher-student interactions. Craftivism can be a

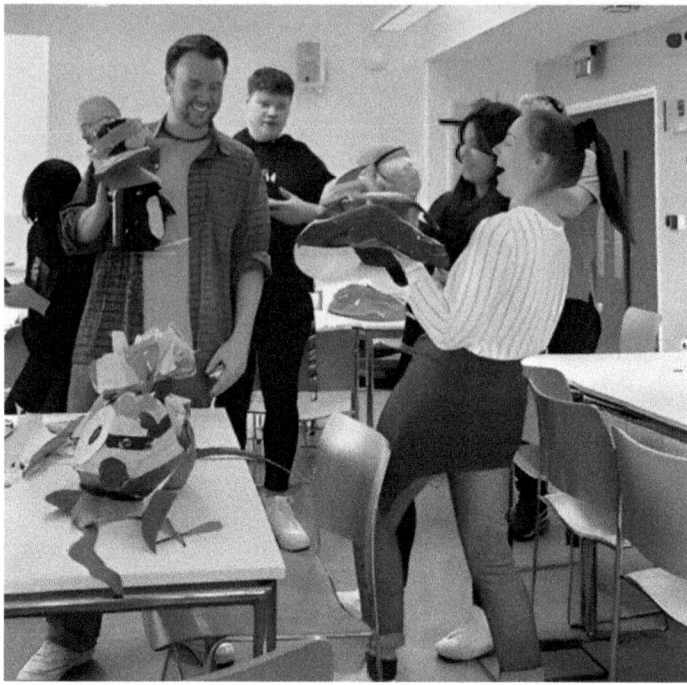

Figure 5.2 Student teachers taking part in a climate craftivism workshop.

T&L method to establish and build dialogue, enabling relationship building with young people in more informal ways. In craftivist workshops elsewhere, similar positive aspects have been noted, e.g., '[t]he quality of intense concentration achieved is experienced as pleasurable, as feelings of worry and self-consciousness fade away, and a sense of time becomes distorted' (Hackney & Setterington, 2022, p. 312).

Craftivism considerations

Three aspects of the craftivist approach emerged as important for T&L on the PGCE course:

1 Student teachers and pupils alike were put at ease through the craft-based, less hierarchical approach and gradually opened up to talk freely in the process of making and creating. All learners were engaged in a making process, and the less formal nature of the talk (i.e., different to a more commonly used direct question and answer format) stimulated a sharing of ideas, which included bringing out personal stories and feelings about climate change. Misconceptions – confusing plastics in the ocean with the

issue of climate change – emerged several times over different craftivism workshops. Student teachers were able to experiment and play with their own responses to pupils' ideas, which gave space for professional growth and reflection.

2 The craft outputs (the 'sea creatures') were used as agents to express the creators' views, i.e., student teachers and pupils were speaking on the creatures' behalf. From the student teachers' perspectives in particular, this strategy enabled more verbal communication between pupils and between student teachers and pupils, which may have otherwise been restricted due to the high-stakes environment for discussion that is often found in teaching spaces (Hodis & Hodis, 2012).

3 The student teachers discussed the practical considerations of utilising such an approach in their own classrooms. Time to set up the resources and to clear away was a concern. Full engagement in the activity, with all pupils taking part, was also recognised as potentially difficult to achieve. Some student teachers also raised a concern of having little time to gather and address misconceptions when working in such individually creative ways, although the quality of conversations held with individuals was said to be noticeably more meaningful.

Creative and critical thinking: reflecting on Examples 1 and 2

Reflecting back on the ideas offered in Table 5.1, split-screen dramatisation (Example 1) involves student teachers *imagining* a classroom setting, the ideas, and the activity which might occur. The dramatisation also involves *doing*, in that a lesson is rehearsed (e.g., with peers), whilst openly *reflecting* on the intended links between the *doing* and the pupil learning that was aimed for. Craftivism (Example 2) involves *doing*, in that there is something made or created, whilst at the same time there is scope for *imagining* (e.g., alternative futures) and *inquiring* (e.g., challenging assumptions). Both examples are set within the context of beginning geography teacher education and focus on the topics of (i) cold environments and (ii) climate change.

Concluding comments

To enable creative and inspiring pedagogies in school environments, these must feature in teacher education courses in university settings. Student teachers can be involved in creative pedagogies that help them understand and experience the value of different ways of T&L, supporting their reflective thinking, e.g., about folk pedagogies (Bruner, 1996), which may be underpinning their notions of how learners learn. Understanding and experiencing creativity during ITE can also build critical resilience towards future 'best practice' educational shifts where impoverished or narrow versions of educational experience may be promoted. Creativity can be achieved in different ways during ITE, and this chapter has provided two examples that show ways to actively engage student teachers in the *doing* and *thinking* of T&L, simultaneously encouraging talk as a means to connect with peers and pupils whilst uncovering the thinking that takes place.

Teacher education can be viewed as a creative journey and a process of *becoming* (Warren-Lee et al., 2024), one which is reflective, ethical, and involves constant renewal. To bring imagination and playfulness into the doing and thinking of T&L can provide fertile ground for navigating the inevitable changes and unknowns in the future of education. This is the kind of teacher education which seeks to 'embody and occasion a creative and, if necessary, subversive approach to meeting central demands' (Warren-Lee et al., 2024, p. 10).

Suggested further reading

Bostad, I. (2012). Existential education and the quest for a new humanism: How to create disturbances and deeper thinking in schools and universities? In L. Wikander, C. Gustafsson, & U. Riis (Eds.), *Enlightenment, creativity and education: Politics, politics, performances* (pp. 45–60). Springer.

Rowsell, J., & Shillitoe, M. (2019). The craftivists: Pushing for affective, materially informed pedagogy. *British Journal of Educational Technology, 50*(4), 1544–1559. https://doi.org/10.1111/bjet.12773

References

Alverman, D., & Hayes, D. (1989). Classroom discussion of content area reading assignments: An intervention study. *Reading Research Quarterly, 24*(3), 305–335. https://doi.org/10.2307/747772

Arnold, M. (1869). *Culture and anarchy: An essay in political and social criticism.* Project Gutenberg.

Ball, S. J., Maguire, M., Braun, A., & Hoskins, K. (2011). Policy subjects and policy actors in schools: Some necessary but insufficient analyses. *Discourse: Studies in the Cultural Politics of Education, 32*(4), 611–624. https://doi.org/10.1080/01596306.2011.601564

Bruner, J. (1996). *The culture of education.* Harvard University Press.

Childs, A., & Ellis, V. (2023). Introduction: Constructing the teacher education crisis in England. In V. Ellis (Ed.), *Teacher education in crisis. The state, the market and universities in England* (pp. 1–26). Bloomsbury.

Claxton, G. (2007). Expanding young people's capacity to learn. *British Journal of Educational Studies, 55*(2), 115–134. https://doi.org/10.1111/j.1467-8527.2007.00369.x

Csikszentmihalyi, M. (1997). *Creativity, flow and the psychology of invention.* HarperPerennial.

Davies, D., Jindal-Snape, D., Collier, C., Digby, R., Hay, P, & Howe, A. (2013). Creative learning environments in education—A systematic literature review. *Thinking Skills and Creativity, 8*, 80–91. https://doi.org/10.1016/j.tsc.2012.07.004

Davis, A. (2018). Evidence-based approaches to education: Direct instruction, anyone? *Management in Education, 32*(3), 135–138. https://doi.org/10.1177/0892020618765421

Deci, E. L., & Ryan, R. M. (2000). The "What" and "Why" of goal pursuits: Human needs and the self-determination of behavior. *Psychological Inquiry*, *11*(4), 227–268. https://doi.org/10.1207/S15327965PLI1104_01

Department for Education (DfE). (2019, 1 November). *Initial teacher training (ITT): core content framework*. DfE. [Online]. https://www.gov.uk/government/publications/initial-teacher-training-itt-core-content-framework

Department for Education (DfE) and Gibb, N. (2019, July 21). *Speech: The importance of a knowledge-rich curriculum*. Gov.uk. [Online]. https://www.gov.uk/government/speeches/the-importance-of-a-knowledge-rich-curriculum

Dewey, J. (1919). Imagination and expression. *Teachers College Bulletin*, *10*(10), 7–15.

Emirates Literature Foundation and University of Exeter. (2023). *We are the ocean*. Emirates Literature Foundation Publishing LLC. [Online]. https://issuu.com/universityofexeter/docs/elf_we_are_the_ocean_2023_11_24

Eraut, M. (2000). Non-formal learning and tacit knowledge in professional work. *British Journal of Educational Psychology*, *70*(1), 113–136. https://doi.org/10.1348/000709900158001

Ethel, R. G., & McMeniman, M. M. (2000). Unlocking the knowledge in action of an expert practitioner. *Journal of Teacher Education*, *51*(2), 87–101. https://doi.org/10.1177/002248710005100203

Firth, R., & Warren-Lee, N. (2022). The use of assessment in sustaining student teachers' engagement in practical theorising to support professional learning. In K. Burn, T. Mutton, & I. Thompson (Eds.), *Practical theorising in teacher education* (pp. 160–178). Routledge.

Hackney, F., & Setterington, L. (2022). Crafting with a purpose, how the 'work' of the workshop makes, promotes and embodies well-being. *Journal of Applied Arts and Health*, *13*(3), 307–324. https://doi.org/10.1386/jaah_00113_1

Hammerness, K., Darling-Hammond, L., & Bransford, J. (2005). How teachers learn and develop. In L. Darling-Hammond & J. Bransford (Eds.), *Preparing teachers for a changing world: What teachers should learn and be able to do* (pp. 358–389). Jossey-Bass.

Hjorth, D., Jones, C., & Gartner, W. B. (2008). Recreating/Recontextualising entrepreneurship. *Scandinavian Journal of Management*, *24*(2), 81–84. https://doi.org/10.1016/j.scaman.2008.03.003

Hodis, G. M., & Hodis, F. A. (2012). Trends in communicative self-efficacy: A comparative analysis. *Basic Communication Course Annual*, *24*(Art.7), 40–80. https://ecommons.udayton.edu/bcca/vol24/iss1/7

Hordern, J., & Brooks, C. (2023). The core content framework and the 'new science' of educational research. *Oxford Review of Education*, *49*(6), 800–818. https://doi.org/10.1080/03054985.2023.2182768

House of Lords. (2023, 12 December). *Secondary education has moved in the wrong direction*. House of Lords Education for 11–16 Year Olds Committee. [Online]. https://ukparliament.shorthandstories.com/11-16-education-future-skills-lords-report/#group-section-A-restricted-programme-of-academic-learning-CA43dV9B3r

Janssen, F., Grossman, P., & Westbroek, H. (2015). Facilitating decomposition and recomposition in practice-based teacher-education: The power of modularity. *Teaching and Teacher Education*, *51*, 137–146. https://doi.org/10.1016/j.tate.2015.06.009

Joint Council for Qualifications (JCQ). (2024). *Examination results*. JCQ. [Online]. https://www.jcq.org.uk/examination-results

Kennedy, M. M. (2010). Knowledge and teaching. *Teachers and Teaching*, *8*(3), 355–370. https://doi.org/10.1080/135406002100000495

Kenrick, D. T., Griskevicius, V., Neuberg, S. L., & Schaller, M. (2010). Renovating the pyramid of needs: Contemporary extensions built upon ancient foundations.

Perspectives on Psychological Science, 5(3), 292–314. https://doi.org/10.1177/1745691610369469

Kind, P. M., & Kind, V. (2007). Creativity in science education: Perspectives and challenges for developing school science. *Studies in Science Education*, 43(1), 1–37. https://doi.org/10.1080/03057260708560225

Kriewaldt, J., & Turnidge, D. (2013). Conceptualising an approach to clinical reasoning in the education profession. *Australian Journal of Teacher Education*, 38(6), 103–115. https://doi.org/10.14221/ajte.2013v38n6.9

Lambert, D. (2011). Reviewing the case for geography, and the 'knowledge turn' in the English national curriculum. *The Curriculum Journal*, 22(2), 243–264. https://doi.org/10.1080/09585176.2011.574991

Lindqvist, H., Weurlander, M., Barman, L., Wernerson, A., & Thornberg, R. (2023). Work-based learning partnerships: mentor-teachers' perceptions of student teachers' challenges. *Educational Research*, 65(3), 392–407. https://doi.org/10.1080/00131881.2023.2234384

Lofthouse, R. (2024). Charting new territories in teacher education. In V. Ellis (Ed.), *Teacher education in crisis: The state, the market and the universities in England* (pp. 133–148). Bloomsbury.

Lorencová, H., Jarošová, E., Avgitidou, S., & Dimitriadou, C. (2019). Critical thinking practices in teacher education programmes: A systematic review. *Studies in Higher Education*, 44(5), 844–859. https://doi.org/10.1080/03075079.2019.1586331

Loughran, J., Keast, S., & Cooper, R. (2016). Pedagogical reasoning in teacher education. In: Loughran, J., & Hamilton, M. (Eds.), *International handbook of teacher education* (pp. 387–421). Springer. https://doi.org/10.1007/978-981-10-0366-0_10

Lucas, B. (2016). A five-dimensional model of creativity and its assessment in schools. *Applied Measurement in Education*, 29(4), 278–290. https://doi.org/10.1080/08957347.2016.1209206

Muijs, D. (2012). Understanding how pupils learn: Theories of learning and intelligence. In V. Brooks, I. Abbott, & x L. Abbott (Eds.), *Preparing to teach in secondary schools: A student teacher's guide to professional issues in secondary education* (2nd ed.) (pp. 45–59). Open University Press. [Online]. https://learningenglandblog.files.wordpress.com/2018/04/preparing-to-teach-in-secondary-schools.pdf

Nygaard, C., Courtney, N., & Holtham, C. (Eds.) (2010). *Teaching Creativity - Creativity in Teaching*. Faringdon: Libri Publishing.

Ojala, M. (2015). Hope in the face of climate change: Associations with environmental engagement and student perceptions of teachers' emotion communication style and future orientation. *The Journal of Environmental Education*, 46(3), 133–148. https://doi.org/10.1080/00958964.2015.1021662

Patston, T. J., Cropley, D. H., Marrone, R. L., & Kaufman, J. C. (2018). Teacher implicit beliefs of creativity, is there an arts bias? *Teaching and Teacher Education*, 75, 366–374. https://doi.org/10.1016/j.tate.2018.08.001

Perryman, J., & Calvert, G. (2020). What motivates people to teach, and why do they leave? Accountability, performativity and teacher retention. *British Journal of Educational Studies*, 68(1), 3–23. https://doi.org/10.1080/00071005.2019.1589417

Piaget, J. (1978). *Behavior and evolution* (Trans. D. Nicholson-Smith). Random House.

Rousseau, J.-J. (2015). *Emile, ou De l'éducation*. Ligaran Primento Digital Publishing. [Online]. http://public.ebookcentral.proquest.com/choice/publicfullrecord.aspx?p=2086528

Rowsell, J., & Shillitoe, M. (2019). The craftivists: Pushing for affective, materially informed pedagogy. *British Journal of Educational Technology*, 50(4), 1544–1559. https://doi.org/10.1111/bjet.12773

Smith, L. (2023). *Creativity in the English curriculum. Historical perspectives and future directions*. Routledge.

Sodha, S. (2023, December 10). Scottish schools have tumbled from top of the class. This is what went wrong. *The Guardian*. [Online]. https://www.theguardian.com/commentisfree/2023/dec/10/scottish-schools-have-tumbled-from-top-of-the-class-this-is-what-went-wrong

Steadman, S. (2024). 'Who is it that can tell me who i am?': What the ITE reforms in England mean for teacher identity (and why it matters). In V. Ellis (Ed.), *Teacher education in crisis, the state, the market and universities in England* (pp. 163–178). Bloomsbury.

Swanzy-Impraim, E., Morris, J. E., Lummis, G. W., & Jones, A. (2022). Promoting creativity, secondary visual art teachers' perceptions and understanding of creativity in Ghana. *Thinking Skills and Creativity, 45*, 1–11. https://doi.org/10.1016/j.tsc.2022.101057

Treffinger, D., Young, G., Selby, E., & Shepardson, C. (2002). *Assessing creativity. A guide for educators*. The National Research Centre on the Gifted and Talented.

Turvey, K. (2024). England's essentialist teacher education policy frameworks as double texts. In V. Ellis (Ed.), *Teacher education in crisis, the state, the market and the universities in England* (pp. 117–132). Bloomsbury.

Universities' Council for the Education of Teachers (UCET). (2020). *Intellectual Base of Teacher Education report (updated February 2020)*. Universities' Council for the Education of Teachers. [Online]. https://www.ucet.ac.uk/11675/ibte-position-statement-updated-february-2020

Vally, Z., Salloum, L., AlQedra, D., El Shazly, S., Albloshi, M., Alsheraifi, S., & Alkaabi, A. (2019). Examining the effects of creativity training on creative production, creative self-efficacy, and neuro-executive functioning. *Thinking Skills and Creativity, 31*, 70–78. https://doi.org/10.1016/j.tsc.2018.11.003

van Velzen, C., van der Klink, M., Swennen, A., & Yaffe, E. (2010). The induction and needs of beginning teacher educators. *Professional Development in Education, 36*(1–2), 61–75. https://doi.org/10.1080/19415250903454817

Vanassche, E., Kidd, W., & Murray, J. (2019). Articulating, reclaiming and celebrating the professionalism of teacher educators in England. *European Journal of Teacher Education, 42*(4), 478–491. https://doi.org/10.1080/02619768.2019.1628211

Vincent-Lancrin, S., González-Sancho, C., Bouckaert, M., de Luca, F., Fernández-Barrerra, M., Jacotin, G., Urgel, J., & Vidal, Q. (2019). *Fostering Students' creativity and critical thinking: What it means in school*. Educational Research and Innovation. OECD Publishing. https://doi.org/10.1787/62212c37-en

Vygotsky, L. S. (1978). *Mind in society: The development of higher psychological processes*. Harvard University Press.

Warren-Lee, N., Smith, L., Orchard, J., Kelly, L., James, J., & Coles, A. (2024). Bracing ourselves: Embracing policy changes through a long-standing University–Schools teacher education partnership in England. *Education Sciences, 14*(2), Art.158, 1–13. https://doi.org/10.3390/educsci14020158

Zimmerman, B. J. (2008). Investigating self-regulation and motivation: Historical background, methodological developments, and future prospects. *American Educational Research Journal, 45*(1), 166–183. https://doi.org/10.3102/0002831207312909

Chapter 6

Part-time distance postgraduate researchers

Establishing a blended community of practice through creativity and collaborative leadership

Janet Orchard, with contributions by Simon Brownhill

Introduction

Building on our previous experience of supporting the professional development of teachers, this chapter reflects on how, through taking a creative and collaborative approach to leadership in Higher Education (HE), we translated a promising and established practice, supported by scholarship, from one educational context (teacher education) to another (doctoral education) for a different purpose. The problem that needed to be solved in this case concerned meeting the needs of part-time, mature, self-funded doctoral students (referred to in this chapter as postgraduate researchers; PGRs), developing them into independent researchers, as required at this advanced level of study, while managing multiple other calls on their time and energy. Consisting of a good number of mid-career professionals, this group needed to typically manage the demands of a responsible job on top of caring duties in their home lives.

The intellectual challenges faced by this group were perceived as being distinctive and significant. Despite the strong practical experience and expertise that PGRs with this profile brought to doctoral research, it also proved a complication due to the fact that it was used to mask relative inexperience and limited expertise regarding their researcher 'self' or 'identity' (Walshaw, 2008). Clearly, a sense of competence and authority on the substantive topic being investigated presents a significant contribution to the project, but this must be weighed up against gaps in knowledge and skills found usually (though not always) in relation to research methodologies and research methods (Lepp et al., 2016).

A non-deficit, but realistic, sense of the challenge of being and becoming a researcher can be difficult to grasp. We believe that PGRs need to understand that educational research is a related but distinct practice into which they are initiated by their doctorate – a thesis (or in the case of an EdD, a dissertation) is doctoral training and not the creation of one's life's work. This may

DOI: 10.4324/9781032633534-9

require, for example, taking instruction from people who are younger, perhaps relatively lacking in terms of practitioner knowledge, yet are more expert in research; these, along with other issues of authority and power relations (see Åberg, 2024), can present significant problems if not handled carefully. Overall, completion rates for this group were consistently lower than those attained by other PGRs, e.g., those undertaking a full-time PhD.

To drive the direction of this chapter, two aims have been established:

- To reflect on how we identified communities of practice (CoPs) as a potential solution to the distinctive challenges identified in this case.
- To explain how we managed to translate an idea and practice in one established setting into a similar but different and unfamiliar context.

By engaging with this chapter, we hope that readers will appreciate that, without being revolutionary, what we did was original. Underpinning the chapter content is an everyday, collegial understanding of being imaginative, which we argue is sadly underrepresented in the writing about creativity.

To provide the reader with some useful context, the chapter opens with a reflective exploration of the background of the principal author.

Background: Janet's story

In 2017, I took over as Director of the University of Bristol School of Education's EdD (professional doctorate) in Hong Kong. My brief was to manage change on the programme, paying specific attention to a 'tail' of students who were struggling to complete dissertations at the doctoral level (Level 8) on top of the demands of their full-time professional responsibilities, these often being in fast-paced and competitive work environments. To add to these considerable challenges, many were at a life stage which brought more caring responsibilities for other family members, relative to those doctoral researchers who were younger and full-time. Perhaps as a result, programme evaluations revealed relatively high numbers of suspension requests.

The practical problems that have been described are common for this category of doctoral researcher (see Block, 2023) and are not exclusive to the Bristol EdD. A related but distinct difficulty for these doctoral researchers specifically concerned the demands of being academically 'critical' on topics close to practice in which one is an expert practitioner (Lindsay et al., 2018). There is typically a gap that needs to be bridged between knowing *how* and knowing *that* in terms of an original contribution to research. It is one thing to be an expert in how to enact a particular aspect of educational practice, and quite another to theorise it in academic English according to those conventions which warrant the award of a doctoral degree. As a result, these already hard-pressed professionals were, at times, unrealistic in their assessment of their progress and the time needed to develop their researcher identity. Like Simon, having been a part-time doctoral researcher myself who found meeting doctoral expectations difficult and demanding (although ultimately rewarding), I particularly empathised with them as best I could as a Programme Director who, in effect, was a poacher turned gamekeeper (someone whose behaviour was now the same as that which I had previously opposed).

By reflecting on a positive part of my own experience as a part-time doctoral researcher, I wondered if developing a close-to-practice research community could help this vulnerable and hard-pressed group of adult learners. Personally, I had previously appreciated being one of a group of experienced practitioners whose needs were met through activities timed to fit around my availability in terms of twilight sessions, and events at the weekend and in the holiday periods. I felt valued and included throughout the long gestation of my own PhD, regarding the respectful and non-judgemental 'team' support I received as being a crucial factor in finally submitting with success. Being mindful as an academic in the field of education of the potential pitfalls of generalising too far from one's own personal experience, I began to ask myself some important questions:

- *Could an ethos of shared endeavour and equality be fostered to support the PGR students for whom I was now responsible?*
- *Moreover, might the informal and supportive atmosphere of such a community help those students, particularly, but not exclusively, from Confucian Heritage Cultural (CHC) backgrounds, feel more comfortable and confident to constructively critique received academic wisdom?*

A more mundane and practical challenge was presented by the learners being situated over 6000 miles away and spread widely across an archipelago,[1] something that the global COVID-19 pandemic merely exacerbated. In the early part of the programme, learners gathered in-person for intensively taught units over three or four weekends for approximately two years of part-time study. This input shifted online during the pandemic with mixed results, some of which were positive, a point for exploration later on in the chapter. However, the provision was far less structured during the dissertation phase of the programme, which could potentially last a further five-to-six years. Experience as a supervisor helped both Simon and me to appreciate just how isolated those registered on the programme might become, particularly if they were not employed in an HE institution themselves. This was the point in their studies at which PGRs could become really disconnected from academic practices, their peers, and academic staff other than their supervisors (principally the first supervisor).

---

1 Defined as 'an area that contains a chain or group of islands scattered in lakes, rivers, or the ocean' (National Oceanic and Atmospheric Administration [NOAA], 2024).

In turn, supervisors (such as Simon) felt under considerable pressure to single-handedly manage the students' needs at a distance, discomforted by the culture of dependence this implied, and running counter to the notion of doctoral research that is self-directed.

Next steps

In this section, we describe the steps we took to introduce new ways to help part-time, at-a-distance doctoral researchers address the specific challenges they faced and which have been identified. Tackling our concerns about isolation and detachment seemed critical to addressing student issues pertaining to the following:

1 demotivation,
2 feeling overwhelmed,
3 feeling detached from the research perspective on their chosen topic, and
4 being immersed in their work and home life.

It was felt that these, combined, could be causing people to struggle, suspend, or withdraw from the programme entirely. Tasked with the challenge of developing their academic identities, it was important to address a couple of key questions:

- *How could we connect these students to research centres and networks, reading groups, and more generic academic support/PGR resources available to their full-time and closer-to-home peers?*
- *How might such changes be introduced without completely restructuring what was in other respects and for other learners, an established, successful, and well-regarded programme?*

This required creativity on our part, as leaders and teachers, respectively. We explain how we went about adopting and adapting the notion of a professional learning community (PLC) for this context. This is one specific kind of CoP whose benefits for in-service teachers are widely recognised (Bolam et al., 2005), yet are underdeveloped in the context of part-time, professional, doctoral researchers.

Taking the familiar and making it strange: creating a CoP for doctoral researchers

Identifying the potential of CoPs

Our idea was to take the familiar notion of a CoP (Lave & Wenger, 1991) and explore what this had to offer our part-time doctoral researchers. The general value of practitioners belonging to a PLC as one kind of CoP has long been recognised (Wenger, 2011), and we decided it was reasonable to think of this group of PGRs as 'practitioners', at least in part, for two reasons:

1 We were looking for a non-deficit approach, one which drew on rather than detracted from their established professional identity (it is important to note that those part-timers we supported were all engaged in professional practice of various kinds in their other working lives, as teachers, tutors, administrators, and leaders).
2 Secondly, we interpreted doctoral training as a form of initiation into skills and capabilities, an exercise in vocational education, with educational research being a practice as well as a site of knowledge creation.

We were also emboldened by the fact that Janet had done something similar with success before, developing 'Philosophy for Teachers' (P4T) (Orchard et al., 2020) with colleagues in a learned society that promotes the philosophy of education. In that particular case, the CoP approach had been adapted to the context of vocational education, also bringing in another familiar pedagogic strategy, that of 'P4C' (Philosophy for Children; see https://p4c.com/), adapting what was appropriate when supporting adult learners. Our challenge was to further experiment by translating the collaborative and experiential form of teaching and learning established with adults within a teacher education context to an understanding of doctoral training as vocational education in HE. *Would this structured peer-support help those experiencing the demands of part-time doctoral training to stay engaged and motivated than if they were alone?*

Key features of CoPs

The more general principles of educational practitioners learning from collective enquiry, through shared reflection on problem-solving and self-correction, are well-established (see Harris & Jones, 2012, p. 10); as such, the key principles which underpin CoPs and PLCs are neither new nor groundbreaking. There were several key ideas which underpinned our thinking and the practice that was implemented:

• Dewey (1929) observed that educational practices themselves may provide the subject matter for problems of educational inquiry,
• Stenhouse (1975) argued for collective enquiry by teachers as school and classroom researchers, and
• Schön (1983) is influential in advocating the notion of the 'reflective practitioner'.

The specific term 'CoP' is attributed to Lave and Wenger (1991). It has since been developed extensively through the later work of Wenger (1998a,

1998b). In defining a CoP, we subscribe to the thinking of Wenger (1998a, p. 1) who states it to be 'communities through which individuals develop and share the capacity to create and use knowledge'. There are clear parallels between this idea and the work that we developed. According to Wenger (1998a, p. 2), CoPs are almost always created 'informally and distinct from formal organizational units' – as such, they may not always be given names. They can exist anywhere in human activity; indeed, readers of this chapter may belong to several, these being in the various contexts in which they interact with others, participating in a CoP either as a core member or on its periphery – think dance teachers in a studio, art historians on *Reddit*, or hobbyists who meet up to improve their skills in photography.

CoPs arise out of the activities which bring people in social groupings together, which might include anything from engaging in lunchtime discussions to solving difficult problems, with the learning coming from mutual engagement in activities. CoPs develop around things that matter to people; subsequently, their practices reflect the members' own understanding of what is important. The communities we encouraged our PGRs to build were certainly organised around what mattered to them, the idea being that by connecting with each other and the projects they were managing, research had a greater chance of being or becoming part of their daily practice as opposed to becoming sidelined.

Membership of a CoP aims to support practitioners in understanding and ideally coping better with the inevitable dilemmas arising from being a doctoral researcher. As Sim (2006, p. 78) identifies, the CoP in which 'members have similar needs and experiences' is an 'effective structure to examine and reflect on these complex situations'. One online activity that PGRs ran by way of peer support was called 'Monday Meet Up' – this simply enabled PGRs to regularly get together for about an hour each week in term time so that, as new and early career researchers (ECRs), they could come together without academic staff being present to share concerns and identify possible solutions and ways forward.

Wenger (1998a) also states that a CoP is defined along three dimensions:

1 What it is about,
2 How it functions, and
3 What capability it has produced.

The essence of what PGR peer support is 'about' in the School of Education (University of Bristol) is the overarching objective of undertaking research training. The way it 'functions' is according to the model of 'action learning sets' (Lofthouse, 2022) which was introduced successfully during one of the research methods training units on the programme. The 'capability' that was 'produced' lies in the development of capabilities to successfully defend an original piece of research in the text submitted (dissertation) and the oral defence (oral examination) towards the very end of the doctoral training process.

The essence of the CoP is its continual renegotiation of aims and agreement among its members on the focus of joint undertaking, which needs reinforcing on a regular basis. PGRs were bound together through mutual engagement in the same activity, with things arising from shared practices and experiences that related, developing understanding and insight perhaps about the research process, but potentially also about the topic being investigated. It was felt that talking about one's own project to others could provoke new ways of seeing that could be hugely insightful.

In the case of PGRs in a doctoral community, this binding together was relatively temporary and short-lived, but strong and intense for the time that the community spent together engaged in enquiry. The practices that developed out of mutual engagement in a common endeavour reflected the members' own understanding of what was important. When the experience of sharing ceased to have an impact, members of the CoP fell away, but this was okay (indeed to be expected) if a critical mass of active members remained. Our aforementioned 'Monday Meet-up' initiative served its time, then fell away, and ended.

Even when a community's actions conform to an external mandate, in this case the university's PGR regulations and how these are interpreted by its officers, it is the community – not the mandate – that produces the practice. In this sense, CoPs are fundamentally 'self-organizing systems' (Wenger, 1998a, p. 2). This was illustrated in our case during the pandemic when we were advised that we should be in touch every week with all people registered on the programme, presumably because very few Schools in the university had around 300 PGRs who they needed to contact. It was too labour-intensive to delegate this responsibility to supervisors (such as Simon who was still developing as a supervisor, experience-wise), and the chance of inconsistent practice across such a large group was also very high. Instead, a weekly PGR email was instituted and sustained throughout the pandemic. Containing news and brief personal reflections to communicate empathy, a consistent mental health check message was communicated to everyone at scale, in the spirit of what the university had intended. Afterwards, PGRs commented positively on how they had received the regular message.

Doctoral training tends to be viewed conventionally as an individual pursuit and one that is potentially isolating (Ali & Kohn, 2006), a perception we sought to challenge by introducing collaborative ways of working. It is argued that CoPs should factor in the needs of the individuals they are comprised of. The theory suggests that they represent the means 'through which individuals develop and share the capacity to create and use knowledge' (Wenger, 1998a, p. 1), the individuals here completing PGR research at a distance and during a pandemic. By emphasising the importance of collaboration and teamwork online through their membership of research centres (such as the one co-created and co-led by Simon[2]) and reading groups, positive numbers of PGRs never-theless have completed, or are completing, often to a higher standard, despite the challenges.

Additional features of a PLC

Earlier in this chapter, we recognised the sensitive power relations in groups with part-time PGRs, particularly in relation to those who had established au-thority in the topic they were investigating in practical terms, this being out of balance with their competence and skill as expert independent researchers. We were mindful of the findings from a study by Jimenez-Silva and Olson (2012) that reported on pre-service teachers, i.e., initiates, who successfully engaged in a CoP with teachers in schools (those more established practitioners) in a collegial way. The study concluded that initiates developed a better under-standing of the relationship between theory and practice, a similar finding reported by Sutherland et al. (2005). By working with colleagues who were supervisors, and across different research centres in the School, we were able to create mutually supportive, non-patronising dynamics of the kind Jimenez-Silva and Olson (2012) reported. Thus, a bespoke practitioner-research group was formed to enable interested doctoral researchers and academics to meet regularly online to share their experiences of the kinds of close-to-practice pro-jects in which they were engaged, including challenges and possible solutions.

The use of ICT, or blended-learning models (developed intensively during the pandemic) proved a leveller across our widely dispersed PGR community in the long term. The virtual 'community of enquiry' (Garrison et al., 2000) that has been established has enabled inter- and trans-national dialogue ex-ploring global educational and research-based concerns. Without the same emphasis on a need to be physically present on campus or in a classroom, part-time doctoral researchers have been included powerfully and in ways that fit well around their work demands and other caring responsibilities.

Finally, we offer a comment on critical reflection, this being identified in the PLC literature as 'justification' for the very premises on which problems are posed or defined initially (see Mezirow, 1990, p. 12). This deeper, less superfi-cial kind of thinking was something that our PGRs needed to master to make an original contribution to the field they were investigating, but it proved to be difficult to sustain beyond the taught units they undertook. Working collabora-tively, members of the CoP were noted as supporting each other to form judge-ments and create new ideas through reflection-*in*-action, reflection-*on*-action, and reflection-*for*-action (Moghaddam et al., 2019; Schön, 1983), processes

---

2 The Centre for Teaching, Learning and Curriculum (TLC) at the School of Education, Univer-sity of Bristol (please visit https://www.bristol.ac.uk/education/research/centres-networks/tlc/).

through which deeper understanding and improvements were likely to occur (Liu, 2015; Smyth, 1989). Indeed, online discussions with their peers meant that PGRs got beyond the single reading of issues, were exposed to a wider range of reading possibilities, and were less quick to reach easy judgements.

Creativity and collaborative leadership in Higher Education

One of the reasons this chapter has been written is to share some specific strategies we used when introducing CoPs extensively onto the doctoral programme, drawing on the reasoning behind them from one established field of vocational education applied to another area of teaching practice that is not always recognised as being 'vocational'. In this final part of the chapter, we unpack a second level of our discussion, one that chimes with the themes of this volume, arguing that our actions have been creative on an everyday understanding of imaginative thinking. We believe that this inclusive, collaborative kind of creativity is too often downplayed or missing entirely in discussions of imaginative and creative practice, particularly regarding leadership.

Of the two main interpretations of creativity that have emerged over the past few decades – 'Big-C' creativity (Csikszentmihalyi, 1998, p. 80) and 'little-c' creativity (Craft, 2001) – it is the latter which is of most relevance to this context. Big-C creativity is linked to 'high' or elite artistic performance, whether it be in fine art, music, dance, or drama (Kaufman & Beghetto, 2009), this being part of a 'cultural canon' which is incongruous to the case described above. Instead, little-c creativity, which relates to everyday aspects of creativity that is available to all (Merrotsy, 2013), is very close to the sense in which we are claiming to have been creative. The aforementioned weekly PGR email was creative in a little-c sense. It was a new practice – the sharing of news and brief personal reflections on a weekly basis – which evolved into something of a custom at the end of each working week. As the weeks passed, it developed into something playful which managed to sustain its own momentum, with in-jokes, regular features, and standard messages as *esprit de corps* built up online during the various lockdowns.

Having imagination can be taken to mean the capacity to suppose, the capacity to think beyond actuality into the sphere of the possible (White, 2002). Kenny (1989) also stresses the importance of originality in relation to accounts of imaginative thinking. What distinguishes being imaginative about something from more general reflections is the capacity to entertain alternative scenarios, thinking beyond conventional responses. Taking a conventional model (in this case, the weekly PGR email, which was like a community news bulletin or newsletter) that is established in one context and applying it to a non-conventional setting is personally deemed to be 'imaginative' because it is based on systems or practices that exist already translated to another acceptable purpose (White, 2002). Suddenly, around the world, around 300 PGRs connected to the UoB SoE were every week receiving a deliberately friendly, informal,[3] and positive community message that was intended to keep their spirits up and feel connected to their university, which in many cases was very far away.

Kaufman and Beghetto (2009, p. 2) introduce two further categories of creativity: 'mini-c' and 'Pro-c'. Given that 'Pro-c' creativity is concerned with increasing competence and enduring skill when considering how a practitioner becomes a master or proponent of Big-C, we feel that this is not of relevance to our case here. However, when considering 'mini-c' creativity, its concern with the value of investing time and effort in 'creativity', inherent both in everyday processes (see Kaufman & Beghetto, 2009, p. 1) as well as the final product, does make a modest contribution to reflection on supporting our part-time PGRs. Take, for example, the process whereby PGRs were taught to write with others, in an organised collaborative writing retreat, in what we creatively (and rather impolitely) named a 'Shut up and Write!' session. This meant that while learning from experience about 'healthy' writing practices in a physical sense, doctoral researchers could also support each other in expressing and channelling emotions connected to the writing process, their own or other people's, with whom they could then better empathise.

On one recent writing retreat, the shared experience prompted a discussion between two mothers about the specific challenges of part-time doctoral research and an exchange of coping strategies that each had found to be helpful. This was reported to academic staff and arguably might not have taken place outside of a peer-to-peer discussion. Whether working as an individual or collectively, Chappell et al. (2016) propose that the creative process can help those involved to develop and express their identity through a dialogue between the internal or personal self, and public shared experiences. Such outcomes, albeit small-scale, represented uniquely valuable opportunities for self-expression, enabling our PGRs to develop through opportunities to experiment. It is argued that these may happen multiple times; sometimes successfully, others not. For our PGRs, being initiated into academic practice where learning to feel dissatisfied with one's creative efforts, and to manage those feelings constructively, was a regular occurrence; we assert that learning from being frustrated is just as important as experiencing a sense of satisfaction.

Having a 'vision'

Imaginative thinking on the lines we have shared in this chapter does not involve particularly unusual or sophisticated mental skill and is certainly not exclusive to special individuals. However, notions of being creative as a leader are often singled out for special attention. In some cases, the language of *vision* or being 'visionary' may be used to describe the qualities of outstandingly

3 The online-doctoral conference that year was organised in a similar spirit.

imaginative and successful leadership in educational settings (Orchard, 2014). However, one difficulty with this interpretation is that the word 'vision' may be attributed to individuals as though they possess privileged powers to perceive the future 'good', a problematic assumption in situations where people are committed to collegiality and do not need such rigid direction. Fullan (1992) goes further, objecting to the way in which notions of vision may be used to promote individualistic, charismatic styles of leadership over more collaborative approaches.

We believe that the capacity to develop a vision for something is concerned with being clear – an ability to articulate a future state for whatever is being managed. For us, creating a vision, or a future case for part-time doctoral researchers going forward, has been about developing a sense of those conditions under which the academic life of those on our programmes, particularly those self-funded part-timers who experience disadvantage, would be tangibly *better*. Having a sense of what would be better overall requires us to consult, survey, and discuss various possibilities – we may have ideas, but we need to 'sense-check' them with the PGR student body who are the experts in what *better* for them might look like. The purpose of the vision is to spell out, ideally, what is needed *and why* to secure the commitment of supervisors, support staff, PGRs, and other individuals. It arises from thinking imaginatively, creatively, and systematically about what is possible and desirable given the situation. By showing how we 'democratise' imaginative and creative thinking in our context, we hope to encourage others to feel similarly empowered.

Concluding comments

We maintain that the mental leap involved in seeing part-time PGRs as initiates into practice, therefore undertaking vocational education of a kind, has been helpful in steering us to the potential of establishing CoPs and PLCs in our support for this group, despite the tendency to see their work as being knowledge-based as opposed to skills-based and driven by the individual. We believe that opportunities to translate established practices for groups of learners into successful new pedagogies for adults have been seized. In the same way that the potential for CoPs to be useful for those in work-based contexts (see Sim, 2006; Sutherland et al., 2005) has been shown to be helpful for us, during the pandemic and beyond, they may be a useful process to carry over into other HE practices and over longer periods.

In drawing on the capacity for imaginative thinking in the positions of educational leadership we occupy, we maintain its value should not be overstated or understood to be a form of thinking or insight confined to special individuals. In our experience working with PGRs, leadership often requires people to think in ways that are imaginative or creative, and responding to and addressing problems at the course level is no exception. We faced a situation for which a non-standard response for the sector was required if PGRs were to support each other more systematically and find much-needed regular and consistent opportunities to reflect more deeply on their doctoral research, which were different from those limited opportunities already established on the doctoral programme. Solutions were generated through collaborative problem-solving in communities of the kind we have described. Throughout, we made sure that PGRs had clear ownership of the issues being examined, which were not imposed by us, through a process of negotiation and discussion. In short, it has been a team effort, and creative as the result of sustained hard work, not individual genius.

Suggested further reading

Cai, L., Dangeni, Elliot, D. L., He, R., Liu, J., Makara, K. A., Pacheco, E-M., Shih, H-Y., Wang, W., & Zhang, J. (2019). A conceptual enquiry into communities of practice as praxis in international doctoral education. *Journal of Praxis in Higher Education*, *1*(1), 11–36. [Online]. https://journals.hb.se/jphe/article/download/74/156/184

Costas Batlle, I., Banks, K., Rodohan, J., Clift, B. C., & Bekker, S. (2023). "Connecting the dots": Developing a doctoral qualitative community of practice. *Qualitative Inquiry*. [Online]. https://doi.org/10.1177/10778004231183943

References

Åberg, J. H. S. (2024). The problem of authority in the supervision process. *Journal of Teaching and Learning in Higher Education*, *5*(1), 1–6. https://doi.org/10.24834/jotl.5.1.1256

Ali, A., & Kohn, F. (2006). Dealing with isolation feelings in IS doctoral programs. *International Journal of Doctoral Studies*, *1*, 21–33. [Online]. http://ijds.org/Volume1/IJDSv1p021-033Ali13.pdf

Block, P. (2023, September 4). Universities continue to fail the non-traditional part-time mature PhD student. *HEPI*. [Online]. https://www.hepi.ac.uk/2023/09/04/universities-continue-to-fail-the-non-traditional-part-time-mature-phd-student/

Bolam, R., McMahon, A., Stoll, L., Thomas, S., & Wallace, M., with Greenwood, A., Hawkey, K., Ingram, M., Atkinson, A., & Smith, M. (2005). *Creating and sustaining professional learning communities* (Research Report Number 637). DfES Publications. [Online]. https://dera.ioe.ac.uk/5622/1/RR637.pdf

Chappell, K. A., Pender, T., Swinford, E., & Ford, K. (2016). Making and being made: Wise humanising creativity in interdisciplinary early years arts education. *International Journal of Early Years Education*, *24*(3), 254–278. https://doi.org/10.1080/09669760.2016.1162704

Craft, A. (2001). Little c creativity. In A. Craft, R. Jeffrey, & M. Leibling (Eds.), *Creativity in education* (pp. 45–61). Continuum.

Csikszentmihalyi, M. (1998). Letters from the field. *Roeper Review: A Journal on Gifted Education*, *21*(1), 80–81.

Dewey, J. (1929). *The sources of a science of education*. Horace Liveright.

Garrison, D. R., Anderson, T., & Archer, W. (2000). Critical inquiry in a text-based environment: Computer conferencing in higher education. *The Internet and Higher Education*, *2*(2-3), 87–105. https://doi.org/10.1016/S1096-7516(00)00016-6

Fullan, M. (1992). Visions that blind. *Educational Leadership*, 49(5), 19–20.

Harris, A., & Jones, M. (2012). *Connecting professional learning: Leading effective collaborative enquiry across teaching school alliances.* National College for School Leadership. [Online]. https://assets.publishing.service.gov.uk/media/5a759d72ed915d506ee802ca/Connecting-professional-learning-leading-effective-collaborative-enquiry-across-teaching-school-alliances.pdf

Jimenez-Silva, M., & Olson, K. (2012). A community of practice in teacher education: Insights and perceptions. *International Journal of Teaching and Learning in Higher Education*, 24(3), 335–348. [Online]. https://files.eric.ed.gov/fulltext/EJ1000686.pdf

Kaufman, J. C., & Beghetto, R. A. (2009). Beyond big and little: The four C model of creativity. *Review of General Psychology*, 13(1), 1–12. https://doi.org/10.1037/a0013688

Kenny, A. (1989). *The metaphysics of mind.* Oxford University Press.

Lave, J., & Wenger, E. (1991). *Situated learning.* University of Cambridge Press.

Lepp, L., Remmik, M., Leijen, Ä, & Leijen, D. A. J. (2016). Doctoral students' research stall: Supervisors' perceptions and intervention strategies. *Sage Open*, 6(3), 1–12. https://doi.org/10.1177/2158244016659116

Lindsay, H., Kerawalla, C., & Floyd, A. (2018). Supporting researching professionals: EdD students' perceptions of their development needs. *Studies in Higher Education*, 43(12), 2321–2335. https://doi.org/10.1080/03075079.2017.1326025

Liu, K. (2015). Critical reflection as a framework for transformative learning in teacher education. *Educational Review*, 67(2), 135–157. https://doi.org/10.1080/00131911.2013.839546

Lofthouse, R. (2022, March 10). *Action learning sets: A pedagogic and professional tool.* Carnegie Education, Leeds Becket University. [Online]. https://www.leedsbeckett.ac.uk/blogs/carnegie-education/2022/03/action-learning-sets-a-pedagogic-and-professional-tool/

Merrotsy, P. (2013). A note on big-C creativity and little-C creativity. *Creativity Research Journal*, 25(4), 474–476. https://doi.org/10.1080/10400419.2013.843921

Mezirow, J. (1990). *Fostering critical reflection in adulthood: A guide to transformative and emancipatory learning.* Jossey-Bass.

Moghaddam, R. G., Davoudi, M., Adel, S. M. R., & Amirian, S. M. R. (2019). Reflective teaching through journal writing: A study on EFL teachers' reflection-for-action, reflection-in-action, and reflection-on-action. *English Teaching & Learning*, 44, 1–20. https://doi.org/10.1007/s42321-019-00041-2

National Oceanic and Atmospheric Administration (NOAA). (2024). *What is an archipelago?* NOAA. [Online]. https://tinyurl.com/mhva2vx5

Orchard, J. (2014). Is good school leadership 'visionary'? In J. Suissa, C. Winstanley, & R. Marples (Eds.), *Education, philosophy and well-being* (pp. 39–53). Routledge.

Orchard, J., Heilbronn, R., & Winstanley, C. (2020). Philosophical conversation with: New and beginning teachers. In A. Fulford, G. Robinson, & R. Smith (Eds.), *Philosophy and community: Theories, practices and possibilities* (pp. 145–162). Bloomsbury.

Schön, D. A. (1983). *The reflective practitioner: How professionals think in action.* Basic Books.

Sim, C. (2006). Preparing for professional experiences – Incorporating pre-service teachers as 'communities of practice. *Teaching and Teacher Education*, 22(1), 76–83. https://doi.org/10.1016/j.tate.2005.07.006

Smyth, J. (1989). Developing and sustaining critical reflection in teacher education. *Journal of Teacher Education*, 40(2), 2–9. https://doi.org/10.1177/002248718904000202

Stenhouse, L. (1975). *An introduction to curriculum research and development.* Heinemann.

Sutherland, L. M., Scanlon, L. A., & Sperring, A. (2005). New directions in preparing professionals: Examining issues in engaging students in communities of practice through a school-university partnership. *Teaching and Teacher Education, 21*(1), 79–92. https://doi.org/10.1016/j.tate.2004.11.007

Walshaw, M. (2008). The concept of identity positioning the self within research. *ICME 11 – Proceedings* (pp. 322–337). [Online]. https://www.mathunion.org/fileadmin/ICMI/files/About_ICMI/Publications_about_ICMI/ICME_11/Walshaw.pdf

Wenger, E. (1998a). Communities of practice: Learning as a social system. *The Systems Thinker, 9*(5), 1–5. [Online]. https://thesystemsthinker.com/wp-content/uploads/pdfs/090501pk.pdf

Wenger, E. (1998b). *Communities of practice: Learning, meaning, and identity.* Cambridge University Press.

Wenger, E. (2011). *Communities of practice: A brief introduction* (pp. 1–7). [Online]. https://scholarsbank.uoregon.edu/xmlui/handle/1794/11736

White, J. (2002). *The child's mind.* Routledge.

Chapter 7

Student innovators

Achieving impact in a connected world through radical creativity

Mark Neild

Introduction

In this chapter, I contrast incremental innovation – 'doing better what we already do' (Norman & Verganti, 2014, p. 82) – with radical innovation – 'doing what we did not do before' (Norman & Verganti, 2014, p. 82). Now, more than ever before, the need for radical creativity (the beginning of a radical innovation process) in human history is acute because our current trajectory does not look promising.[1] Climate crises, societal discontent, and technological acceleration all require that we change current practices and not do what we have done before. Bringing about that change needs radical creativity. This chapter draws heavily on a research project involving master's students studying for a degree in innovation. The examples and student reflections cited in this chapter are primarily drawn from the study.

Innovation and creativity are often used almost interchangeably in organisation and business contexts. Innovation gives more focus to execution (Sawyer, 2012), whereas creativity features heavily in its early stages – the so-called *fuzzy front end* (O'Brien, 2020) – hinting at how poorly the genesis of innovation is generally understood among scholars. Two different metaphors (Moran, 2009) describe the creativity process:

- A common one refers to breaking through a barrier to develop some hitherto impossible outcome.
- A less common one refers to a more organic or emergent process.

Although breakthroughs do occur in the creative process (Sawyer, 2012), Moran (2009) argues that these are only identified in hindsight, offering no clearly repeatable process, thus limiting their value to researchers or practitioners. Emergence (as per the second bullet point above) describes the property where a complex entity has properties or behaviours that its constituent parts do not have on their own (Newman, 1996). Although conceptually esoteric,

---

1 See, for example, the *Global Risks Report 2024* by the World Economic Forum (2024).

DOI: 10.4324/9781032633534-10

emergence provides a better explanation for how radical creativity (conceiving of completely new concepts) happens.

Two succinct aims have been established to drive the direction of this chapter:

• To explain the radical creativity process, and
• To illustrate the radical creativity process with examples from Higher Education practice.

The chapter opens with an exploration as to why we need radical creativity.

We need radical creativity

Cast your mind back half a century: *how much has changed?* At first glance, everything. But if we look below the surface, maybe not so much. Fifty years ago, people had travelled through space, cars (and traffic jams) were commonplace, supersonic passenger travel was possible, and consumer electronics were commonplace in most homes, as were labour-saving devices. Nuclear power made the same claims for abundant cheap electricity as today's renewables. Then, as now, we worked around 40 hours a week, and the promise that technology (even AI) would free us from the drudgery of everyday life seems even less likely now than it did then. I am not saying nothing has changed – TVs have gone from a big box with a small monochrome screen to a huge screen in gloriously high-resolution colour, aggregating enormous content choices – but the essential job is much the same. Cars go faster and more safely on less fuel, but they retain their form and still only fly in movies. Most of the change above has been incremental, broadly predictable (at least in the short term), and with precious few real surprises. *Where is the creativity in that?*

Radical creativity is difficult

Human brains are not naturally good at radical creativity (coming up with ideas completely outside of previous experience) because they filter sensory perceptions through a lens of practice, sometimes referred to as 'cultural mediation' (Cole, 1996, p. 119). This situated cognition (explained in the next section) powerfully surfaces a deeper and more widespread phenomenon than most of us are aware of. Recent studies of neuroplasticity show that the brain reinforces neural pathways for frequently recurring activities while pruning synapses that are not triggered, a process persisting well into adulthood (Tierney & Nelson, 2009). Usually, this serves us well as we get better at things we regularly practice, but it has an impact on creativity, hindering learners' ability to conceive wholly new ways of being. The further we deviate from our experience, the more fallible our judgement becomes (Tversky & Kahneman, 1974). To make matters worse, novelty alone is insufficient (Sawyer, 2012).

Creative ideas need to resonate with people if they are to have an impact (Neild, 2023b). The fundamental difference between a vandal's graffiti and street art is the context; while both are criminal, the latter is highly valued by some people. The challenge for radical creativity is to conceive wholly new things that intended users, who have never experienced anything like them, will love. The contradictions in achieving this should be self-evident, hence why it is described by some as *fuzzy*.

In the coming sections, I will share, via different examples, how student innovators have overcome these challenges, showing how divergent thinking escapes the limitations of the obvious, while convergent thinking grounds creative ideas in contexts that intended users find both valuable and appropriate. It is based on my research in Higher Education where students learn how to foster radically different ways of being. Let me ask an important question:

What aspects of students' developing skills and practice best enable them to conceive the inconceivable and then transform it into products so compellingly obvious in their benefits that people naturally adopt them?

To answer this, let us start by turning to socio-cultural theory and within it, situated cognition.

Socio-cultural theory and situated cognition

Our brains store individual experiences in a unique way – there is no systemic or objectively rational basis for subconscious decisions, it is just what we do *every day* (Vygotsky, 1978). We find it difficult to explain them to others who have not shared our experiences because there is no common ground. To do so requires some shared mechanism that enables both parties to view the situation in a comparable way. This shared situation definition, or intersubjectivity (Wertsch, 1985), is important in innovation to help people make sense of something they may have never encountered before. Shared situation definitions occur naturally in communities that work together – think communities of practice (CoP) (Lave & Wenger, 1991). They have a shorthand, a local vernacular, implicitly understood by community members, but typically making little sense to outsiders. In academia, for example, the word 'chair' is sometimes used to denote a professor, whereas its meaning is quite distinct from 'chair' (of a meeting) that is used in other contexts. Lave and Wenger's (1991) work on situated learning in CoP broadly describes an apprenticeship style of learning where implicit skills are passed from those who have mastered them to those seeking to learn. But Lemke (1997) asks about the limitations of learning wholly within a CoP: *can these CoPs foster radical creativity?*

Years of innovation consulting have shown me that hierarchies of specialists in large organisations, far from accelerating change, actually impede it. Their cognition becomes so situated in current practice that they find it impossible to escape its constraints to imagine wholly new ways of being. Understandably, deep expertise is the basis for social capital within the community. It is not easy for experts to embrace the impending redundancy of their life's work; unsurprisingly, they resist it. Well-known examples of this happening include *Nokia* (mobile phones) and *Kodak* (photography) (Gassmann, 2014).

Escaping situatedness

How do we free our brains from the shackles of situatedness to enable radical creativity? Fodor's (1980) discussion of this learning paradox and the resolutions of other scholars offer some useful insights. Fodor (1980, p. 142) describes the learning paradox as follows:

> Asking about something implies that you already know what you seek. So, you do not need to learn about it. But, unless you know what knowledge you seek, you will not know where to look, so will never learn about it.

This circularity shows why learning completely new things seems impossible. Bereiter (1997) addresses the paradox above by drawing on Popper's (1978) *immaterial knowledge objects* that are neither subjective nor objective, enabling them to transcend context. By way of illustration, one of my students' projects adapted theoretical models from academic literature, 'bending' them using AI to accelerate the production of video animation, a context in which such processes had never hitherto been attempted. The result was a sevenfold improvement in the time taken to produce video assets, which could never have been achieved by improving the existing processes.

Boom (1991) draws on Vygotsky's (1978) distinction between *intermental* (social learning) and *intramental* (individual learning) to argue that if two or more individuals know (or have experience of) phenomena unique to each of them on the intramental plane, then through intermental dialogue they can gain knowledge of things they have not themselves experienced and may not even know to ask about. Boom's (1991) approach supports inclusive innovation, this being recognised as developing products to meet the specific needs of minority communities. Intermental dialogue, which relies on intersubjectivity to properly make sense of the lived experience of underserved communities, has helped my innovation students develop appropriate new products for the visually impaired, wheelchair users, and adults who have difficulty feeding themselves. I was shocked to see how adults with diminished motor control in their hands were forced to use baby spoons until one of my students designed cutlery that restored their dignity. Mainstream products often prove inappropriate to those with specific needs, but it is not until we see the world through their eyes that we appreciate their feelings. Particular care is needed

---

Case Study 7.1

A student changed the meaning of 'urinal' to include facilities for women at outdoor events. The female founders had observed the far longer queues of women than men at festivals for the toilets. The word 'urinal' symbolised the reason why women queued more for the toilet than men did. By reframing 'urinal' to include a product designed specifically to accommodate the way women urinate, it became a symbol of '*peequality*' (as the founders described it, a play on the venture's brand *Peequal*).

Cultural meanings need to evolve in tandem with the emergence of a new product, otherwise, the new product risks making no sense to its audience and being rejected. *Peequal*'s founders designed a product that emulated how women 'wild pee'. By legitimising the covert 'behind the bushes' behaviour of desperate women through the creation of proper facilities, the process felt natural, even in an entirely new and formal setting.

---

when establishing intersubjectivity with those with very different backgrounds to avoid making assumptions unsupported by evidence (Neild, 2023a).

A key limitation of the approaches described above is that knowledge or experience was already out there and are thus examples of *P-creativity* – things that have been done previously albeit elsewhere or in different contexts, but are new to the person (Boden, 1996). *What about* H-creativity – *things which have never been done before?*[2] The most plausible resolution to the learning paradox for wholly new ideas comes from *emergence* (Sawyer, 1999). He develops Mead's (1932) conception of the emergence of the novel using his own research into improvisational theatre, describing a process of *collaborative emergence* between the actors. Sawyer's paper distinguishes between intersubjectivity in the static sense (as described by Wertsch, 1985) and a more dynamic and emergent relationship in which meanings and culture evolve. This is a useful distinction for radical creativity. In collaborative emergence, even as a product evolves, its surrounding environment evolves with it, ensuring that the new product remains appropriate for its intended audience. This is evidenced in Case Study 7.1.

Does cognitive diversity drive creativity?

The three resolutions to the learning paradox described above rely on an element *of* cognitive diversity – brains developed through substantially different prior experiences – working together. Intuitively, cognitive diversity should

---

2 For more on *Psychological (P)-* and *Historical (H)-creativity*, please see Boden (2004).

reduce situatedness by drawing together multiple contexts. There is empirical support for this view, but the causal factors between diversity and creativity are complex, non-linear, and sometimes even negative (Hundschell et al., 2022). Having different perspectives around a table is only as useful as the team's ability to harness them. Duhigg (2016) describes how it is the interplay between various team members rather than their individual capabilities that most contribute to team performance. He cites examples of the hit US TV show *Saturday Night Live* and *Google's* project to find what makes the perfect team, this being in contrast to how poor teamwork between highly qualified aircrew led a perfectly serviceable commercial airliner to fly into the sea, killing all onboard. Limited functional diversity within a single CoP can lead to *groupthink* – this is where dominant individuals drive a consensus, which fails to take into account all the facts. In a previous career that saw me teaching problem-solving skills to junior management consultants, I found that often the more creative, but less vocal members of the group contributed nothing until somebody asked them to, which never occurred to those who were more vocal. Instruction on effective teamwork helps here, with Edmondson's (1999) paper on *psychological safety* highlighting effective behaviours, e.g., encouraging students to explore their different personalities through online personality tests and agreeing on ways of working together through Team Charters (that encourage everyone to contribute without fear). Collectively, these demonstrably improve team effectiveness (Aaron et al., 2014) by operationalising constructive behaviours among teammates and research participants, a point I will elaborate on in the next section. Examination of students' summative reflections [from Edmondson's work] highlight the value of (a) recognising and (b) making full use of the power of diverse thinking in their teams, and that different perspectives enable them to review their research findings more robustly, thus driving better decisions. Other students report better productivity through effective delegation of tasks. While these are valuable outcomes, the link to team creativity is less clear. My observations, based on six years of teaching innovation in Higher Education, borne out by the examples described in this chapter, suggest that general team diversity does not overcome situated cognition sufficiently to inspire radical creativity; it requires something more.

On co-creation

While briefly mentioning *multi-disciplinarity* (effective interfaces between disciplines) and *interdisciplinarity* (which synthesises different disciplines into a coherent whole), I have not explicitly mentioned *transdisciplinarity*. It is transdisciplinary working that really drives radical creativity, particularly where it involves joint problem-solving. The student examples cited earlier and in this section were the result of transdisciplinary problem-solving. Solutions to customer problems, along with the definition of the problems themselves, were co-created in virtual teams of up to 100 people. Co-creation is an interesting phenomenon and one which is often held up as 'the answer', although there is a paucity of literature that describes how it works at a cognitive and creative level (Stier & Smit, 2021). In the sections that follow, I will build on the theory already shared and show how well-executed co-creation[3] can lead to the emergence of radical creativity, this being the start of an effective innovation process.

Co-creating the emergence of radical creativity

Cognitive diversity contributes to overcoming the constraints imposed by situated cognition, but just having more and different people involved or lots of different ideas (Torrance, 1984) is not the whole answer. Despite accepted measures of creativity including *divergent thinking* (a quantity and variety of raw ideas), Sawyer (2012) observed that the link between divergent thinking and creativity is tenuous. *What if we reframe creativity as diverging from situatedness?* Earlier on in the chapter, I described some of the mechanisms through which cognitive diversity helps to escape the situatedness imposed by cultural mediation and the learning paradox. But just coming up with something completely new is not in itself creative. For many creativity researchers, think Bruner (1962) and Runco and Jaeger (2012), appropriateness or meaningfulness is at least as important a measure of creativity as novelty or originality. Logically, we might conclude that the most appropriate idea is the one we already have, this being situated in the original context, pitting appropriateness against moving beyond the constraints of context. Variants of the current solution are what most people typically come up with. *But what if the current trajectory is sub-optimal?* No matter how hard we try, situated cognition keeps bringing us back to our current ways of doing or being. In the animation example mentioned earlier, it required a completely different approach to achieve a sevenfold improvement in speed; tinkering with the original approach could at best achieve a fraction of this. We need radical creativity to lead us to a better trajectory, a more attractive destination, more sustainable or more socially just, for example, or even simply quicker, cheaper, less effort, or more satisfying than current practice. *But how is a better trajectory to be found if it is so difficult to imagine things we have never experienced?* Aardman Animations (see https://www.aardman.com/), who supported our student animators, had no interest in AI – *what relevance does AI have to the plasticine made famous by Wallace and Gromit?* So, forget the means and focus on the end.

---

3 Collaboration and co-creation are often used interchangeably, but the relationships between actors can be quite different. For a longer discussion on co-creation in innovation, please see Neild (2023a).

Reframing divergent and convergent thinking

The clue lies in the word 'destination'. Thinking in terms of *outcome* (the 'what?') rather than *output* (the 'how?') enables thinking beyond the context. Our student animators would have struggled to sell AI-powered animation to Aardman, but offering to speed up the process sounded a lot more interesting (Neild & Tan, 2022). I would like to use an innovation cliché about 'better mouse traps' – slight improvements that are not worth the effort of changing – to illustrate the point. Often, I will ask my innovation students to think about how they might come up with a better mouse trap. They struggle, which is the point of the exercise. If I then ask what we are trying to achieve, the answer 'Fewer or no mice!' is quickly suggested. If we then reframe the question to ask 'How might we achieve fewer or no mice?', a far broader field of options presents itself, and it is not long before someone suggests getting a cat. A cat is an obvious solution to the no-mice problem but is a radical solution to the 'better mouse trap' problem because it involves a much bigger cognitive leap from the wood, cheese, and springs in the traditional trap. For people brought up with cat and mouse cartoons (think *Tom and Jerry*), cats catching mice feels culturally familiar, which is why it makes a good example. It shows three important things:

1 Reframing a problem in terms of *what* or *outcome* is a useful way to kickstart thinking about a problem from a different perspective – diverging from the original context.
2 *Appropriateness* can be understood in terms of cultural or cognitive fit. For a new idea to gain acceptance, it is necessary to converge it towards a cultural norm. Such norms may be completely unrelated to the original context, but close enough to existing habits that adoption makes sense or feels intuitive.
3 For radical creativity to be accepted, there is always a tension between diverging far enough to escape situated thinking, but not so far that the new idea makes no sense to those who intended to adopt it.

Reframing *divergent thinking* as divergence from context and *convergent thinking* as convergence towards the culturally familiar runs counter to accepted views of creativity. It better aligns with emerging views of ambidextrous leadership (Rosing et al., 2011) and allied concepts that describe divergence and convergence in terms of increasing and reducing variation respectively (Gupta et al., 2006). It casts light on how co-created innovation overcomes the apparent contradiction of radical appropriateness, the key to innovations being used. When *Peequal* were designing their urinal (Case Study 7.1), they paid a lot of attention to how women squatted. With carefully positioned hand holds and a hook for their bags, the stance felt natural and familiar with all needs catered for, making it far easier to be comfortable with a product that nobody had seen before.

Having compared *what?* thinking to *how?* thinking, let us now consider another divergent technique: *why?* thinking.

Co-creating the problem

Many nascent entrepreneurs using creative problem-solving techniques overlook the challenge of discovering the real problem.[4] Being trained in school to solve problems has increased skills, but problem definition is much less well-practiced. Students are so used to being given problems to solve as an academic exercise in management and engineering that they rarely question whether it is the right problem, so keen are they to start on the solution. Techniques like the *five-whys* aim to get to the root cause of a problem by repeatedly asking why?[5] Typically, by the fifth *why?*, the root cause problem is very different from the original context, making a seemingly radically creative solution seem the obvious path to follow. This technique works well with people too, although with science problems, cause and effect can be more easily linked than with people.

The reasons for human habits are often far from obvious to other people, their origins lying in long-forgotten experiences. Students asking research participants why they do certain things is typically met with a shrug and 'It's obvious!', a reply revealing how rarely people question custom and practice. Bourdieu (1977) describes this phenomenon as *habitus*. Here is where co-creation proves incredibly useful. Tacit practice (van Houten, 2023), sometimes referred to as *second nature*, is both invisible and obvious to individuals. To anyone else, its effects are neither. You and I may gaze at an object (think an analogue wall clock) and agree on its explicit (objective) attributes such as colour, weight, and shape, but fundamentally disagree on its tacit (subjective) attributes such as value to us and its appropriateness to our needs. The point here is that other people's subjectivities are hidden and require effort to make these known (explicit). With non-physical products such as media or services, the challenge becomes more acute as this next student example shows (Case Study 7.2).

This example of reframing through convergent thinking took several weeks of discussion and only happened when one person suggested it and others quickly agreed. The example also shows the power of co-creation, which I will discuss in more detail later. Such insights are rarely published and easy to miss in interviews because of their tacit and often personal nature. But in a trusted environment of peers with psychological safety and motivation to seek something better than the products currently on offer, insights often emerge

---

4 For a valuable resource discussing this, take a look at the article by Maurya (2024).
5 For an excellent and engaging illustration of this technique, please visit: https://youtu.be/N7cR2gArCFE?si=l_NPJyw1ztChCnpf

---

Case Study 7.2

Young adults are reported to be increasingly susceptible to mental health issues. Two students were keen on tackling mental health as they had lived experience of the debilitating effects it can have. *Why did problems persist despite the availability of a well-known product?* * *Why were students not engaging with it?* A focus group – a facilitated discussion among fellow young adults representing potential buyers of the planned product – revealed that the stigma of 'issues' [the word *issue* signified a sense of personal failure among the group] put people off. Reframing the problem away from mental health issues, through mental wellbeing and on to mental fitness, substantially improved engagement. The group understood the benefits of physical fitness. The cognitive leap to investing similar effort in mental fitness was not excessive, enabling people to view engagement in a more positive way.

* Most students in this example were aware of *Headspace*, a meditation app(lication). But for many, it did not seem to offer the solution they hoped for.

---

that would not in a one-to-one interview. A fuller explanation of the reasons for this is in the next section.

It is disconcerting to think that progress thus far – defining a problem worth solving – marks just the first milestone for an innovation journey. A problem definition co-created with a representative sample of the target audience is a good indicator of its desirability. Given that around half of all products launched by leading companies are not desirable (Simester, 2016; Victory et al., 2021), then identifying a problem that enough people will put effort into solving is still a good achievement. The real challenge, developing a valuable and appropriate solution that addresses the identified problem, begins here.

Complexity and emergence

Support for an emergent view of the early (creativity) stage of innovation comes from Sarasvathy's (2001) ethnographic study on the process followed by successful entrepreneurs. At the earliest stage of an entrepreneurial journey, there is no organisation, which means no resources or relationships to rely on. Her findings uncovered a logic based on *contingency* (start with just the resources immediately to hand) and *locality* (work with the people that are easy to reach) that *carefully manages risk* (validate demand before committing resources further). This *effectual logic* (Sarasvathy, 2001) explained a seemingly random process. Driven by a lack of resources and no clear market demand (for a product yet to exist), the entrepreneurs in her study (and indeed student entrepreneurs in the examples shared in this chapter) were unable to follow a typical management causal process in which the end is defined, and the means acquired from the surrounding organisation to achieve it. Instead, by starting with whatever means are at hand to entrepreneurs, (typically what they know and who they know), allows the end to emerge, this being contingent on their ability to gather the necessary support and resources to develop it further. Student innovators face the same challenges, with limited resources and no clear indication of any demand for a product idea until a 'problem worth solving' emerges (as illustrated in the example offered at the end of the last section).

Emergence can be compared with a Darwinian process of natural selection. But instead of the random variation caused by an accidental genetic mutation, entrepreneurs deliberately adapt their ideas to fit with the external environment in what is referred to as a Complex Adaptive System (CAS).[6] A CAS has four interesting features:

1 Its path cannot be predicted from the initial conditions because the possible interactions within the system that influence its future direction are too numerous to model – what emerges is original and surprising. Complexity arises in markets because, contrary to neo-classical economics, humans are neither rational nor are their behaviours reducible to predictable utility maximisation theories (Simon, 1955).
2 Without feedback, the system does not adapt. Innovators deliberately elicit feedback, incorporate it into their designs, and push the adaptations out for further feedback to maximise the desirability of their emerging product.
3 The rate of adaptation needs to be regulated. The system spirals into chaos if the rate is too fast or goes in too many directions at once. Memes 'going viral' remains the exception on social media rather than the rule – if too many had explosive growth, it would rapidly get overwhelming (for people and possibly also for the technical infrastructure), resulting in chaos.
4 Finally, *emergence* is a feature of a CAS. When lots of local independent agents interact around a common topic, a consensus emerges, which no individual could predict, but all broadly agree on. This is exactly what an innovator wants as this heralds the birth of a brand-new market, undiscovered by anyone else.

Driving the emergence of radical creativity

Can emergence be driven? Studies show that *attractors* are the states to which CAS tends, even in cultural evolution (Falandays & Smaldino, 2022). In natural selection, attractors define what characterises the 'fittest', engendering its

6 For an approachable companion to complexity theory, see Theise (2023) who shows how complexity theory can be applied to Biology, Physics, and even religions.

survival (Darwin, 1869); in cultural selection, a similar process is at work (Mesoudi, 2021) except that innovators drive the feedback loops as described in the second point regarding a CAS above (Galkina & Atkova, 2020). Innovators do not define attractors any more than social media influencers do. Influence is bestowed by consensus and it is consensus that the innovator really wants. A group of cognitively diverse individuals, united by a common desire to solve a specific problem, creates a motivated market (Neild, 2023b). *Peequal* emerged because enough women were sufficiently motivated to reduce queuing times for the toilet (Case Study 7.1). *Remap* similarly found enough people motivated to improve mental fitness (Case Study 7.2). In both cases, people were willing to share intimate and personal details for no reward other than the promise of a product that they liked the idea of. The entrepreneur's objective is to orchestrate the emergence of both a motivated market and new products to satisfy the desires of that market. Contrary to some views on innovation (Sarasvathy et al., 2003), it is not the entrepreneurs' task to define or create a market, but instead to facilitate convergence so that a consensus definition emerges.

Participants in a motivated market are not picked by student entrepreneurs but self-selected into it (Neild, 2023b), thus creating a deliberately biased sample. Unlike in academic research where the objective is to find broadly generalisable knowledge, in innovation research, the question is more about whether there is sufficiently widespread bias with a broad consensus around addressing a specific issue. This 'problem worth solving' (Neild, 2023a) is what constitutes an opportunity to create a new market. Student groups assemble looking for interesting ideas to progress into projects. As a practising instructor, I encourage my students to think of high-level topic areas representing problems or opportunities, and then promote conversations among peers to see which topic areas resonate. They may use a survey on social media to reach more people and gather some preliminary data on general preferences (this is useful for market sizing), and then invite any respondents who are interested in offering more detailed insights by giving them the opportunity to opt in by providing their contact details. Surveys, because of their highly structured nature, do not offer deep insights and are limited to the questions the researcher plans to ask (Queirós et al., 2017). Semi-structured interviews and observations enable the discovery of areas that may not have occurred to the researcher, helping them explore beyond boundaries imposed by previous experience. This is the beginning of the co-creation process as insights from participants increasingly shape the research process, as illustrated in Figure 7.1.

Attracting cognitive alignment

Sarasvathy's (2001) work on effectuation distinguishes between predicting the future and creating it, arguing that successful innovators do the latter because the former is notoriously difficult. Indeed, the reader can probably

Community Engagement / Primary Research Plan

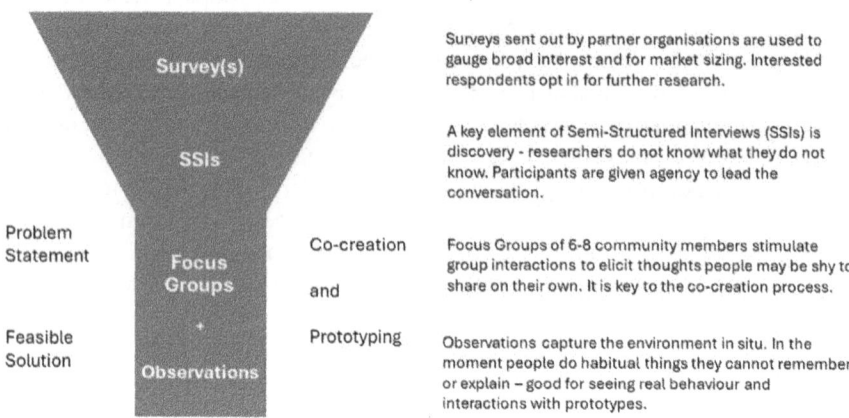

Surveys sent out by partner organisations are used to gauge broad interest and for market sizing. Interested respondents opt in for further research.

A key element of Semi-Structured Interviews (SSIs) is discovery - researchers do not know what they do not know. Participants are given agency to lead the conversation.

Focus Groups of 6-8 community members stimulate group interactions to elicit thoughts people may be shy to share on their own. It is key to the co-creation process.

Observations capture the environment in situ. In the moment people do habitual things they cannot remember or explain – good for seeing real behaviour and interactions with prototypes.

Figure 7.1 Eliciting the emergence of radical creativity.

think of products that have substantially changed the course of history – the printing press, the steam engine, the car, and the Internet are but a few examples. Recalling the earlier definition of creativity that included appropriateness and value suggests that not every idea can become an attractor. There needs to be some mutually beneficial symbiosis between the outer environment (including culture) and the idea before it can start to drive the direction of emergence. The idea needs to resonate with its intended audience before cultural evolution can occur. The implication, that the process of creative innovation is a combination of both the discovery and creation of opportunities, accords with a study examining entrepreneurship as information processing (Vaghely & Julien, 2010). So, what is really meant when referring to innovation as behaving like a CAS is that its adoption depends on cultural evolution. For a brand-new product to be culturally appropriate and thus understood in a culturally mediated world, culture needs to change in step with the emerging product.

Previous work on cultural evolution includes the role innovation plays in driving it, illustrative examples of which include Tomasello (1999) and Mesoudi (2021). Similarly, the role of cultural attractors in driving cultural evolution is well documented (Falandays & Smaldino, 2022), but the literature is sparse in describing how cultural attractors cause innovation to emerge. Instead, based on the properties of CAS, the nature of emergence within them, and my own professional observations of how student innovators bring about cultural change, I will propose a model for the emergence of radical creativity as the first step in identifying new products that customers will adopt.

Mesoudi's (2021) process of *cultural selection* closely mirrors natural selection, except that intentional agents (in a motivated market) deliberately select more beneficial variants, enabling cultural selection to evolve far quicker than natural selection. For example, in scarcely a human biological generation, the meaning of the signifier 'telephone' has evolved from a tethered single-function voice communication device to an untethered (mobile) device capable of thousands of functions, with voice calls rapidly diminishing. This is cultural evolution at work and shows how quickly our ways of being can change given the right innovation.

An important question to ask is: *what makes innovation so appropriate that it can bring about such a large-scale behaviour shift? And why* (as I shared at the beginning) *have other things changed so little?* Here again, the definition of creativity introduced in this chapter sheds some light. Beyond novelty, creativity must be valuable and appropriate. Valuable innovation offers tangible benefits; appropriate innovation makes sense to us. We appreciate it because it makes those benefits obvious in the contexts and situations of our everyday lives. Often, innovation needs to reframe a product to make it meaningful (Norman & Verganti, 2014). Henry Ford's genius in the early 20th century was to reframe the meaning of a car from being a rich person's plaything to a working person's tool. The only way he could achieve this was by a radical innovation in manufacturing, this being the first-ever production line. A century later, Elon Musk's perceived genius was to reframe electric cars from the humble golf buggy to exciting high-performance cars. Nobody bought a Toyota Prius because it was fun or sporty, but when Tesla showed that the fastest production car in the world could be electric, even confirmed internal combustion fans started to take notice, and with them, high-end car makers. The point here is that radical creativity achieves impact when it helps enough people achieve what they desire yet struggle to accomplish. *So, how do we develop these 'motivated markets'?*

Students' social lives exist in a CAS. At any one time they can be interacting with multiple sub-groups, relating in various capacities with family, people they study with, people they live with, and those with whom they pursue leisure activities. These groups are all self-selecting: people opt in to them. A motivated market is just the same – it is simply a group that opts in or interacts with others that share a special interest. This might be an aspiration or 'job to be done' (Klement, 2018) rather than the more traditional demographic segmentation (e.g., age or income bracket) typically used by marketing firms. In line with effectual reasoning, entrepreneurs float ideas through social groups to see which ones resonate. They start off quite broad, but over time cognitive alignment occurs because the random choice of phrasing caused by the diversity of participants' backgrounds starts to converge as they collectively share a common reference frame or intersubjectivity. Innovators push for intersubjectivity by expressing a common intrinsic motivator and then probing for specific signs and signifiers that provoke the optimal feedback. In the case of *Peequal* (Case Study 7.1), participants initially disliked the term 'urinal' because it symbolised male dominance in toilet design. Over time though, as they started to understand what the product was intended to do, they saw a female-only urinal as representing equality. For *Remap* (Case Study 7.2), the discovery that mental fitness resonated much better with their intended audience (and their emerging product) than dealing with issues proved to be instrumental in attracting initial customers. Both examples show how important semiotics can be for a radically creative concept to be perceived as appropriate. Shared meanings emerge when group members clumsily or evocatively express similar sentiments until the group starts to converge around the most evocative signifiers. Often these emergent signifiers (be they words, pictures, or actions) are not the natural starting point for participants, but when perceived, they resonate more strongly and are adopted in preference to the original. Thus, new meanings emerge and self-reinforce within the group and the group collectively starts adopting a common parlance. Instructors encourage the use of prototypes to provide visual and activity-based interactions surfacing different dimensions of meaning. At the simplest (low fidelity) level, prototypes might be basic drawings. They gain sophistication through the process as the group aligns on the feature set until they become (high fidelity) detailed simulations of the user experience in interacting with the prototypes to optimise the user interface.

Concluding comments

This chapter opened with a conundrum: neuroscience and situated cognition appear to conspire against radical creativity. Yet by reframing creativity from 'coming up with the new' to discovering what is culturally appropriate, the paradox of learning wholly new things can be countered. The last decade or so has marked a significant shift in our understanding of systems thinking (CAS). It is in the interactions between people that radical creativity emerges, not necessarily just in the heads of individuals or in individual communities. By broadening our view of diversity beyond the woke view of equality, diversity, and inclusion to celebrate and seek to understand *otherness* rather than fearing or ignoring it, radical and inclusive creativity will flourish.

However, it is important to remember that we cannot force it. Innovation does not happen by telling people they need to behave differently, but by helping them to behave in ways that they believe to be better. The current generation of students is naturally more digitally connected. For them, reaching out to a hundred people and finding communities of interest online is far easier than for previous generations. Our task as educators is to open their eyes to the possibilities that connectedness enables. Large language models like *ChatGPT* may be powerful at finding what already is, but for the foreseeable future, radical creativity, powered by human diversity, is far better at determining what should be.

Acknowledgements

I am indebted to my students, especially those whose examples are shared in this chapter as they have taught me a lot about how to start a high-impact business with very few resources. Three years on and they are all thriving, picking up awards and growing recognition for the benefits they bring their customers. I am also indebted to the editor of this volume, Simon Brownhill, and my peer reviewers, Alison Oldfield and Andrew Collins, for helping to order my jumbled tacit thoughts into the more explicit narrative you see here.

Suggested further reading

Sarasvathy, S. D. (2001). *What makes entrepreneurs entrepreneurial?* (pp. 1–9). [Online]. https://22657557.fs1.hubspotusercontent-na1.net/hubfs/22657557/Public%20 Documents%20For%20Site/what-makes-entrepreneurs-entrepreneurial-sarasvathy.pdf

Theise, N. (2023). *Notes on complexity: A scientific theory of connection, consciousness, and being.* Spiegel & Grau.

References

Aaron, J. R., McDowell, W. C., & Herdman, A. O. (2014). The effects of a team charter on student team behaviors. *Journal of Education for Business, 89*(2), 90–97. https://doi.org/10.1080/08832323.2013.763753

Bereiter, C. (1997). Situated cognition and how to overcome it. In D. Kirshner & J. A. Whitson (Eds.), *Situated cognition: Social, semiotic, and psychological perspectives* (pp. 281–300). Erlbaum.

Boden, M. A. (1996). Creativity. In M. A. Boden (Ed.), *Artificial intelligence: Handbook of perception and cognition* (pp. 267–291). Academic Press. https://doi.org/10.1016/B978-012161964-0/50011-X

Boden, M. A. (2004). *The creative mind: Myths and mechanisms* (2nd ed.). Routledge.

Boom, J. (1991). Collective development and the learning paradox. *Human Development, 34*(5), 273–287. https://doi.org/10.1159/000277061

Bourdieu, P. (1977). *Outline of a theory of practice* (R. Nice, trans.). Cambridge University Press.

Bruner, J. S. (1962). The conditions of creativity. In H. Gruber, G. Terrell, & M. Wertheimer (Eds.), *Contemporary approaches to creative thinking: A symposium held at the university of Colorado* (pp. 1–30). Atherton Press. https://doi.org/10.1037/13117-001

Cole, M. (1996). *Cultural psychology: A once and future discipline.* Belknap Press of Harvard University Press.

Darwin, C. (1869). *On the origin of species by means of natural selection, or the preservation of favoured races in the struggle for life* (5th ed.). John Murray.

Duhigg, C. (2016). *Smarter, faster, better: The new science of productivity.* Penguin Random House.

Edmondson, A. (1999). Psychological safety and learning behavior in work teams. *Administrative Science Quarterly, 44*(2), 350–383. https://content.lesaffaires.com/LAF/lacom/psychological_safety.pdf

Falandays, J. B., & Smaldino, P. E. (2022). The emergence of cultural attractors: How dynamic populations of learners achieve collective cognitive alignment. *Cognitive Science, 46*(8), 1–34. https://doi.org/10.1111/cogs.13183

Fodor, J. (1980). On the impossibility of acquiring 'More Powerful' structures. In M. Piattelli-Palmarini (Ed.), *Language and learning the debate between Jean Piaget and Noam Chomsky* (pp. 142–162). Routledge.

Galkina, T., & Atkova, I. (2020). Effectual networks as complex adaptive systems: Exploring dynamic and structural factors of emergence. *Entrepreneurship Theory and Practice, 44*(5), 964–995. https://doi.org/10.1177/1042258719879670

Gassmann, O. (2014, September 14). The danger in missing the innovation moment. *Financial Times.* [Online]. https://www.ft.com/content/b2ef363c-31c4-11e4-b377-00144feabdc0

Gupta, A. K., Smith, K. G., & Shalley, C. E. (2006). The interplay between exploration and exploitation. *Academy of Management Journal, 49*(4), 693–706. https://doi.org/10.5465/AMJ.2006.22083026

Hundschell, A., Razinskas, S., Backmann, J., & Hoegl, M. (2022). The effects of diversity on creativity: A literature review and synthesis. *Applied Psychology, 71*(4), 1598–1634. https://doi.org/10.1111/apps.12365

Klement, A. (2018, January 18). Know the Two Very Different Interpretations of Jobs to be Done. *Jobs to Be Done.* [Online]. https://jtbd.info/know-the-two-very-different-interpretations-of-jobs-to-be-done-5a18b748bd89

Lave, J., & Wenger, E. (1991). *Situated learning: Legitimate peripheral participation.* Cambridge University Press.

Lemke, J. (1997). Cognition, context and learning: A social semiotic perspective. In D. Kirshner & J. A. Whitson (Eds.), *Situated cognition theory: Social, neurological and semiotic perspectives* (pp. 97–149). Erlbaum.

Maurya, A. (2024). Love the Problem, Not Your Solution. *LeanFoundary.com.* [Online]. https://www.leanfoundry.com/articles/love-the-problem-not-your-solution

Mead, G. H. (1932). *The philosophy of the present.* The Open Court Publishing Company.

Mesoudi, A. (2021). Cultural selection and biased transformation: Two dynamics of cultural evolution. *Philosophical Transactions of the Royal Society B: Biological Sciences, 376*(1828), 20200053 (1–12). https://doi.org/10.1098/rstb.2020.0053

Moran, S. (2009). Metaphor foundations in creativity research: Boundary vs. organism. *The Journal of Creative Behavior, 43*(1), 1–28. https://doi.org/10.1002/J.2162-6057.2009.TB01303.X

Neild, M. (2023a). The collaboration pyramid – Inspiring radical innovation that people are more willing to adopt. *The Open Review, 8,* 207–224.https://doi.org/10.47967/TOR2022COL/VOL8.17

Neild, M. (2023b). The motivated market theory – How intersubjective relationships distributed across networks enable higher value innovation. In K. R. Jensen, S. Kaudela-Baum, & R. Sheffield (Eds.), *Innovation leadership in practice: How leaders turn ideas into value in a changing world* (pp. 349–366). Emerald Publishing Limited. https://doi.org/10.1108/978-1-83753-396-120231018

Neild, M., & Tan, R. (2022). Innovation initiatives in enterprises: Advancing learning at work. In K. Evans & L. Wing On (Eds.), *Third international handbook of lifelong learning* (pp. 1–22). Springer.

Newman, D. (1996). Emergence and strange attractors. *Philosophy of Science, 63*(2), 245–261. https://www.jstor.org/stable/188472

Norman, D. A., & Verganti, R. (2014). Incremental and radical innovation: Design research vs. technology and meaning change. *Design Issues, 30*(1), 78–96. https://doi.org/10.1162/DESI_a_00250

O'Brien, K. (2020). Innovation types and the search for new ideas at the fuzzy front end: Where to look and how often? *Journal of Business Research, 107,* 13–24. https://doi.org/10.1016/j.jbusres.2019.09.007

Popper, K. R. (1978). *Three worlds. The tanner lecture on human values.* The University of Michigan.

Queirós, A., Faria, D., & Almeida, F. (2017). Strengths and limitations of qualitative and quantitative research methods. *European Journal of Education Studies, 3*(9), 359–387.

Rosing, K., Freseba, M., & Bausch, A. (2011). Explaining the heterogeneity of the leadership-innovation relationship: Ambidextrous leadership. *The Leadership Quarterly, 22*(5), 956–974. https://doi.org/10.1016/j.leaqua.2011.07.014

Runco, M. A., & Jaeger, G. J. (2012). The standard definition of creativity. *Creativity Research Journal, 24*(1), 92–96. https://doi.org/10.1080/10400419.2012.650092

Sarasvathy, S. D. (2001). *What makes entrepreneurs entrepreneurial?* (pp. 1–9). [Online]. https://22657557.fs1.hubspotusercontent-na1.net/hubfs/22657557/Public%20Documents%20For%20Site/what-makes-entrepreneurs-entrepreneurial-sarasvathy.pdf

Sarasvathy, S. D., Dew, N., Velamuri, S. R., & Venkataraman, S. (2003). Three views of entrepreneurial opportunity. In Z. J. Acs & D. B. Audretsch (Eds.), *Handbook of entrepreneurship research: International handbook series on entrepreneurship, vol 1* (pp. 141–160). Springer. https://doi.org/10.1007/0-387-24519-7_7

Sawyer, K. (1999). The emergence of creativity. *Philosophical Psychology, 12*(4), 447–469. https://doi.org/10.1080/095150899105684

Sawyer, K. (2012). *Explaining creativity: The science of human innovation* (2nd ed.). Oxford University Press.

Simester, D. (2016, March 15). Why great new products fail. *MIT Sloan Management Review.* [Online]. https://sloanreview.mit.edu/article/why-great-new-products-fail/

Simon, H. A. (1955). A behavioral model of rational choice. *The Quarterly Journal of Economics, 69*(1), 99–118. https://doi.org/10.2307/1884852

Stier, J., & Smit, S. E. (2021). Co-creation as an innovative setting to improve the uptake of scientific knowledge: Overcoming obstacles, understanding considerations and applying enablers to improve scientific impact in society. *Journal of Innovation and Entrepreneurship, 10*(35), 1–14. https://doi.org/10.1186/s13731-021-00176-2

Theise, N. (2023). *Notes on complexity: A scientific theory of connection, consciousness, and being.* Spiegel & Grau.

Tierney, A. L., & Nelson, C. A. (2009). Brain development and the role of experience in the early years. *Zero to Three, 30*(2), 9–13. https://www.ncbi.nlm.nih.gov/pmc/articles/PMC3722610/

Tomasello, M. (1999). *The cultural origins of human cognition.* Harvard University Press.

Torrance, E. P. (1984). *The Torrance tests of creative thinking: Norms-technical manual* (3rd ed.). Personnel Press.

Tversky, A., & Kahneman, D. (1974). Judgment under uncertainty: Heuristics and biases. *Science, 185*(4157), 1124–1131. https://doi.org/10.1126/science.185.4157.1124

Vaghely, I. P., & Julien, P. A. (2010). Are opportunities recognized or constructed? An information perspective on entrepreneurial opportunity identification. *Journal of Business Venturing, 25*(1), 73–86. https://doi.org/10.1016/J.JBUSVENT.2008.06.004

van Houten, M. M. (2023). Professional tacit knowledge sharing in practice. Agency, boundaries, and commitment. *Journal of Workplace Learning, 35*(9), 197–217. https://www.emerald.com/insight/content/doi/10.1108/jwl-02-2023-0025/full/pdf

Victory, K., Nenycz-Thiel, M., Dawes, J., Tanusondjaja, A., & Maria Corsi, A. (2021). How common is new product failure and when does it vary? *Marketing Letters, 32*, 17–32. https://doi.org/10.1007/s11002-021-09555-x

Vygotsky, L. S. (1978). *Mind in society: Development of higher psychological processes* (M. Cole, V. Jolm-Steiner, S. Scribner, & E. Souberman, Eds.). Harvard University Press. https://doi.org/10.2307/j.ctvjf9vz4
Wertsch, J. (1985). *Vygotsky and the social formation of mind.* Harvard University Press.
World Economic Forum. (2024). *Global risks report 2024.* World Economic Forum. [Online]. https://www.weforum.org/publications/global-risks-report-2024/digest/

Chapter 8

Adult Asian learners

Characteristics, challenges, and creative strategies of instruction to engage

Antonia Yu and Eugene Li

Introduction

Learners from different countries exhibit different learning qualities known as personal characteristics (Drachsler & Kirschner, 2012). These can be shaped by a person's culture, age, maturity, gender, or socio-economic status. In this chapter, we will consider the personal characteristics in the context of adult Asian learners,[1] along with creative strategies that instructors can implement to cater to their learning needs. We have found that little of the existing literature concerned with engaging adult learners in Higher Education (HE) has been written in the context of the East. The characteristics of adult Asian learners are often perceived to be quiet, passive, reliant on indirect communication, and dependent on rote memorisation, as compared with those learners from the West (Champagne & Walter, 2000). Based on these characteristics, instructors face a suite of common challenges when they are teaching adult Asian learners. In response to this, this chapter aims to:

- recognise current strategies used to help instructors better understand how to engage adult Asian learners in the HE classroom, and
- recommend creative instructional strategies to engage adult Asian learners based on their personal characteristics.

The chapter opens with a brief discussion about creative teaching and a recognition of the common characteristics of adult Asian learners.

Considering creative teaching and the characteristics of adult Asian learners

Creative teaching has the intention to help students learn new materials by transferring what they have learned to new problems, the success of which

---

1 For clarification, in this chapter 'adult Asian learners' refers to those who are deemed to be young (individuals who are aged between 18 and 24).

DOI: 10.4324/9781032633534-11

rests on the interactions between instructors and students (Lam & Chung, 2021; Mayer, 1989). For us, moving away from a traditional teacher-centred approach and helping Asian learners to be less reliant on rote memorisation can be fuelled by creative teaching. Our goal as creative teachers is to help adult Asian learners shed their label of being quiet/passive learners by teaching them transferrable soft skills such as time management, goal setting, and planning.

Maximising the potential of this learning process is dependent on the personal characteristics of students. Differences in geographical and cultural backgrounds contribute to the variance in learner characteristics, these ranging from active to passive, and proactive to reactive. Embracing creative teaching practices when working with adult learners requires educators *and* adult learners to take active roles and have a positive attitude in transforming their abilities to think, particularly creative thinking, this being commonly referred to as 'thinking outside the box' (Tsai, 2012). To understand how we as educators can creatively engage adult Asian learners through our teaching, one way is to recognise their characteristics, matching them with the best approaches to teaching so that adult learners can thrive.

Learner culture and the mode of education which they have previously received must be considered when instructors make choices in the teaching approaches they use in the classroom. The 'matching' we hinted at above is perceived as being of real value as it can help learners to build their active and creative behaviours (Oprea, 2014). Through such an approach, creative teaching (on the part of the educator) specifically enables learners to transfer what they have learned to new problems (Mayer, 1989). Knowledge of the common characteristics of adult Asian learners can help instructors to promote creativity which is essential for fostering openness, flexibility, and the ability to withstand uncertainty in the vast changing world (Galbraith & Jones, 2012). We recognise three common characteristics of adult Asian learners – these are categorised in Table 8.1.

Although some of the characteristics in Table 8.1 contribute to the perception of adult Asian learners being less creative, it is crucial to be mindful of these alongside positive characteristics that they exhibit, such as perseverance in getting high marks and good grades. Instructors need to remember this, embracing the right methods in teaching based on the learning characteristics of adult Asian learners (Kaplina, 2015). By using a selection of suitable approaches, such as developing adult knowledge in a practical situation (Bai, 2022), this can yield a positive and direct effect in terms of the motivational orientation of learners.

The perceived challenges of teaching adult Asian learners

There are three major perceived challenges for instructors teaching adult Asian learners. The first is the language proficiency of both lecturers and students. Instructors who are advanced in their subject knowledge may not have the language proficiency to teach and explain the technical language applicable

Table 8.1 Three common characteristics of adult Asian learners

Learner characteristic	Description
Quiet and passive	Adult Asian learners are commonly perceived as quiet, passive, and shy learners; as such, they rarely give verbal opinions (Champagne & Walter, 2000). In traditional Asian classrooms, with instructors exercising full control in a uni-directional teaching environment, this practice keeps Asian learners silent in the learning process (Lam & Chung, 2021). This passiveness fuels their reticence to engage in critical thinking, discussion, and argument (Urban & Jirsakova, 2022). With being silent as one of the obvious problems of student resistance (Graeme, 2003), the right teaching methods are needed in Asian classrooms to actively engage students in the learning process.
Indirect communication	Adult Asian learners tend to communicate less with other students, expressing themselves indirectly rather than sharing their ideas verbally. Hodgson (2019) highlights that they are reluctant in working as a group for projects and assignments. Graeme (2003) emphasises that the right tools can facilitate more direct communication and interactions with others. In order to encourage adult Asian learners to communicate with others during the learning process, instructors should create an interactive learning environment as a catalyst to help this group (Vongsila & Reinders, 2016).
Rote memorisation	The mode of learning principally used by adult Asian learners focuses on memorisation, with the retention of content being deemed to be a preferred approach to learning. For clarification purposes, rote memorisation refers to the process of learning through repetition, new knowledge being *remembered* but not necessarily *understood*. By way of an example, in the Hong Kong context, their education system focuses only on memorisation, with learners treating learning as a memory game, only having to memorise the teaching notes they have been given (Law, 2019). Champagne and Walter (2000) claim that this preferred approach to learning makes adult Asian learners less creative.

to their subject (Vu & Burns, 2014). This is a problem that can be attributed to their language development in their formative years and the language used during their technical training. Although these instructors may be able to communicate in conversational English, this does not mean they will have the language proficiency to communicate their technical subject matter. Students who are brought up in an environment where English is not their first language are likely to struggle with the sudden transition to a formal English medium of instruction (Vu & Burns, 2014). Not only is the language unfamiliar, but the technical language also poses a challenge. English for academic purposes and discipline-specific language are commonly cited as major barriers for adult Asian learners (see Pun & Jin, 2021). Students may be perceived as being uninterested or passive, whereas their language proficiency in fact could be the source of difficulty (Penfold & van der Veen, 2014).

The second challenge is the diversity within the student body. The tertiary education sector in Asia has been rapidly growing (Walkinshaw et al., 2017). It is no longer just a source of students but is also becoming a destination for international learners from all over the world. This growing diversity in the student body brings with it a new set of challenges for instructors to cater to different learner characteristics. In addition to the rising admission of international students in Hong Kong (Tse, 2023), students with a Chinese background are made up of at least two major groups:

- Hong Kong students, and
- mainland Chinese students.

Although mainland Chinese students share the same ethnic background, they are viewed as being culturally different because of variations in upbringing, learning environments, and school experiences (Yu & Zhang, 2016; Yu et al., 2019). This diversity makes engaging adult Asian learners in the classroom more difficult as individuals have different learner expectations and learning needs.

The final challenge that instructors face is the fast-evolving education landscape, this being dictated by new policies (Cheng, 2009; Walkinshaw et al., 2017) and a lack of resources to support policy implementation. Lam and Chung (2021) found that institutions did not provide adequate training for instructors to keep abreast with the changes to education policy. If training were provided, it was not made mandatory or it clashed with instructors' busy schedules. Instructors only began understanding the new teaching strategies (as advocated in the policy) when enough teaching experience had been gained. While using new technology in their teaching, Singaporean instructors reported a lack of skill in using the tools to help students fulfil their learning needs (Majal, 2020). Instructors shared that they were not confident in using the technology so opted to use simpler practices such as uploading their face-to-face lectures as videos, using polling applications, and sharing presentation slides online. While conducting a study in Vietnam, Vu and Burns (2014) found that instructors only needed subject knowledge and the ability to speak English. However, many of the experienced instructors were trained in Russian, while those who were skilled English users lacked experience in teaching. Hiring lecturers from international contexts was an option but it increased the cost for the university. In addition, the study found that the university also struggled to provide adequate reference materials, classroom equipment, and sustainable internet access to staff and students. We assert that it is important to not only be aware of these challenges and research findings but also consider effective ways to practically address them. We encourage readers to select one of the three suggested readings below, extracting from it suggested ways to address one or more of the challenges above:

1 Jiang, X., Yang, X., & Zhou, Y. (2017). Chinese international students' perceptions of their language issues in U.S. universities: A comparative study. *Journal of Interdisciplinary Studies in Education*, *6*(1), 63–80. [Online]. https://files.eric.ed.gov/fulltext/EJ1332755.pdf
2 Shea Sanger, C., & Gleason, N. W. (Eds.) (2020). *Diversity and inclusion in global higher education: Lessons from across Asia*. Palgrave Macmillan.
3 Horta, H. (2023). Emerging and near future challenges of higher education in East Asia. *Asian Economic Policy Review*, *18*(2), 171–191. https://doi.org/10.1111/aepr.12416

Common strategies for teaching adult Asian learners

We recognise that there are four common strategies for teaching adult Asian learners (see Figure 8.1), these being also referred to as 'approaches' and 'methods'.

An important question to ask is: *which of these is best for adult Asian learners?* To answer this, we need to consider if/how associated pedagogical practices of each strategy can be adapted for learners from a different culture. According to Biggs (1999, as cited in Penfold & van der Veen, 2014), there are three associated approaches, implementation-wise, that can be adopted: *Assimilation,*

The *traditional teacher-centred approach* is described by Lathan (n.d.) as one where 'the teacher functions in the familiar role of classroom lecturer, presenting information to the students, who are expected to passively receive the knowledge being presented'. Of interest is the common misconception of this serving as the preferred approach of adult Asian learners.	The *electronic self-directed strategy* is deemed to be appropriate for mature, highly motivated, independent students. This strategy uses modern e-learning platforms to deliver information to students. The largest benefit of this strategy allows students to learn at their own preferred pace.
The *student-approach* has the instructor play the role of facilitator in guiding and assisting students through the learning process. In this role, the educator focuses on briefing and debriefing, rather than transferring information to students (Kaplina, 2015). Students rely on their various skills to gather in-depth information on a particular subject matter.	The *project-based method* uses real-world problems to engage students in learning transferrable skills such as collaboration, resource management, and critical thinking through problem-solving (Almulla, 2020).

Figure 8.1 Four common strategies for teaching adult learners in Asia.

Accommodation, or *Teaching as education*. The bullet points below are offered by way of a succinct explanation:

1 *Assimilation* focuses on having students adapt to Western methods of learning and teaching.
2 *Accommodation* focuses on an educator's understanding of the target culture and adapting teaching strategies to suit the needs of the students.
3 *Teaching as education* does not focus on the differences in culture but on the learning process, emphasising good teaching practices that teach students appropriate learning behaviours and habits.

In relation to the third bullet point above, Hodgson (2019) identifies six characteristics of good teaching practices which are summarised in Table 8.2 for reader reflection.

By way of an explanation, to support those students who are struggling with the language or those who are easily distracted, Hodgson (2019) suggests using a variety of instruction modes to help students focus on the task (Table 8.2, no. 1). These strategies may affect the instructional style necessary to be successful in teaching adult Asian learners. One strategy is to teach transferrable skills and behaviours such as communication, time management, and problem-solving (no. 2), the assertion being that students find these helpful as a general form of self-improvement. Instructors should also model scholarship by bringing research into the classroom, supporting claims they make with reference to external studies (no. 4) – this shows students how they can approach scholarship and academia from a role model perspective. Prompt feedback is an important part of the learning process as it can help to address the needs of different individuals (no. 5). The timeliness of the feedback will make it more

Table 8.2 Characteristics of good teaching practices (adapted from Hodgson, 2019)

No.	Characteristics of good teaching practices	Examples
1	Attend to short attention spans	Use of multimodalities – think VARK (see Introduction, p. 9)
2	Enable the development of transferrable skills	Use of problem-solving and leadership skills
3	Engage student interest in assessment tasks	Use of real-world case studies and role play
4	Link research and teaching	Support students when working with academic sources
5	Provide prompt feedback to students	Provide opportunities for students to seek feedback before submission deadlines
6	Pay attention to the feedback from students	Use observations of student engagement in classroom tasks to inform future practice

useful for students to recall and reflect on their work. Instructors should not only give feedback but also consider the feedback from students (non-verbal, verbal, written) to help instructors adjust and continually improve their teaching practices (no. 6).

We appreciate that engaging adult Asian learners in a classroom setting can be difficult; as such it requires a combination of existing and creative methods to encourage their participation. It is to this that the chapter turns its attention.

Current and creative ways of engaging adult Asian learners

While rapid growth and the adoption of new educational policies in Asia have been observed, the general tendency is for the classroom to be run as traditional teacher-centred. This is the case in Japan, Singapore, and Hong Kong. Although there have been efforts to shift the focus of the classroom from instructor to student (Filatova, 2015; Hallinger & Lu, 2013; Wastila, 2019; Yeung, 2009), the cultures of these countries still have a propensity for a teacher-centred approach.

In Japan, college classrooms still gravitate towards the teacher-centred approach even though the benefits of the student-centred approach are known (Demir et al., 2012). Crosby and Woollock (2019) have proposed a creative method for engaging Japanese students while attempting to move away from the teacher-centred classroom. They experimented with the use of visual methods in HE classrooms, examples of which include comic book analysis and model-making (construction). The use of comic books showed these adult learners cultural similarities and differences, giving students stimulating content to discuss. Model-making was chosen as a project for students to research and produce during the class. They were asked to discuss what the subject of their model was and answer questions throughout the lesson to further reinforce ideas through repetition. The idea is that through this, students would be able to transfer knowledge from their short-term memory to their long-term memory. By incorporating visual methods, Crosby and Woollock (2019) found that students were more intrinsically motivated to engage with the materials offered to them. While hidden, the primary learning objectives were achieved through analysis, discussion, and the presentation of these visual mediums. The use of these unconventional materials (at least in the Japanese context) shifted the classroom from being teacher-centred to being student-centred.

In Singapore, instructors have been adjusting to the use of technology to aid their engagement with adult learners (Majal, 2020). Although some believe that technology would not help to engage adult learners, others believe there are real benefits to the incorporation of technology, e.g., online platforms. A robust online platform can encourage new creative modes of teaching that promote new forms of learning such as blended or self-directed learning. Blended learning mixes up the modes in which students engage with materials. Unlike the traditional teacher-centred classroom, blended learning gives students more control over what materials they are using to achieve their lesson objectives. Regardless of the content, blended learning can be used to teach students transferrable skills such as digital literacy, critical and creative thinking, and information curation. Self-directed learning gives instructors opportunities to motivate students to engage with creative materials outside of traditional class time (see Morris, 2020). Students who are more comfortable working at their own pace and managing their own learning may prefer this over the traditional teacher-centred approach. However, Asian students are not typically self-motivated because of the tradition of having an instructor provide them with knowledge. As such, this may not be the best approach for adult Asian learners.

In an effort to shift classrooms away from the traditional teacher-centred approach, some HE instructors in Hong Kong have adopted different creative approaches to teaching such as motivation and engagement based on the 'Motivation and Engagement Wheel' (see Yin, 2018) and active learning methods (see Hallinger & Lu, 2013). Adaptive motivation and engagement aim to amplify students' positive attitudes and behaviours towards learning, while maladaptive motivation and engagement hinder student learning with fears of uncertainty and self-sabotage. To maximise adaptive motivation and engagement, Yin (2018) argues that instructors need to allocate lessons to train students in planning, self-motivation, and time management. These skills teach students to build confidence and an appreciation for learning. To minimise maladaptive motivation and engagement, instructors are required to give clear instructions to lessen the fear of uncertainty and create an inclusive environment to ease student anxiety. Instructors should make students aware of the negative emotions that lead to anxiety and a fear of failure in an effort to mitigate the impacts of maladaptive engagement (we argue that it is okay to be wrong, especially if you learn from it!). Yin's (2018) promotion of a student-centred shift in the classroom requires modification in instructor mentality. Currently, this is not widely adopted, but the concepts bring new insight into the possibilities of ways to engage adult Asian learners in HE.

Hallinger and Lu (2013) suggest instructors adopt active learning methods to motivate adult learners at the tertiary level in Hong Kong. They provide three suggestions:

- The first suggestion is for instructors to have clear intended learning outcomes. These can give students direction and purpose. Due to cultural influences, Hong Kong students are uncomfortable with uncertainty, so clear learning outcomes eliminate this. We argue that this suggestion actually has less to do with active learning (see Chapter 1) and is more related to what students will learn and how that learning will be assessed, making course/unit/module design, assessing student learning progress, and the facilitation of learning activities easier and more effective (see Stanford University, n.d.).

- The second suggestion relates to assessment *for* learning (A*f*L) which helps to draw the focus away from summative assessment (A*o*L) and put it more on learning. The shift in mentality (starting with the instructor and then students) is no longer just overcoming an assessment but thinking more about how assessments can be used to make improvements. We support this from an active learning perspective, recognising that A*f*L 'enables learners to become less passive in the classroom', especially when they 'develop the ability to assess themselves and to take responsibility for their own learning' (Cambridge International Education Teaching and Learning Team, n.d.).
- The third suggestion is to work collaboratively to mitigate the effects of a diverse student body. Instead of rote learning, as observed by Law (2019), collaborative work gives students an opportunity to reinforce their learning through peer feedback and negotiation of meaning. This means that those who do not share the same experiences are not disadvantaged. We value the work of Major (2020, p. 19) who sees collaborative learning as a 'tried and true active learning method for the college [university] classroom'.

Strategies for instruction

Strategies for instruction refer to teaching approaches an educator uses to help students meet learning objectives. The use of appropriate strategies for instruction can help educators teach creatively in the HE sector (Joseph et al., 2013) and help students learn new material (Mayer, 1989). Different styles of instruction can lead to creativity, not just to benefit educators but also to sustain interest and interaction between instructors and learners (Galbraith & Jones, 2012; Lam & Chung, 2021). As such, using strategies for instruction can help create an interactive classroom, one which can motivate adult learners during the learning process (Sogunro, 2015). In order to choose the right strategy for instruction, educators need to take into account the prior knowledge of learners (Hast, 2020). Instructors also need to be aware of how learners can bring their knowledge and informal experiences to formal learning settings (such as the university classroom) when learning new knowledge.

For adult Asian learners, who are generally quiet and passive, instructional strategies which promote interaction between instructors and learners can help them build confidence and create mutual respect (Maulana, 2020). The interactive approach to instruction is, therefore, recommended for use as it can motivate them to participate more during the learning process. Seaman and Fellenz (1989) suggested that the interactive approach to instruction offers learners more opportunities for others to react to their ideas, insights, knowledge, and experiences; this also helps learners to organise their thoughts. Role play, debates, peer practice, and co-operative learning groups are just some of the strategies for instruction which can promote creative teaching in the classroom by motivating learners to use their experiences to advance learning (Peerters et al., 2014; Saskatchewan Education, 1991). The suggested strategies for instruction can promote creative teaching in a number of ways (see Table 8.3).

Table 8.3 Suggested strategies for instruction to promote creative teaching (drawing on the work of Community Training and Assistance Centre and Washoe County School District, 2016)

Scenario	Suggested instructional strategy	Rationale
Instructors want to engage learners by encouraging them to creatively recall their experiences by getting them to work in different roles.	Role play	Role play can help learners use various ways of representing knowledge – be it physically and/or orally – by recalling their experiences and prompting their curiosity and exploration.
Instructors would like to engage a group of shy learners who are able to express themselves creatively in writing but are less inclined to express their ideas orally in a creative way.	Debates	Learning through debates allows students to engage in the research of knowledge and creative thinking. This strategy of instruction can specifically help students to contribute to the development of learning content from different perspectives.
Instructors would like to help learners feel comfortable in working as a group to consolidate or build knowledge.	Peer practice	Peer practice involves peer teaching and collaboration among learners. Students may be grouped in pairs or small groups to solve problems together or discuss concepts. This provides an opportunity for learners to support each other, especially with active learners helping those who are more passive.
Instructors would like to build a support group for students who are passive and rely on indirect communication.	Co-operative learning groups	A co-operative learning group is a heterogeneous (mixed) one, which allows learners to take different roles in the group and share tasks and knowledge with groupmates. Passive learners can first serve as silent members to observe the interactions of other members. Such observations may lead them to contribute to the group at a later stage. Learners in the same group can build positive levels of interdependence and interaction to facilitate learning.

Irrespective of which strategy of instruction is embraced (as per Table 8.3), Ong (2021) suggests that instructors need to pay closer attention to the design of clear instruction that can cater to the different needs of adult learners, this being purposeful in improving learners' engagement and motivation. Giving clear instruction depends heavily on the teaching behaviours of instructors and also the learning behaviours of learners. As adult Asian learners tend not to express their thoughts directly, instructors giving clear instructions can aid learners understanding and provide them with a model of clarity and conciseness to express themselves with direction and with a degree of ease as part of the learning process. This can be achieved by offering learners concise explanations, articulate demonstrations, and comprehensive questioning (Saskatchewan Education, 1991). Concise explanations allow adult learners to deepen their understanding of a concept from a succinct baseline, whereas articulate demonstrations help them to experience and understand the learning process, with the comprehensive questioning skills of an educator helping adult learners to foster their knowledge through role play, for example (for adaptable ideas, see NCCA, 2015).

Concluding comments

This chapter has characterised some of the common learner characteristics of adult Asian learners, e.g., quiet, passive, indirect communicators, and rote memorisers. It is not the intention of this chapter to perpetuate these stereotypes; instead, it is important for instructors to understand the learning characteristics of their students to better cater to their learning needs. The chapter also collates some of the common challenges that tertiary instructors have when teaching adult Asian learners. The three major challenges – language proficiency of both student and instructor, diversity in the student body, and a lack of resources to support instructors in meeting the aforementioned challenges – demand careful and creative consideration if these are to be effectively managed in the HE classroom.

Examples from Japan, Singapore, and Hong Kong have been shared in recognition of some of the current innovations embraced by the Asian tertiary sector to engage adult learners. This includes visual methods, the use of technology to stimulate blended or self-directed learning, the use of the 'Motivation and Engagement Wheel' as a creative approach to engage adult learners (Yin, 2018), and active learning methods (also see Chapter 1). We argue that more needs to be done to bring creative instruction into the HE classroom, especially in Asia. We have found that a responsive style of instruction is required to engage adult Asian learners, this being direct and clear for quiet/passive learners, the use of which can reduce fear of failure and uncertainty. Strategies of instruction such as role play can be used to promote direct communication in those who favour indirect communication. For passive learners, peer practice could be an effective way to get them more involved. We believe that the HE classroom needs to be student-centred, comfortable, and non-hierarchical. A creative approach to teaching is one that we advocate as it moves the classroom away from the traditional teacher-centred approach. A student-centred classroom will emphasise student accountability for their own learning, and teach them positive and valuable learning behaviours like time management. Creative teaching will also help to eradicate the Asian stereotype of quiet/passive learners, giving students more opportunities to showcase their personal characteristics.

Acknowledgements

Simon Brownhill for his advice and guidance throughout the writing process, along with the enrichment contributions he made to the chapter. Ibrahim Berksoy and Nako Abdullah for their comments and feedback in the planning stage and on an earlier draft.

Suggested further reading

Koh, C. (Ed.) (2020). *Diversifying learner experience: A kaleidoscope of instructional approaches and strategies.* Springer. https://doi.org/10.1007/978-981-15-9861-6
Wong, T. M. (2018). Teaching innovations in Asian higher education: Perspectives of educators. *Asian Association of Open Universities, 13*(2), 179–190. [Online]. https://www.emerald.com/insight/content/doi/10.1108/AAOUJ-12-2018-0032/full/html

References

Almulla, M. A. (2020). The effectiveness of the project-based learning (PBL) approach as a way to engage students in learning. *Sage Open, 10*(3), 1–15. https://doi.org/10.1177/2158244020938702
Bai, M. (2022). The characteristics of adult learners and second language teaching strategies. *Proceedings of the 2022 International Conference on Science Education and Art Appreciation (SEAA 2022)* (pp. 980–987), Chengdu, China. [Online]. https://www.atlantis-press.com/proceedings/seaa-22/125976980
Biggs, J. B. (1999). *Teaching for quality learning at university.* Society for Research into Higher Education and Open University Press.
Cambridge International Education Teaching and Learning Team (n.d.). Getting started with Assessment for Learning. *Cambridge Assessment International Education.* [Online]. https://cambridge-community.org.uk/professional-development/gswafl/index.html#:~:text=AFL%20increases%20independence,responsibility%20for%20their%20own%20learning
Champagne, M., & Walter, P. (2000). A Bourdieuian perspective on differences in adult learning styles: deconstructing Asian learners. *Adult Education Research Conference.* [Online]. https://newprairiepress.org/aerc/2000/roundtables/9
Cheng, Y. C. (2009). Hong Kong educational reforms in the last decade: Reform syndrome and new developments. *International Journal of Educational Management, 23*(1), 65–86. https://doi.org/10.1108/09513540910926439

Community Training and Assistance Centre and Washoe County School District. (2016). *Student Learning Objectives – Instructional Strategies List*. [Online]. https://www.washoeschools.net/cms/lib/NV01912265/Centricity/Domain/228/WCSD%20Instructional%20Strategies%20List%2006.06.2016.pdf

Crosby, R., & Woollock, A. R. (2019). Creative approaches to education in the Japanese tertiary sector: Two case studies using applied visual enquiry (AVE). *The Annals of Gifu Shotoku Gakuen University, Faculty of Education, 58*, 45–56. [Online]. https://shotoku.repo.nii.ac.jp/record/2144/files/07-Creative%20approaches%20to%20education%20in%20the%20Japanese%20tertiary%20sector.pdf

Demir, K., Sutton-Brown, C., & Czerniak, C. (2012). Constraints to changing pedagogical practices in higher education: An example from Japanese lesson study. *International Journal of Science Education, 34*(11), 1709–1739. https://doi.org/10.1080/09500693.2011.645514

Drachsler, H., & Kirschner, P. A. (2012). Learner characteristics. In N. M. Seel (Ed.), *Encyclopaedia of the sciences of learning* (2012 ed.) (pp. 1743–1745). Springer. https://doi.org/10.1007/978-1-4419-1428-6_347

Filatova, O. A. (2015). Cultural attributes of students to make student-centered approach successful. *International Journal of Languages, Literature and Linguistics, 1*(1), 20–24. https://doi.org/10.7763/IJLLL.2015.V1.5

Galbraith, M. W., & Jones, M. S. (2012). Creativity: Essential for the adult education instructor and learner. *PAACE Journal of Lifelong Learning, 21*(2012), 51–59. [Online]. https://www.iup.edu/pse/files/programs/graduate_programs_r/instructional_design_and_technology_ma/paace_journal_of_lifelong_learning/volume_21/galbraith-jones.pdf

Graeme, S. (2003). Comparing online and traditional teaching – A different approach. *Campus-Wide Information Systems, 20*(4), 137–145. https://doi.org/10.1108/10650740310491306

Hallinger, P., & Lu, J. (2013). Learner centered higher education in East Asia: Assessing the effects on student engagement. *International Journal of Educational Management, 27*(6), 594–612. https://doi.org/10.1108/IJEM-06-2012-0072

Hast, M. (2020). "It is there but you need to dig a little deeper for it to become evident to them": Tacit knowledge assessment in the primary science classroom. In C. Koh (Ed.), *Diversifying learner experience* (pp. 13–28). Springer. https://doi.org/10.1007/978-981-15-9861-6_2

Hodgson, P. (2019). Opportunities, challenges and creative teaching practices of new international and local recruits in Hong Kong. *Athens Journal of Education, 6*(2), 111–125. [Online]. https://www.athensjournals.gr/education/2019-6-2-2-Hodgson.pdf

Joseph, S., Thomas, M., Simonette, G., & Ramsook, L. (2013). The impact of differentiated instruction in a teacher education setting: Successes and challenges. *International Journal of Higher Education, 2*(3), 28–40. https://doi.org/10.5430/ijhe.v2n3p28

Kaplina, S. E. (2015). Innovative methods in teaching English to adults. *Journal of Siberian Federal University, Humanities & Social Sciences, 11*(8), 2437–2447. https://doi.org/10.17516/1997-1370-2015-8-11-2437-2447

Lam, P. C., & Chung, H. H. Y. (2021). Teaching creatively in Hong Kong higher education sector: Transition from the teacher-centered approach to the creative teaching approach. *Journal of Communication and Education, 5*(1), 57–73. http://www.hkaect.org/jce/5(1)/Lam&Chung_2021_JCE_5(1)_pp57-73.pdf

Lathan, J. (n.d.). Complete Guide To Teacher-centered Vs Student-centered Learning. *University of San Diego*. [Online]. https://tinyurl.com/yzskax2d

Law, V. (2019, August 13). The Spoon-feeding Education. Genaction blog. *UNICEF Hong Kong*. [Online]. https://genaction.unicef.org.hk/en/blog/detail/22/

Majal, P. (2020). *Teaching Adult Learners Online: A Case Study in Singapore* (Doctoral dissertation, The University of Western Australia). [Online]. https://research-repository.uwa.edu.au/en/publications/teaching-adult-learners-online-a-case-study-in-singapore

Major, C. (2020). Collaborative learning: A tried and true active learning method for the college classroom. In K. C. Culver & T. L. Trolian (Eds.), *New directions for teaching and learning: Special issue – Effective instruction in college classrooms: Research-based approaches to college and university teaching, 164,* 19–28. Wiley. https://doi.org/10.1002/tl.20420

Maulana, M. F. (2020). Instructional strategies for foreign languages learning: A practical approach of Mahmud Yunus' thought. *Tadris: Jurnal Keguruan dan Ilmu Tarbiyah, 5*(1), 87–96. https://doi.org/10.24042/tadris.v5i1.5942

Mayer, R. (1989). Cognitive views of creativity: Creative teaching for creative learning. *Contemporary Educational Psychology, 14*(3), 203–211. https://doi.org/10.1016/0361-476X(89)90010-6

Morris, T. H. (2020). Creativity through self-directed learning: Three distinct dimensions of teacher support. *International Journal of Lifelong Education, 39*(2), 168–178. https://doi.org/10.1080/02601370.2020.1727577

National Council for Curriculum and Assessment (NCCA). (2015). *Workshop 02: Focus on learning – Effective questioning.* NCCA. [Online]. https://ncca.ie/media/1924/assessment-booklet-2_en.pdf

Ong, I. (2021). Play and flow: Harnessing flow through the power of play in adult learning. Koh, C. (Ed.), In *Diversifying learner experience – A kaleidoscope of instructional approaches and strategies* (pp. 137–156). Springer.

Oprea, C. L. (2014). Interactive and creative learning of the adults. *Procedia – Social and Behavioral Sciences, 142,* 493–498.https://doi.org/10.1016/j.sbspro.2014.07.654

Peerters, J., Backer, F., Buffel, T., Kindekens, A., Struyven, K., Zhu, C., & Lombaerts, K. (2014). Adult learners' informal learning experiences in formal education setting. *Journal of Adult Development, 21,* 181–192. https://doi.org/10.1007/s10804-014-9190-1

Penfold, P., & van der Veen, R. (2014). Investigating learning approaches of Confucian heritage culture students and teachers' perspectives in Hong Kong. *Journal of Teaching in Travel & Tourism, 14*(1), 69–86. https://doi.org/10.1080/15313220.2014.872903

Pun, J., & Jin, X. (2021). Student challenges and learning strategies at Hong Kong EMI universities. *PLoS ONE, 16*(5), e0251564. https://doi.org/10.1371/journal.pone.0251564

Saskatchewan Education. (1991). *Instructional approaches: A framework for professional practice.* Saskatchewan Education. [Online]. https://pubsaskdev.blob.core.windows.net/pubsask-prod/15320/15320-instructional-approaches.pdf

Seaman, D., & Fellenz, R. (1989). *Effective strategies for teaching adults.* Merrill Publishing Company.

Sogunro, O. A. (2015). Motivating factors for adult learners in higher education. *International Journal of Higher Education, 4*(1), 22–37. http://dx.doi.org/10.5430/ijhe.v4n1p22

Stanford University. (n.d.). Creating Learning Outcomes. *Stanford Teaching Commons.* [Online]. https://teachingcommons.stanford.edu/teaching-guides/foundations-course-design/course-planning/creating-learning-outcomes

Tsai, K. C. (2012). The value of teaching creativity in adult education. *International Journal of Higher Education, 1*(2), 84–91. https://doi.org/10.5430/ijhe.v1n2p84

Tse, H. (2023, October 18). Hong Kong to raise non-local university student intake ceiling to 40%. *Hong Kong Free Press.* [Online]. https://hongkongfp.com/2023/10/18/hong-kong-to-raise-non-local-university-student-intake-ceiling-to-40-reports/

Urban, K., & Jirsakova, J. (2022). Motivation and personality traits in adult learners. *Journal of Adult and Continuing Education*, *28*(1), 151–166. https://doi.org/10.1177/14779714211000361

Vongsila, V., & Reinders, H. (2016). Making Asian learners talk: Encouraging willingness to communicate. *RELC Journal*, *47*(3), 331–347. https://doi.org/10.1177/0033688216645641

Vu, N. T., & Burns, A. (2014). English as a medium of instruction: Challenges for Vietnamese tertiary lecturers. *Journal of Asia TEFL*, *11*(3), 1–31. [Online]. https://tinyurl.com/8xtjajaa

Walkinshaw, I., Fenton-Smith, B., & Humphreys, P. (2017). EMI issues and challenges in Asia-Pacific higher education: An introduction. In B. Fenton-Smith, P. Humphreys, & I. Walkinshaw (Eds.), *English medium instruction in higher education in Asia-Pacific: From policy to pedagogy* (pp. 1–18). Springer. https://doi.org/10.1007/978-3-319-51976-0_1

Wastila, J. (2019). The student-centered classroom in EFL classes in Japan: A team-based approach. *Meisei International Communication Research Journal*, *11*(1), 45–55. [Online]. https://meisei.repo.nii.ac.jp/record/1611/files/J-kcNo11a04.pdf

Yeung, S. Y. S. (2009). Is student-centered pedagogy impossible in Hong Kong? The case of inquiry in classrooms. *Asia Pacific Education Review*, *10*(3), 377–386. [Online]. https://link.springer.com/article/10.1007/s12564-009-9028-x

Yin, H. (2018). What motivates Chinese undergraduates to engage in learning? Insights from a psychological approach to student engagement research. *Higher Education*, *76*(5), 827–847. [Online]. https://link.springer.com/article/10.1007/s10734-018-0239-0

Yu, B., Mak, A. S., & Bodycott, P. (2019). Psychological and academic adaptation of mainland Chinese students in Hong Kong universities. *Studies in Higher Education*, *46*(8), 1552–1564. https://doi.org/10.1080/03075079.2019.1693991

Yu, B., & Zhang, K. (2016). 'It's more foreign than a foreign country': Adaptation and experience of mainland Chinese students in Hong Kong. *Tertiary Education and Management*, *22*(4), 300–315. https://doi.org/10.1080/13583883.2016.1226944

Part III

Engaging tools

Chapter 9

Poetic methods

Creatively examining stories and voice in Higher Education

Rachel Helme

A shifting emotional journey – a poem

It starts with the sadness of 'not'
  Not planned
  Not sure how I feel
  Mourning
  Trying to let go
  Not able
  Second best

Then became self-centred
  Why do I?
  Do I feel?
  Out of control
  What if no one?
  What if no one?
  I am scared
  I am nervous of letting go
  I have to control

But then there is a shift
  Isn't that the point?
  Allowing what may happen
  What might emerge
  Silence is a right
  Resistance and compliance
  Not equals if they have to
  With and alongside
  How do they feel?
  How is it for them?

DOI: 10.4324/9781032633534-13

Introduction

I created the poem on page 147 from an entry in my own research diary that I wrote during my doctoral study (Helme, 2023). It was April 2020 – a pivotal moment in the study. It was the point at which I, as a researcher, had to make a decision about whether to continue the study or postpone it due to restrictions imposed during the COVID-19 pandemic. I felt it was necessary to re-examine my own voice that I felt had become lost in the prose of the research diary. The notion of voice is a prominent feature in Higher Education (HE) that is often encapsulated in different forms of prose, including, for example, students' written comments from feedback activities, encouraging the development of academic voice through writing and reflexivity, as well as listening to the voices of others when creating literature reviews. However, there has been much debate around practices in HE that are said to favour Western and European principles, seen by some as elitist in structure. In her book, *How Higher Education Feels*, Quinlan (2016) argues that HE can often be seen as being objective, with a focus mostly on the logical and rational voice. Emotional responses are seen as being irrational, primitive, and out-of-control (Postareff & Lindblom-Ylänne, 2011). This is exemplified by Trinh et al. (2021, p. 27) who argue that having to conform suggested that 'my creativity, my culture, my poems, my lived experience and my stories were not important'. Canagarajah (2024, p. 280) calls for the decolonisation of writing practices that they see as rejecting 'embodiment and relationality that are significant for indigenous and Southern communities'. In order to disrupt the reliance on academic prose, there is a need to introduce creative ways of examining and developing voice that do not ignore 'the struggle for recognition, voice and legitimacy' (Burke, 2008, p. 208). I argue that the ways of working in HE should acknowledge the emotive realm, for which arts-based methods, and more specifically (for this chapter) poetry, are particularly suited.

The content of this chapter is driven by two aims:

- To demonstrate the use of poetry as a means to engage with voice in HE.
- To introduce readers to poetic structures that can be used to engage creativity with voice-related reading and writing practices.

I begin by talking about the relationship between poetry and language.

Using structures to find poetry within language

The question here is *Why poetry? What does the use of poetry and methods drawn from poetic inquiry afford over the use of prose alone?* When used in research, poetry is said to communicate thoughts evocatively, both conveying and engaging with emotions. Butler-Kisber (2020) describes this as new ways of knowing, creatively playing with the form of language to convey meaning that may not be evident when using prose alone. There is the opportunity to go beyond the meaning of words towards experiencing or feeling language, attending to what Fitzpatrick and Fitzpatrick (2020, p. 9) describe as 'aesthetic knowledges' found in the form of language. From a feminist perspective, the use of poetry is a powerful way to foreground the voices of those that see themselves as marginalised by dominant academic practice, inviting the speaker and/or listener to make connections with and through embodied stories (Lindemann, 2019; Ward, 2011).

The use of the term 'poetry' in this chapter goes beyond the type of poetry that might be experienced in school, such as lyrical first-person poems. There is a focus on the *poeticity* of language, repetitions in the verbal structure, and semiotics of spoken or written language found in the following:

phrases   syntax   metaphors

sounds   vocalisation   rhythm

salient   vivid   poignant words

(Butler-Kisber, 2020; Jakobson, 1960; Staats, 2021)

In Figure 9.1, the use of repeated, similar phrases and metaphors as devices can be seen in the creation of a poem. The figure reveals the first two verses of a transcript poem drawn from narrative data where two participants, a student (left-hand side) and a teacher (right-hand side), talk about their experiences of teaching and learning mathematics. The focus is on one particular student called Claire (a pseudonym), who had recently begun studying at a post-16

A weak grade 3
Not confident with number
Potentially over graded
Muddled like a maze
Always wanting to be the first to speak
Shouting out
Disrupting the take up time
Overcompensating for potential lack of ability
The wrong kind of attention
Going to have a difficult job to do

Like a maze
Not straight at all
A very long way I had to go
There were mistakes
Wasn't easy for me
A difficult start
Plans all over the place
A daily struggle
Hurdles of maths
I couldn't understand

Figure 9.1 A poem about the teaching and learning of mathematics (Helme, 2023).

college in the Southwest of England. Claire was allocated a grade 3 (equivalent grade D-E) in her mathematics GCSE by her school at the end of her secondary education and therefore had to continue to study mathematics in college in order to improve her grade.

The first four lines of the teacher's verse are structured around phrases that the teacher used in their evaluation of Claire's ability: *weak; not confident; over graded; muddled*. The poetic repetition used is focused on phrases with similar meanings that suggest the teacher beliefs about Claire and what is inferred to be a misallocation of a grade 3. The subsequent lines relate to observed classroom behaviours: *first to speak; shouting out; disrupting; the wrong kind of attention*. In the original narrative, the teacher suggested that these behaviours related to the fact she (Claire) had been over graded and, as such, they appear in the same verse. Claire's own verse is structured around her use of metaphors of barriers to learning: *a maze; not straight; a long way; all over the place; hurdles*. The metaphors that she used seemed physical in nature and, hence, required personal effort to overcome. The verses created draw on the poeticity in the language: less sonnet and more symphony, less rhyme and more rhythm. There is no prescribed approach for creating the poems, with poetic creators using both existing poetic structures, for example, drawing on the form of dramatic dialogues, such as scripted plays or monologues, spoken from the point of view of a character, or, alternatively, some develop their own poetic structures (Butler-Kisber, 2020; Faulkner, 2019).

Voicing a poem

Voice in writing and poems will often refer to who spoke or authored the original words (that is, whose voice is being listened to). Prendergast (2009) talks about three categories of voice when creating poems:

1 The *autobiographical voice*, where a person will be talking about themselves and their own experiences;
2 *Participant voice*, either created from prose, e.g., transcripts or feedback activities, or poems created by the participants themselves; and
3 *Literature voiced*, written from, or in response to, theory or literature reviews.

In another form of categorisation, Butler-Kisber (2020) describes poems in terms of how the words and phrases are sourced or created:

- *Found poems* are crafted by another person using the original words from, for example, interview transcripts and literature reviews. The words and phrases are reordered or reframed to draw attention to particular themes and insights.
- *Generated poetry* is self-authored, using one's own words to craft poetry that, by way of two examples, represents interpretations of personal experiences or draws attention to reflexivity.

The two forms of categorisation above are interconnected:

i The autobiographical voice is generated, this being written about the self by the self;
ii The participant voice can be found or generated, this being drawn from transcripts or written as poems by the participants themselves;
iii The literature voiced is found out of the words of other authors.

Creativity in HE

In order to begin to disrupt a world dominated by objectivity and prose, it is necessary to incorporate creative approaches in the way that voice is engaged with in HE (Fitzpatrick & Fitzpatrick, 2020; Quinlan, 2016). For this chapter, creativity is defined by Kleiman (2008, p. 209) as involving 'notions of novelty and originality combined with notions of utility and value'. To engage creatively involves opportunities to be creative, at the meeting point of originality and utility, in a sense poetry with a purpose. In a study into conceptions of creativity in HE, Kleiman (2008) noted the following five main categories for academics' perceptions of creativity:

- A *constraint-focused experience*, e.g., being constrained by the system or lack of experience,
- A *process-focused experience*, e.g., leading to explicit outcomes or making connections,
- A *product-focused experience*, e.g., the production of something or of significant originality,
- A *transformation-focused experience*, e.g., undertaken with the intention to be transformative or exploiting risk-taking, and
- A *fulfilment-focused experience*, e.g., personal or professional fulfilment.

Kleiman (2008) states that transformation and fulfilment are central but are not often seen as part of everyday academic practices. In this chapter, I will examine the use of poetry as both original and novel, and having value and utility, with the potential for transformation and fulfilment within the emotional experiences of examining and developing voice within HE.

Poems and HE

Listening to experiences found in prose

The use of poems is a means to start to listen for or understand another's experience, either as a student or academic. Prendergast (2009) talks about a focus on feelings as an arena for introducing poems into analysis, for example, *How does it feel to be a new student? What are the feelings invoked by*

Table 9.1 Examples of poetic structures used to examine voice in Higher Education

Source	Purpose	Poetic structure	Details
Demir-Yildiz (2020)	Students' feedback on the physical environment at university.	Wish poems	• Sentence starters that students complete: 'I wish…'. • Statements analysed using thematic analysis, grouped around how students might change their environment.
Kaukko et al. (2024)	The stories of asylum-seeking students in Australian HE.	Pronoun poems	• Extracting phrases around the speakers' use of a pronoun, verb, and other seemingly important words. • Analysed for coexisting voices within the pronoun poem.
Zambo and Zambo (2013)	Examining the complexity of experience for students completing their Doctorate in Education (EdD).	I poems	• Similar to the details in the entry above, extracting the speakers' use of the I pronoun, verb, and other seemingly important words. • Analysed for nuances in the way students talk about themselves.

imposter syndrome? When creating poems from prose, the listener takes the original narrative and creates poems, following rhythms, repeats, and salient words, in order to listen in new ways to the narrative; it is participant voiced and found poetry. For an experienced poem creator, it is possible to manipulate the language, identifying key themes, language, or metaphors being used. However, in some examples of giving attention to voice in HE, structures have been offered to draw out poeticity which could be a helpful starting point for the less confident, both as a support for an instructor and a student. In Table 9.1, examples of poetic structures are offered, these being organised around the use of a phrase, both to generate and to examine narrative.

Both sentence starters and extracting pronoun phrases provide creative structures to begin the work of becoming a poem creator. There is scope for additional creativity, with 'I wish' becoming, for example, 'I notice' or 'I think', and extracted pronoun phrases being identified from 'they' or 'she/he', or even other words such as 'the course' or 'the teaching'.

Case studies: the use of pronoun poems within the Listening Guide

The case studies offered in this chapter draw on a small-scale project looking at students' identity work within the context of low attainment in mathematics (see Helme, 2023). The study investigated ways to give attention to voice, to listening carefully to the way students talked about themselves, as well as how others, such as their teacher, talked about them. The study was located within a post-16 college; however, it must be stressed that ways of listening carefully to voice are applicable to many settings, especially HE.

The study used a poetic inquiry method called the Listening Guide (Gilligan et al., 2006). This method of creating and examining poetic structures is a voice-centred, relational method that is said to bring the listener into a relationship with the speaker, reflecting on the multilayered nature of a person's lived experience. The Listening Guide is said to replace judgement with curiosity (Gilligan & Eddy, 2021), reflecting on the nuances of coexisting voices that may reside within the same narrative. The method asks the listener to consider the following questions:

- *What does the narrative sound like?*
- *What words, rhythms, and silences does it have?*
- *What does it feel like to listen to?*

The speaker's voices are seen as fluid as well as situated, multivocal in the same ways as an orchestra of instruments produce individual melodies that, together, create a symphony of music. The method gives explicit attention to the listener's subjectivities in a complex choreography between speaker and listener (Davis, 1997; Gilligan et al., 2006). The Listening Guide method comprises four sequential steps or *listenings* (see Figure 9.2).

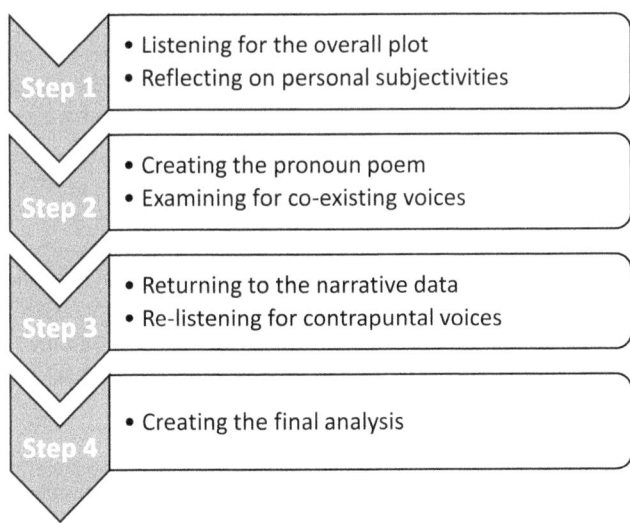

Figure 9.2 Steps in the Listening Guide method of analysis (adapted from Gilligan et al., 2006).

The first step of the Listening Guide involves two parts. The first part begins with reading the complete text, getting a sense of the landscape of the narrative, attending to both what stories are being told and how they are being told: *What metaphors are used? What is not told?* In the second part of this first step, the listener is invited to explicitly reflect on the impact of their own subjectivities on the listening interpretation process.

The second step of the Listening Guide focuses on the first-person voice of the speaker, through the creation and inspection of a poetic structure called an 'I poem'. The pronoun I poem focuses on a person's use of their first-person voice,[1] constructed by extracting the pronoun and related verbs, as well as other seemingly important words, arranging the phrases in the order that they appear in the narrative. The listener then examines the pronoun poem for nuances that are seen as speakers' coexisting voices.[2]

The third step of the Listening Guide involves returning to the full narrative to examine how the nuances found in the pronoun poem appear in the narrative, before bringing together all of the listening in the previous steps to compose a final analysis (fourth and final step). Exemplification of the above can be found in Case Study 9.1.

Grouping poems

The method of clustering or grouping poems under a common theme is said to provide a nuanced, holistic understanding of a particular situation or experience that might not be apparent in a single poem (Butler-Kisber, 2020). There are examples of studies that have grouped participant-voiced poems, created from different participants' transcripts, as well as clustering found poems with autobiographical, generated poems of the researchers' own experiences (see Görlich, 2016; Ohito & Nyachae, 2019; Zambo & Zambo, 2013). In Case Study 9.2, I demonstrate how using more than one poem enables the listener to hear changes over time.

Reflexivity

The notion of using poems to examine voice and affect in HE goes beyond the analysis of others' transcripts or narratives from feedback. There are benefits to including autobiographical generated poems, and poems written by students and academics to convey (and in some cases process) experiences.

---

1 Important caveat: I acknowledge that, in some languages, the first-person pronoun is not used in the same way as it is in English; speakers will use different pronouns depending on the audience (see, for example, Ng and Choi, 2009).
2 A number of authors have extended the use of the first-person voice to include other pronouns and therefore the term 'I poem' is often replaced with the term 'pronoun poem' (see Helme, 2021; Kaukko et al., 2024).

Case Study 9.1

Darren's story

Darren (pseudonym) was a student who had been attending a post-16 college in the Southwest of England and was in his third year of having to retake his mathematics GCSE examination. Darren spoke about an incident in class where he had been able to give an answer but was not able to explain his mathematical thinking. He went on to talk about the impact more generally as he was attempting to explain his mathematics. Here is the poem from this section of narrative:

> *I do it in my head*
> *I know how to*
> *if I have to explain*
> *I know how I am*
> *I just leave it*
> *I know how to*
> *I need to*
> *I need to*
> *I know how I am doing it*
> *if I have to*
> *I can't really explain*
> *I knew*
> *I just leave it*
> *I know how I got*

I invite the reader to read this poem multiple times, both silently and out loud – *can you feel the frustration as Darren wrestles between 'I have to' and 'I can't'?* By isolating the statements that Darren uses has afforded the opportunity to not only read the words but also *feel* the words, thus hearing the poignant struggle. Darren's previous and current teachers had labelled Darren as lazy or a student who would not record his working out in maths. They suggested that Darren was being defiant, choosing not to record in his exercise book. Using a poetic structure has suggested another story here, one of both struggle and frustration.

Quinlan (2016) describes the transition to and within HE as the reshaping of one's identity, a navigation of unfamiliar cultures in order to gain a sense of belonging. The author uses poems written by students and academics as a way to engage the listener–reader in the collaborative work, an embodied response to hearing the experience of HE conveyed in the poems. Promoting

Case Study 9.2

Claire's story

Claire (pseudonym) was a student who was attending a post-16 college in the Southwest of England during the COVID-19 pandemic. The impact of the pandemic on education in England, as it was globally, meant that teaching was either face-to-face or online, this being dependant on government policy at the time. Students did not sit examinations, due to COVID-19 restrictions, but were allocated a grade by their college, this being based on teachers' continued assessment of their work. Claire was interviewed at three points over the academic year, from December 2020 to June 2021, using images as a stimulus for the discussions. The images were chosen by Claire to represent her experiences of learning mathematics. The data was mostly collected via e-mail; however, the final interview used online conferencing software for a virtual verbal sharing of views. Below are the poems created from sections of the first interview:

> *I have chosen*
> *I had to go to achieve*
> *as I struggled*
> *how I felt about*
> *that I am in*
> *I am finally understanding*
> *like I couldn't understand*
> *I kept trying*
> *I felt like*
> *I could finally answer*
> *I didn't get much help*
> *therefore I struggled*
> *I asked*
> *I wouldn't get*

Now compare the section of her first poem above with a poem created from the third interview near the end of the academic year:

> *now I have*
> *I can do*
> *I can access*
> *I'm much more confident*
> *I see it as*
> *I had*

where I am now
I'm actually finding
when I was really stuck
I said to
I'm meeting
I have come through
further than I expected

What do you notice about the way Claire talks about herself over time? By grouping these poems together, as a listener you can examine the change in the way that she talks about herself. Claire's tone seems to have changed – from struggle to confidence, from 'I didn't' to 'I can'.

emotional wellbeing within university campuses is particularly important in light of the current discourses around mental health (Majorana & VanDeusen, 2022). The potential issue for the poem creators, students, and academics is the sense of *I am not a poet*. As with listening to experiences, the use of guidance in the form of a poetic structure can support this process. In one such example, Majorana and VanDeusen (2022) describe a course where they used an 'AutoBio' poetic structure as a window to wellbeing in contrast to the usual tradition of providing an introductory paragraph on a discussion board. They suggest initially using the poetic structure which is offered in Figure 9.3.

Providing a structure gave those students who had less experience with poetic form a format to follow; however, Majorana and VanDeusen (2022) go on to suggest that students should be encouraged to reflect using a wide range of poetic forms. Alternatively, poem creators might use other known structures such as a haiku, traditionally three phrases, with syllables in a five–seven–five pattern, or the four rhyming couplets of poems such as 'Roses are red, violets are blue...'. Using poetry as reflective practice, both by providing a structure

(Line 1) First name
(Line 2) Four adjectives that describe you
(Line 3) Important relationships (daughter of ..., mother of ..., etc.)
(Line 4) Three things, people, or ideas you love
(Line 5) Three feelings you have experienced
(Line 6) Three fears you have experienced
(Line 7) Three things you give to others
(Line 8) Accomplishments (who composes ..., who discovers ..., etc.)
(Line 9) Three things you want to see happen or want to experience
(Line 10) Residence
(Line 11) Last name

Figure 9.3 A structure for reflexive practice (adapted from Majorana & VanDeusen, 2022).

and by encouraging students to find or develop their own, has been described as going some way in fostering creativity, independence, and criticality (Threlfall, 2013). Although this may be particularly pertinent to courses that use reflective journals, such as Initial Teacher Training (ITT), there is scope for any course that uses forms of self-reflection or critical analysis.

Writing creatively

It is common for students to have concerns about academic writing in HE, and this anxiety may be more prevalent for students who see themselves as non-traditional, through either educational experience, nationality, or family history of attending university (Cronin & Hawthorne, 2019; Quinlan, 2016). Exploring poems can be a useful tool to promote creative writing in HE, involving both examining found poems and creating generated poems. Poems are said to foster personal involvement in written tasks, especially for those students who are learning to use a language in which they are unfamiliar, English as an additional language (EAL) being one such example. Kirkgöz (2014) explains how the 'writing-using' model was a powerful and playful strategy for encouraging poem construction as a way to aid students with creative thinking for their academic writing. The 'writing-using' involves providing a poem, often on a closely related theme, which will elicit a response from the listeners. The poem is used as a model, and the structure, meaning, and emotive language are examined before students are encouraged to produce a poem from their own point of view. Kirkgöz (2014) goes on to suggest that the process of learning to manipulate language increases confidence and generates imaginative responses. In a related example, Cronin and Hawthorne (2019) discuss introducing images alongside poems to evoke responses from nursing students. The students were then invited to respond by writing their own poem, looking at key themes such as communication at work. The authors suggest that 'getting students writing' (Cronin & Hawthorne, 2019, p. 76) is an important first stage; however, they also argue that poetry writing might help to develop higher-level academic writing skills, such as breaking down and distilling complex ideas. They suggest the freedom of poetic writing supports thinking around language and form in writing, which is transferable to more traditional prose forms of academic writing.

Reading literature

As well as writing activities, the use of literature voiced, found poetry can support the synthesis of theory and research literature. Similar to creating poems from narrative, poetry can focus the reader on the important discussions and themes in a text. Sulastri et al. (2023) advocate techniques such as 'blackout poetry' to facilitate the engagement of students in the text. Blackout poetry involves obscuring most of the source text, literally taking a marker pen and blacking out the *noise* of unneeded words. As a result, the listener exposes a handful of key, salient words, which can be extracted as a rewriting of the original written text. Using this process, the writing of the blackout poem becomes a re-reading of the original text, focusing on what seems most important by covering the *noise* of additional words. Sulastri et al. (2023) suggest that using blackout poetry develops the ability to skim and scan when reading literature. In a different example, Prendergast (2006) transformed her literature review by employing poetry and grouping the poems as a form of synthesis of sources. She cited the original words from the texts but played with page breaks and patterns, using repetition for emphases. The different poems were grouped or clustered in order to capture and present the range of theoretical perspectives on contemporary continental aesthetic philosophy and theatre/performance theory, this being the focus of her doctoral work. These processes have similarities to the strategies discussed previously when listening to experiences in that the poem creator is tasked with identifying the words and phrases that seem most significant; of course, significance will be different for each listener. However, this is the beauty of poetry – not necessary seen as objective but embracing subjectivity and world view.

Concluding comments

In this chapter, I have discussed the use of poetry – this not being routinely present in academic discourse – as a means to engage with the emotive experiences of HE. I have introduced some structures to support the reader to start to become a poem creator by offering them a way into the craft and practice. One of the purposes of this chapter was to whet the reader's appetite, showing the power of poetry as a creative method that adds value to practice in HE. Quinlan (2016, p. 265) states that 'emotion matters in HE because education is relational and emotions are central to relationships'. I argue that strategies that acknowledge, support, and process the role of emotions are pivotal to educational practice.

I will finish with an original poem, one that I wrote as a response to completing this chapter. I hope it will go some way to inspire or challenge, or at least make the reader think.

> *The poem and me*
>
> *At first I turned away*
> *the poetic form, at odds with academia*
> *the expectations of structure and rules*
> *of prose and research*
>   *the rigor is absent*
>   *the rational thinking*
>   *the objectivity*

but
The poem did not turn away
the ebb and flow, repetition and rhyme
the musicality of language and words
of emotions and meaning
the words became a verse
the verse became data
the data a poem
and then the poem became me

Acknowledgements

Thank you to the poetic creators who came before me and will come afterwards, as well as the participants who most generously provided their words.

Suggested further reading

Faulkner, S. L. (2019). *Poetic inquiry: Craft, method and practice* (2nd ed.). Routledge.
Quinlan, K. M. (2016). *How higher education feels: Commentaries on poems that illuminate emotions in learning and teaching.* Sense Publishers.

References

Burke, P. J. (2008). Writing, power and voice: Access to and participation in higher education. *Changing English, 15*(2), 199–210. https://doi.org/10.1080/135868 40802052419
Butler-Kisber, L. (2020). Poetic inquiry. In E. Fitzpatrick & K. Fitzpatrick (Eds.), *Poetry, method and education research: Doing critical, decolonising and political inquiry* (pp. 21–40). Routledge.
Canagarajah, S. (2024). Decolonizing academic writing pedagogies for multilingual students. *TESOL, 58*, 280–306. https://doi.org/10.1002/tesq.3231
Cronin, C., & Hawthorne, C. (2019). 'Poetry in motion' a place in the classroom: Using poetry to develop writing confidence and reflective skills. *Nurse Education Today, 76*, 73–77. https://doi.org/10.1016/j.nedt.2019.01.026
Davis, B. (1997). Listening for differences: An evolving conception of mathematics teaching. *Journal for Research in Mathematics Education, 28*(3), 355–376. https://doi.org/10.2307/749785
Demir-Yildiz, C. (2020). Wish poems of undergraduate students related to physical environment of educational faculty. *International Journal of Higher Education, 9*(2), 258–269. [Online]. https://www.sciedupress.com/journal/index.php/ijhe/issue/view/866
Faulkner, S. L. (2019). *Poetic inquiry: Craft, method and practice* (2nd ed.). Routledge.
Fitzpatrick, E., & Fitzpatrick, K. (2020). *Poetry, method and education research: Doing critical, decolonising and political inquiry.* Routledge.
Gilligan, C., & Eddy, J. (2021). The listening guide: Replacing judgment with curiosity. *Qualitative Psychology, 8*(2), 141–151. https://doi.org/10.1037/qup0000213
Gilligan, C., Spencer, R., Weinberg, M. K., & Bertsch, T. (2006). On the Listening Guide: A voice-centered relational method. In S. N. Hesse-Biber & P. Leavy (Eds.), *Emergent methods in social research* (pp. 253–271). SAGE Publications, Inc.

Görlich, A. (2016). Poetic inquiry: Understanding youth on the margins of education. *International Journal of Qualitative Studies in Education, 29*(4), 520–535. https://doi.org/10.1080/09518398.2015.1063734

Helme, R. (2021). I and THEY poetic voices in learning to listen to a student labelled as low attaining in mathematics. *For the Learning of Mathematics, 41*(1), 2–7.

Helme, R. (2023). *Foregrounding the voices of students: Extending the Listening Guide in a feminist poetic inquiry into identity work in the context of low attainment in mathematics* [Doctoral thesis, University of Bristol].

Jakobson, R. (1960). Closing statements: Linguistics and poetics. In T. Sebeok (Ed.), *Style in language* (pp. 350–377). MIT Press.

Kaukko, M., Macaulay, L., Reimer, K., Dunwoodie, K., Webb, S., & Wilkinson, J. (2024). 'It is a university where I felt welcome': Poems of asylum-seeking students' sense of coherence in Australian higher education. *Higher Education Research & Development, 43*(4), 889–905. https://doi.org/10.1080/07294360.2023.2280746

Kirkgöz, Y. (2014). Exploring poems to promote language learners' creative writing. *Procedia-Social and Behavioral Sciences, 158,* 394–401.https://doi.org/10.1016/j.sbspro.2014.12.106

Kleiman, P. (2008). Towards transformation: Conceptions of creativity in higher education. *Innovations in Education and Teaching International, 45*(3), 209–217. https://doi.org/10.1080/14703290802175966

Lindemann, H. (2019). *An invitation to feminist ethics* (2nd ed.). Oxford University Press.

Majorana, J., & VanDeusen, E. (2022). Promoting emotional wellbeing in the university classroom through poetry. *About Campus, 27*(2), 26–34. https://doi.org/10.1177/10864822221100251

Ng, J., & Choi, I. (2009). Culture and first-person pronouns. *Personality and Social Psychology Bulletin, 35*(11), 1492–1499. https://doi.org/10.1177/0146167209343810

Ohito, E. O., & Nyachae, T. M. (2019). Poetically poking at language and power: Using black feminist poetry to conduct rigorous feminist critical discourse analysis. *Qualitative Inquiry, 25*(9–10), 839–850. https://doi.org/10.1177/1077800418786303

Postareff, L., & Lindblom-Ylänne, S. (2011). Emotions and confidence within teaching in higher education. *Studies in Higher Education, 36*(7), 799–813. https://doi.org/10.1080/03075079.2010.483279

Prendergast, M. (2006). Found poetry as literature review: Research poems on audience and performance. *Qualitative Inquiry, 12*(2), 369–388. https://doi.org/10.1177/1077800405284601

Prendergast, M. (2009). Poem is what? Poetic inquiry in qualitative social science research. *International Review of Qualitative Research, 1*(4), 541–568. https://doi.org/10.1525/irqr.2009.1.4.541

Quinlan, K. M. (2016). *How higher education feels: Commentaries on poems that illuminate emotions in learning and teaching.* Sense Publishers.

Staats, S. (2021). Mathematical poetic structures: The sound shape of collaboration. *Journal of Mathematical Behavior, 62*(100846), 1–15. https://doi.org/10.1016/j.jmathb.2021.100846

Sulastri, F., Sri, M., & Belkis, S. A. (2023). Killing two birds with a stone: Merging reading and writing activities through blackout poetry. *Premise: Journal of English Education and Applied Linguistics, 12*(2), 580–593. https://doi.org/10.24127/pj.v12i2.7008

Threlfall, S. J. (2013). Poetry in action [*research*]. An innovative means to a reflective learner in higher education (HE). *Reflective Practice, 14*(3), 360–367. https://doi.org/10.1080/14623943.2013.767232

Trinh, E. & Pentón Herrera, L. J. (2021). Writing as an art of rebellion: Scholars of color using literacy to find spaces of identity and belonging in academia. In J. Sablan &

J. Van Galen (Eds.), *Amplified voices, intersecting identities: Volume 2. first-generation PhDs navigating institutional power in early academic careers* (pp. 25–34). Brill/ Sense. https://doi.org/10.1163/9789004445253_003

Ward, A. (2011). "Bringing the message forward": Using poetic re-presentation to solve research dilemmas. *Qualitative Inquiry, 17*(4), 355–363. https://doi.org/ 10.1177/1077800411401198

Zambo, R., & Zambo, D. (2013). Using I poems to hear the voices and understand the actions of EdD students conducting action research. *The Qualitative Report, 18*(42), 1–17. https://doi.org/10.46743/2160-3715/2013.1453

Chapter 10

Digital portfolios

Considering creativity in relation to the summative assessment of Higher Education learners

Alison Oldfield

Introduction

Digital technology is often presented as a catalyst in reshaping many aspects of education, including processes and practices of assessment (Selwyn, 2021; Timmis et al., 2016; Weller, 2020). At a time when many Higher Education (HE) settings are also prioritising '21st Century skills' such as 'creativity' (Tight, 2021), digital technologies are often framed as ways for re-imagining and re-approaching assessment in novel and creative ways (Ibarra-Sáiz et al., 2020; Richardson & Clesham, 2021). This chapter critically examines these claims alongside a case study where digital portfolios were introduced as a mode of summative assessment in an English HE class focused on the design of learning technologies. Through this example, the chapter considers what digitally mediated, creative approaches to summative assessment look like in reality, how technology-enhanced assessment can enable creativity in assessment, and what challenges materialise in such approaches. Thus, this chapter aims to:

- Consider the importance and challenge of supporting students' creativity within a HE context that is highly influenced by summative assessment, and
- Examine the potential of technology-enhanced assessment in supporting creativity within assessment, reflecting on a case study involving intentional design and the use of a 'creative' approach to assessment through digital portfolios on a UK postgraduate course.

The chapter begins with a discussion regarding the importance of assessment in HE, before further considering the current role of digital technologies in shaping creative approaches to assessment.

Setting the scene: the importance of assessment

Assessment is a critically important aspect of education that permeates teaching and learning processes at all levels, including HE (Cumming & Wyatt-Smith,

DOI: 10.4324/9781032633534-14

2009; Sambell et al., 2013). This importance is demonstrated, at one level, by a huge increase over the past 70 years in scholarly interest and debate about assessment practices (Heil & Ifenthaler, 2023). Assessment is a process that aims to gather and evaluate evidence of learning or understanding of knowledge or skills and usually takes place in educational settings on an individual basis (Boud & Bearman, 2024). It may have various purposes – from supporting student progress to qualification requirements and evaluation of performance – with most HE assessments being designed in alignment with the intended learning outcomes of a course, i.e., what knowledge, skills, and understanding are hoped that students will gain through the learning experience (Black, 1998; Sambell et al., 2013).

However, assessment in practice is complex and multi-faceted, as depicted through the wide variety of terms and concepts related to assessment. Two such concepts – formative assessment (or Assessment *for* Learning) and summative assessment (or Assessment *of* Learning) – demarcate distinctions in purposes and forms of assessment that continue to undergo scrutiny and debate (Black & Wiliam, 2009; Heil & Ifenthaler, 2023). The term 'assessment' in this chapter primarily refers to summative assessment, which in HE usually takes place at the end of a learning experience and relates to the intended learning outcomes of a class (Perry et al., 2022). However, the development of assessment in the case study presented later on in this chapter also prioritised and valued formative feedback and activity within assessment practices, recognising the interlinking and value of both aspects of assessment for distinct purposes (Newton, 2007).

It is also important to recognise that the use of and approaches to summative assessment can have wider implications than simply evaluating and measuring student learning. As such, scholars have argued that how assessment is conducted can also demonstrate the broader aspirations, culture, and conceptualisations of learning in an institution or a programme. For example, Care and Kim (2018, p. 22) state that the form and focus of assessment is a 'driver of teaching and learning', showing what knowledge and skills are valued and seen to be important by educators or an institution. French et al. (2023, p. 2) state that '[t]he way in which students are assessed..., arguably more than any other aspect of teaching, signals to students what is valued by their teachers, the discipline, and the institution'. Furthermore, assessment practices have been shown to have implications on wider aspects of an educational experience, such as student motivation (Kickert et al., 2022) and wellbeing (Jones et al., 2021). In sum, the practices and approaches of assessment hold significant sway over many aspects of education and thus deserve serious consideration in HE planning and delivery.

Given this importance, assessment practices and approaches regularly attract research, policy, and public attention and critique, as demonstrated in recent debates which highlight how more conventional methods of assessment – such as exam-based or high-stakes assessment – are increasingly 'unfit for purpose', and new and innovative approaches are needed (French et al., 2023; Gee & Shaffer, 2010; Schwartz & Arena, 2013; Timmis et al., 2016). While a full examination of the various forms and efficacies of assessment is beyond the scope of this chapter, what is presented below is an exploration of what digitally mediated and creative approaches might offer to summative assessment in HE in the UK.

Digital technologies and assessment

The increasing ubiquity and use of digital technologies within education have long drawn the interest and attention of many scholars (Kearsley, 1998; Selwyn, 2021; Weller, 2020). Described in many ways, digital technologies incorporate a wide range of emerging and new technologies that are seen to offer the potential to shape various educational practices at local and national levels (Becta, 2007). Evidence for the effectiveness of such technologies to improve education and learning outcomes is variable, wide-ranging, and often inconclusive (Livingstone, 2014; Yeung et al., 2021), yet technologies remain influential and prominent in considering educational provision, practice, and innovation. This chapter considers technology use in relation to assessment, an area that itself has warranted significant attention (Timmis et al., 2016) and become prominent in current debates on the use of AI for adaptive learning, personalised learning, and aided teaching systems (Guan et al., 2020).

Digital technologies have been designed and are increasingly used to manage and create assessments in many ways: from making existing methods more efficient or easier to administer (as in computer-based assessments such as on-screen tests) to more fundamental changes in the ways that learning is captured, shared, and evaluated (as in the use of multimedia or different sensory stimuli) (Perry et al., 2022). Finger and Jamieson-Proctor (2009) suggest a categorisation of the use of information and communication technologies (ICT) for assessment; these are recognised in Table 10.1.

This chapter focuses its attention on the final category – how digital technologies are used for digital or *e-portfolio purposes* – with a specific emphasis on how this can support creativity within assessment approaches, as considered in the next section.

Creativity and creative approaches to assessment using digital technologies

Alongside the increasing prevalence of digital technologies within education, debates have arisen in relation to what skills should be prioritised and considered in contemporary HE classrooms. In recent decades, these skill sets have been known by various monikers such as 21st-century skills, employability skills, or transferable skills, and have become commonplace in educational discussions (Tight, 2021). The increased emphasis on these skills as educational priorities

Table 10.1 Ways that ICT can be used to support assessment, as categorised by Finger and Jamieson-Proctor (2009, pp. 67–70)

How ICT is used	Example
ICT use and skills are the focus	ICT is a tool that students use for and in their learning. Learning is understood by collecting data on students' ICT use, skills, and competencies.
ICT supports learning of content, which is the focus	ICT supports instructional delivery, communication or information searching, or delivery. Student learning is measured on their mastery of content objectives.
ICT as a data collection tool	ICT develops tests or examinations that collect data, such as computer adaptive tests or online quizzes.
ICT as a recording, analysis, and communication tool	ICT assists teachers or lecturers with record keeping and reporting of student learning, including attendance, grade calculation, and observations.
ICT as a plagiarism detector	ICT applications and processes detect plagiarism and issues related to academic integrity (i.e., Turnitin).
ICT as used for e-portfolio purposes	ICT applications and tools support the collecting and recording of information through a variety of media or range of evidence; these serve as a 'powerful means for developing stories of deep learning' (p. 69).

suggests that knowledge acquisition itself is no longer sufficient as a sole outcome of education; it should also invest in developing 'softer' skills that support citizens to participate in the so-called knowledge economy and associated national/global economic success (Facer, 2012). Shute et al. (2010) relate this to assessment, arguing that typical forms of assessment like examinations are unsatisfactory means of supporting learning and aiding individuals to thrive in a dynamic and uncertain world. However, it is important to note that skill-based curricula and frameworks have faced their own critiques, which include a lack of clarity, and other pedagogical and assessment challenges (see Tight, 2021).

While the definition of these skills and how they are developed differ across borders and initiatives,[1] they tend to include concepts like problem-solving, complex decision-making, innovation, collaboration, global awareness, digital literacy, communication, and (as is of relevance to this chapter) creativity (Tight,

---

1 The development and naming of these skills tend to come from countries found in the Global North, these being written about, adopted, and adapted in other countries around the world. This is illustrated by the following:

- Discussions on such skills development in the United States – see P21's Partnership for 21st Century Skills (Battelle for Kids; visit https://www.battelleforkids.org/insights/p21-resources/),
- The '7 "C"s Skills of 21st Century Learning' (Trilling and Fadel, 2009),
- The European Union's (2019) *Key Competences for Lifelong Learning* (see https://data.europa.eu/doi/10.2766/569540), and
- A discussion about 21st-century skills in Pakistan (Khan et al., 2019).

2021). Creativity as a concept and as a skill ('being creative') is notoriously difficult to define, this being described as 'a vast topic' that crosses contemporary discourse and academic debates (Kaufman & Glăveanu, 2019, p. 27). This may partly be due to it being regarded as a multi-disciplinary concept, often situated within the domain of psychology (Thomson & Sefton-Green, 2011), but also within the fields of design, education, and digital technologies.

Creativity can be broadly synonymised with newness or innovation, but many current definitions of the word combine these attributes of newness or novelty with appropriateness to the task at hand (Kaufman & Glăveanu, 2019; Sternberg & Lubart, 1998), recognising that creativity is more than just doing something new for its own sake. Creativity has been central in scholarship related to education, both in considering digital and technology-enhanced learning in informal learning settings and youth media cultures (Ito et al., 2010), and also in more formal classroom settings, as in constructionist approaches to learning such as making and creating (Papert, 1993).

But, as highlighted above, it has been considered and interpreted in various ways. Indeed, Thomson and Sefton-Green (2011, p. 1) contend that

> Creativity – in an educational context – can mean many things: turning classrooms into more exciting experiences, curriculum into more thoughtful challenges, teachers into different kinds of instructors, assessment into more authentic processes, and putting young people's voice at the heart of learning.

This education-oriented interest in creativity is driven by two main factors: to support meaningful engagement in educational activity and to support learners' abilities to contribute to the 'creative' or 'knowledge economy' in our contemporary world (Gilmore & Comunian, 2016; Loveless & Williamson, 2013). However, a noted challenge of incorporating creativity and other '21st Century skills' is the difficulty in assessing or evaluating them. Creative activities are 'inherently uncertain' (Beghetto & Schmidt, 2023, p. 498) and can be laden with setbacks, failures, or unexpected turns, which sit at odds with assessment structures and approaches. Furthermore, the assessment of creativity as a skill or capability is particularly difficult because of the ambiguity and complexity which surrounds it as a concept. Of interest is the thinking of Care and Kim (2018, p. 23) who suggest that

> Challenges in assessing twenty-first century skills lie in our lack of comprehensive understanding of the nature and development of the skills, about their multidimensionality, and about how to partition variance in behaviour that is attributable to knowledge, or attributable to skill.

These challenges have been seen to occur in digitally enhanced and intentionally creative learning spaces too. For example, a recent study by Walen and Gericke (2023, p. 1765) examined the role that 'makerspaces'[2] played in a classroom. In this study, the participating teachers said that makerspaces could 'stimulate creativity' but were less articulate about what they understood 'creativity' to be. Indeed, teachers in this study identified a significant challenge of intentionally including creativity through makerspaces in their classroom, this being how to assess the concept: 'The challenge was not for the students to develop creativity during makerspace activities, but for the teachers to know how to assess this development ... teachers were confused about what creativity actually is and what assessment criteria to use' (Walen & Gericke, 2023, p. 1765).

This example highlights the tensions between aspirations of incorporating creativity into classroom activities alongside the constraints of more traditional assessment methods. Research examining how to assess these less-defined skills does exist, as per the work of Shute and Ventura (2013) on 'stealth assessment' or assessment that takes place without the learner noticing. However, in the main, a dilemma remains: *how can instructors introduce and develop uncertain, more flexible, and potentially riskier aspects of learning, like creativity, alongside current educational assessment practices?*

This chapter provides an examination of one such approach. It is important to note that the example did not aim to measure or evaluate the skill or competency of 'creativity' itself, this being due to the reasons previously mentioned. Instead, it considered a different role for 'creativity' – beyond how it can be assessed as a discrete skill, but rather how creative and digitally mediated approaches might offer different and valuable ways for students to reflect on and demonstrate learning. Thus the intention was to develop an assessment task and approach that invited more creativity into students' modes of expression. Examining this relationship between creativity and digital technology, that is, how digitally mediated creative approaches can support and enable learning within assessment, serves as an important consideration in the discussion below. To begin with, an overview of the approach is summarised in Case Study 10.1.

An exploratory examination of the content of Case Study 10.1 is used to drive the direction of the remainder of this chapter.

Digital portfolios as a creative approach to assessment

The choice of introducing digital portfolios, as per Case Study 10.1, was developed from my own research into e-assessment practices and technologies, this being undertaken alongside a rather long history of the use of digital or

---

2 A 'makerspace' is a physical space that is developed in educational or community locations (public libraries, for example) which aim to support creative or collaborative activity through making or creative endeavours.

Case Study 10.1

This case study examines the ways in which one type of digital technology – digital portfolios – was introduced to support creative forms of demonstrating knowledge and reflection in assessment. It took place in a Postgraduate Taught unit I have taught as part of a team for five years. The unit focus is on designing technologies for learning and aims to support students to gain a broad understanding of technology design processes, particularly considering how these might be undertaken to develop technologies that are specifically aimed to support or enhance learning. Across the unit, individual students develop their own technology design ideas – from conceptualisation through to low-fidelity prototype stages. Along the way, students are supported to

- consider a problem area or issue related to learning or education and design a technology idea related to that area,
- identify and work with a relevant conceptualisation of learning, and
- consider what design stages and design activities they would use in designing their own idea, and who they would involve along the way.

While the design ideas are individually generated, students also work in peer groups and so receive regular feedback on ideas and progress, sharing digital links to their portfolios on a shared repository. Additional formative feedback is offered through regular classroom sharing, with formal written feedback being provided on portfolio drafts halfway through the term.

The incorporation of a portfolio into the unit assessment was developed during a review of the unit, in which the teaching team decided to broaden the original assessment of a single essay at the end of the unit by adding the portfolio as a second and earlier point of assessment. The aim of the portfolio was to record, document, and reflect upon the design activities and ideas across the unit. The rationale for choosing this format was multi-faceted and we hoped it would

- act as a record for class-based activities and readings each week to support students in compiling their design progress across the term,
- prompt reflection and consideration of design ideas and decisions made,
- align with the conceptual use of portfolios in professional design contexts and also various forms of digital representation and media more broadly, lending authenticity to the task, and
- offer novel and appropriate means for students to demonstrate their developing understanding and learning in the unit in broader ways, moving away from a single high-stakes written assessment.

e-portfolios[3] in the field (Oldfield et al., 2013; Timmis et al., 2016). Indeed, the use of digital or e-portfolios has been one way that digital technologies are often used to diversify and re-shape assessment, or even as one way to 'transform teaching, learning and assessment' (Walland & Shaw, 2022, p. 363). This is further demonstrated in their inclusion in Finger and Jamieson-Proctor's (2009) categorisation (see Table 10.1).

The Joint Information Systems Committee (JISC) (2008, p. 3) defines an e-portfolio as 'a collection of digital artefacts articulating experiences, achievements and learning'. Such portfolios aim to collect, reflect, and demonstrate processes involved in learning as much as the final product (JISC, 2008, p. 3). Digital or e-portfolios generally refer to an online or digital personalised space that an individual can use to record, document, or develop ideas through various types of representation or media. In the case of the unit (as per Case Study 10.1), students had the option to use web-based portfolios, word processing or presentation software, note-taking software, or other types of digital web-based tools of their choosing. The portfolios could include graphics, photos, drawings, notes, sketches, or typed information. We hoped such a range of options provided meaningful choices for students in how their learning and reflection could be demonstrated. A key aspect of the portfolio assessment was that it was more than just a collection of activities, but that it also incorporated student reflection on aspects of the design process and what they had learned across the unit. In this way, it resembled what Finger and Jamieson-Proctor (2009, p. 72) call a 'student learning portfolio': a 'purposeful collection of examples of student work annotated (ideally) with students' reflective commentary'.

The qualities and opportunities that e-portfolios offer also complemented the ways in which we wanted to develop assessment in the unit. Their value is partly held in the 'fusion' that e-portfolios offer between process and product, whereby the 'process' of compiling, selecting, and reflecting on aspects of the portfolio sit alongside the product that results from these aspects (Winsor & Ellefson, 1995, pp. 68–69). As the aim of the unit was focused on the development of, and reflections on, the process of designing the technology for learning (more than the actual resulting product), we hoped that e-portfolios would offer students the potential to demonstrate these processes in diverse multi-modal ways. The task of creating a multi-modal portfolio was also more 'authentic' to future professional fields like design, which emphasises iteration and reflection. By supporting activities like reflection, digital portfolios have been called a 'bridge' (Cabau, 2017, p. 309) and 'synergy tool' (Cabau, 2017, p. 144) between the worlds of academia and professional practice. In developing the assessment approach for this unit, we drew from research

---

3 As both 'digital portfolio' and 'e-portfolio' are used in the literature to describe this type of digital technology, these terms are used interchangeably in the remainder of this chapter.

suggesting that digital portfolios can support creativity and offer diversity in assessment, as well as enabling reflective thinking, a key learning aim of this unit (Becta, 2007).

Returning to the focus of this chapter, we also explicitly wanted the assignment to invoke and support students' creativity and creative learning. But within the framing of the unit, this was not simply adhering to the idea of creativity as novelty and innovation; it was, instead, closer to the word's original roots, emanating from the Latin word *creare*, which means to bring something forth – in essence to make and produce something (Glăveanu & Kaufman, 2019). The portfolio was intended to be a way to encourage students to use a variety of different (yet still meaningful) ways to express their ideas, merging together the qualities of newness and appropriateness as described above (Sternberg & Lubart, 1998). We also wanted to introduce a wider range of ways that students could use to demonstrate their knowledge and understanding, so that they could choose and work with approaches and media that were particularly meaningful for them. This intention is echoed in Thomson and Sefton-Green (2011, p. 16) discussion of creative learning, in terms of how it 'allows students to use their imaginations, have ideas, generate multiple possible solutions to problems, communicate in a variety of media, and in general "think outside the box"'.

Furthermore, we were also motivated by the potential for the use of digital portfolios to support feedback conversations across a term, thus moving away from single points of teacher-delivered feedback, and veering more towards a feedback relationship where 'students actively decode feedback information, internalise it and use it to make judgments of their own work' (Whitelock & Watt, 2008, p. 152). To summarise, the purpose of the portfolio as a piece of assessment was to offer flexible, novel, and shareable ways for students to demonstrate and express their learning and knowledge in relation to the design process and their technology design ideas.

Supporting creativity in technology-enhanced assessment: realities and challenges

In the initial introduction of using digital portfolios as part of the assessment process, we were energised and excited about the potential this offered, and what avenues it might open up for students beyond the standard written essay. Over the ensuing years that the portfolio has been part of the unit assessment, the student portfolios have often been valuable and meaningful ways of gauging students' progress, reflections, and engagement with/understanding of design processes and activities across an entire term, rather than just a single point after the unit conclusion. But the introduction and use of portfolios has not been without its own challenges.

Since its establishment, student feedback on the use of portfolios has been mixed. Through unit evaluations, students have said that they appreciate the portfolio and assessment approach, with different students writing that the portfolio and assessment approach is 'interesting', 'beneficial', 'makes me realize what I have learned in the sessions', and has offered an opportunity to 'learn how to make a suitable portfolio to show my design thinking and promote my products'. Others have identified difficulties in the portfolio as an assessment method, suggesting it took some getting used to and was not always easy to navigate. This was partly due to it being perceived as a novel form of assessment, with students commenting that they 'had never done that before' and that the instructions were too 'vague to motivate creativity'. While many commented that the feedback from peers and tutors was helpful, others wished for 'continual feedback' to gain more regular support on its development or felt that more detailed instructions on suitable portfolio formats were needed. In response to this, we developed a feedback mechanism of providing written comments on a portfolio draft and shared these on a classroom forum so other students could comment on or examine each other's portfolios. In this way, the portfolio itself acted as an enabling device for feedback which supported further reflection and development of student knowledge (Wiliam, 2011).

As suggested above, the use of portfolios as an assessment method on this unit was unique to the programme, as other unit assessments tended to be long-form essays related to a specific task or question on an educational topic of relevance to a unit. While the portfolio assignment remained rooted in the demonstration of knowledge, critical thinking, and engagement with academic literature, it also introduced new elements. Specifically, the portfolio as a task was relatively unstructured, flexible in terms of modality and expression, and openly embraced ideas of creativity and reflection, qualities that also resonate with recent research emphasising the importance of learners' ownership and agency in choosing the format and 'look and feel' of portfolios (Meth et al., 2020, p. 1812). It is fair to say that this type of assessment opened up new possibilities, uncertainties, and also potential risks for students. Other research has recognised that tools and approaches such as portfolios can ask students to engage in critical reflection on their own learning in more active and self-directed ways than more traditional forms of assessment might (Marinho et al., 2021). Our experience was that some students approached this novel task with enthusiasm while for others it raised questions and concerns about what would be acceptable and 'right' within the assessment and the existing evaluative criteria, which may have negatively influenced their willingness to be more creative in their portfolio approach. McCardle et al. (2018) discuss related research in which students in a UK design programme often approached design proposals in risk-averse ways in an effort to get higher grades. In response to such questions in our unit, and in recognition of the concerns raised by novel forms of assessment, we developed substantial guidance for students on what might go in the portfolio, how to demonstrate different aspects of the criteria, and possible areas of content and media forms. Perhaps somewhat ironically, what was intended as a more creative, flexible mode of assessment to support students' choice of the modality of expression resulted in the generation of higher quantities of material to support students' assessment, e.g., structured guidance, discussions, and student support, than was found in previous modes.

Furthermore, the unit approached creative modes of expression through the portfolio development as a socially supported activity, building in time across the term for informal and structured feedback on portfolio development from both peers and tutors. However, its situatedness as an individual form of assessment meant that feedback discussions tended to centre on whether or not the portfolio content and form were the 'right' ones in relation to evaluative criteria, rather than what they substantively or conceptually demonstrated in relation to their design process. This aligns with the argument proffered by Boud and Bearman (2024, p. 467) who demonstrate how 'individualistic assumptions underpinning assessment in higher education' sit in tension with social aspects of learning. The student approach to assessment also remained attuned to the evaluation of a certain body of knowledge or the 'right' way of doing things rather than substantive reflection of their design work, which often felt at odds with the intended purpose of using portfolios. The importance of the graded and evaluative aspects of the task was perhaps unsurprisingly insurmountable.

Finally, the use of digital portfolios as a way to widen the modes of expression and demonstration of knowledge, understanding, and reflection was complex and multi-faceted to administer and manage. While our intention was to support students to use a range of media or platforms to showcase their understanding, it soon became clear that issues of interoperability across existing platforms would constrain the width of this range. A number of practical constraints required solving; these included:

- how to provide access to web-based portfolios,
- ensure submissions were not edited post-deadline,
- assure access to various multimedia forms,
- integrate portfolios with university plagiarism and marking software, and
- manage portfolio size across multiple platforms to ensure fairness and consistency.

The digital portfolios were themselves embedded in a nest of other technologies that shaped their use and usefulness. While this form of media allowed for some flexibility, it was also constrained by other digital technologies associated with assessment, which therefore limited the actual scope for creativity. These practical and technological issues added other layers of administration and constraint. For example, it further implicated student administration teams and colleagues, who collectively helped to create new assignment cover sheets, submission points, and instructions for students to manage the portfolio submission requirements.

This experience encourages further reflection on the categorisation of ICT uses, as offered by Finger and Jamieson-Proctor (2009; see Table 10.1). While Case Study 10.1 aligns with their category of ICT use within an e-portfolio, it also demonstrates how the singular use of a digital or e-portfolio is not separate from other uses of ICT – including for plagiarism purposes or learning management systems – nor from other material or social aspects of the learning experience. Instead, the introduction of this technology to support assessment is intertwined with a network of other things and people and enacts a range of new practices, activities, and ad hoc solutions to technical hitches generated by the introduction of this creative approach. Such entanglements demonstrate how technological innovations in education are embedded within social, material, and institutional contexts that further influence how their implementation takes shape. In this way, technologies themselves do not hold essential qualities or pre-determined outcomes (Selwyn, 2021). These issues highlighted that, while worthwhile and valuable in demonstrating learning and reflection for this unit, supporting creative approaches through digital portfolios was neither straightforward nor easy to implement. In this case, taking a creative approach required more than a singular innovative teacher or technological innovation, but came to be alongside a landscape of other social, technological, and material actors. Creativity, as a mode of novel and appropriate expression, is demonstrated as being intimately intertwined with existing technological systems, social relationships, and assessment experiences.

Concluding comments

Assessment remains a fundamental driver of education. Amid ongoing calls for more innovative assessment in HE, this chapter set out to consider how creative digital approaches could support students' demonstration of skills and knowledge in one postgraduate unit. As is true for many such initiatives, the pedagogical purposes of introducing new technologies become entangled in complex ways with existing practices, relationships, and technology use, particularly when summative assessment is involved (Garrett, 2011; Selwyn, 2021). As shown here, the introduction of digital portfolios may have sparked new ways of working and catalysed different modes of expression or reflection on learning, but the technology was not a determinant itself in bringing about creativity or more creative outputs. One resulting question from Case Study 10.1 then may be *how might we further examine the socially and materially situated aspects of creativity within assessment?*

Furthermore, if creativity is, indeed, deeply important to 'success in almost all areas of life, personal and professional' (Glăveanu & Kaufman, 2019, p. 7) and should be part of an educational experience, then it should be considered alongside current assessment practices, institutional requirements, and existing affordances of digital technologies. In Case Study 10.1, the digital portfolio was important to both the process and the product for demonstrating learning, as it offered opportunities for feedback and reflection throughout the iterative design process and across the term. However, the alignment of the portfolio with summative assessment remained an integral factor for students in terms of approaches to and experience of creating portfolios, something also recognised by Garrett (2011) who suggests that pedagogical intentions of e-portfolios to support reflection in learning can be co-opted into the production of assessment data. While he argues for a return to the intended pedagogical purposes of the tool, this can be challenging within HE environments that remain wedded to compulsory summative assessment. Therefore, Case Study 10.1 has demonstrated both how creative expression and modalities can bring novel, flexible, and multi-modal approaches to learning, and how these can simultaneously lie in tension with assessment requirements. A further point for consideration then is how HE assessment practices, both with and without digital technologies, might accept, normalise, and even neutralise the risks associated with the uncertainty, opening possibilities that more creative approaches encourage.

Acknowledgements

I am grateful to Mark Neild for his comments on an early draft, and to Simon Brownhill for his supportive editorship.

Suggested further reading

Selwyn, N. (2021). *Education and technology: Key issues and debates.* Bloomsbury Publishing.

Wyatt-Smith, C., & Cumming, J. (Eds.). (2009). *Educational assessment in the 21st century: Connecting theory and practice.* Springer.

References

Becta. (2007). *Impact study of e-portfolios on learning.* Becta. [Online]. https://dera.ioe.ac.uk/id/eprint/1469/7/becta_2007_eportfolios_report_Redacted.pdf

Beghetto, R. A., & Schmidt, A. C. (2023). Creative curricular experiences: Navigating uncertainties and emotions toward creative expression. In Z. Ivcevic, J. D. Hoffman, & J. C. Kaufman (Eds.), *The Cambridge handbook of creativity and emotions* (pp. 498–520). Cambridge University Press.

Black, P. J. (1998). *Testing: Friend or foe? The theory and practice of assessment and testing.* Falmer Press.

Black, P., & Wiliam, D. (2009). Developing the theory of formative assessment. *Educational Assessment, Evaluation and Accountability, 21*(1), 5–31. https://doi.org/10.1007/s11092-008-9068-5

Boud, D., & Bearman, M. (2024). The assessment challenge of social and collaborative learning in higher education. *Educational Philosophy and Theory, 56*(5), 459–468. https://doi.org/10.1080/00131857.2022.2114346

Cabau, B. (2017). E-portfolio as a tool to respond higher education ambitions and societal expectations. In T. Chaudhuri & B. Cabau (Eds.), *E-portfolios in higher education* (pp. 141–154). Springer. https://doi.org/10.1007/978-981-10-3803-7_10

Care, E., & Kim, H. (2018). Assessment of twenty-first century skills: The issue of authenticity. In E. Care, P. Griffin, & M. Wilson (Eds.), *Assessment and teaching of twenty-first century teaching skills: Research and applications* (pp. 21–39). Springer.

Cumming, J. J., & Wyatt-Smith, C. (2009). Framing assessment today for the future: Issues and challenges. In C. Wyatt-Smith & J. J. Cumming (Eds.), *Educational assessment in the 21st century* (pp. 1–16). Springer.

Facer, K. (2012). Taking the 21st century seriously: Young people, education and socio-technical futures. *Oxford Review of Education, 38*(1), 97–113. https://www.jstor.org/stable/23119474

Finger, G., & Jamieson-Proctor, R. (2009). Assessment issues and new technologies: E-portfolio possibilities. In C. Wyatt-Smith & J. J. Cumming (Eds.), *Educational assessment in the 21st century* (pp. 63–81). Springer.

French, S., Dickerson, A., & Mulder, R. A. (2023). A review of the benefits and drawbacks of high-stakes final examinations in higher education. *Higher Education,* 1–26. https://doi.org/10.1007/s10734-023-01148-z

Garrett, N. (2011). An e-portfolio design supporting ownership, social learning and ease of use. *Educational Technology & Society, 14*(1), 187–202. https://www.jstor.org/stable/jeductechsoci.14.1.187

Gee, J. P., & Shaffer, D. W. (2010). Looking where the light is bad: Video games and the future of assessment. *Phi Delta Kappa International EDge, 6*(1), 3–19.

Gilmore, A., & Comunian, R. (2016). Beyond the campus: Higher education, cultural policy and the creative economy. *International Journal of Cultural Policy, 22*(1), 1–9. http://doi.org/10.1080/10286632.2015.1101089

Glăveanu, V. P., & Kaufman, J. C. (2019). Creativity: A historical perspective. In J. C. Kaufman & R. J. Sternberg (Eds.), *The Cambridge handbook of creativity* (pp. 9–26). Cambridge University Press.

Guan, C., Mou, J., & Jiang, Z. (2020). Artificial intelligence innovation in education: A twenty-year data-driven historical analysis. *International Journal of Innovation Studies, 4*(4), 134–147. https://doi.org/10.1016/j.ijis.2020.09.001

Heil, J., & Ifenthaler, D. (2023). Online assessment in higher education: A systematic review. *Online Learning, 27*(1), 187–218. https://doi.org/10.24059/olj.v27i1.3398

Ibarra-Sáiz, M. S., Rodríguez-Gómez, G., Boud, D., Rotsaert, T., Brown, S., Salinas-Salazar, M. L., & Rodríguez-Gómez, H. M. (2020). The future of assessment in higher education. *RELIEVE, 26*(1), Art. M1. http://doi.org/10.7203/relieve.26.1.17323

Ito, M., with Antin, J., Finn, M., Law, A., Manion, A., Mitnick, S., Schlossberg, D., Yardi, S., & Horst, H. A. (2010). *Hanging out, messing around, and geeking out: Kids living and learning with new media.* MIT Press.

Joint Information Systems Committee (JISC). (2008). *Effective practice with e-portfolios: Supporting 21st century learning.* JISC. [Online]. https://research.qut.edu.au/eportfolio/wp-content/uploads/sites/186/2018/04/JISC_effective_practice_e-portfolios.pdf

Jones, E., Priestley, M., Brewster, L., Wilbraham, S. J., Hughes, G., & Spanner, L. (2021). Student wellbeing and assessment in higher education: The balancing act. *Assessment & Evaluation in Higher Education, 46*(3), 438–450. https://doi.org/10.1080/02602938.2020.1782344

Kaufman, J. C., & Glăveanu, V. P. (2019). A review of creativity theories: What questions are we trying to answer? In J. C. Kaufman & R. J. Sternberg (Eds.), *The Cambridge handbook of creativity* (pp. 27–43). Cambridge University Press.

Kearsley, G. (1998). Educational technology: A critique. *Educational Technology, 38*(2), 47–51. http://www.jstor.org/stable/44428437

Khan, H., Jumani, N. B., & Gul, N. (2019). Implementation of 21st century skills in higher education of Pakistan. *Global Regional Review*, 4(3), 223–233. https://doi.org/10.31703/grr.2019(IV-III).25

Kickert, R., Meeuwisse, M., & Stegers-Jager, K. M. (2022). Curricular fit perspective on motivation in higher education. *Higher Education*, *83*, 729–745. https://doi.org/10.1007/s10734-021-00699-3

Livingstone, S. (2014). Critical reflections on the benefits of ICT in education. In C. Davies, J. Coleman, & S. Livingstone (Eds.), *Digital technologies in the lives of young people* (pp. 9–24). Routledge.

Loveless, A., & Williamson, B. (2013). *Learning identities in a digital age*. Routledge.

Marinho, P., Fernandes, P., & Pimentel, F. (2021). The digital portfolio as an assessment strategy for learning in higher education. *Distance Education*, 42(2), 253–267. https://doi.org/10.1080/01587919.2021.1911628

McCardle, J. R., Huskisson, A., & Perry, S. (2018*). Performance metrics: Are the risks too high to be creative?* Proceedings of the 20th International Conference on Engineering and Product Design Education (E&PDE 2018), Dyson School of Engineering, Imperial College, London, 6–7 September. [Online]. https://repository.lboro.ac.uk/articles/conference_contribution/Performance_metrics_Are_the_risks_too_high_to_be_creative_/9339809?file=16948490

Meth, D., Finger, M., & Brough, D. (2020). The graduate professional portfolio as 'synergy tool': Navigating the complex role of portfolios in future-focused design education. In Boess, S., Cheung, M., & Cain, R. (Eds.), *Proceedings of DRS 2020 synergy: Volume 4 Education* (pp. 1803–1816). [Online]. https://dl.designresearchsociety.org/cgi/viewcontent.cgi?article=1195&context=drs-conference-papers

Newton, P. E. (2007). Clarifying the purposes of educational assessment. *Assessment in Education*, 14(2), 149–170. https://doi.org/10.1080/09695940701478321

Oldfield, A., Broadfoot, P., Sutherland, R., & Timmis, S. (2013). *Assessment in a digital age: A research review*. Stellar Project Report. [Online]. https://www.bristol.ac.uk/media-library/sites/education/documents/researchreview.pdf

Papert, S. (1993). *The children's machine: Rethinking school in the age of the computer*. Harvester Wheatsheaf.

Perry, K., Meissel, K., & Hill, M. F. (2022). Rebooting assessment. Exploring the challenges and benefits of shifting from pen-and-paper to computer in summative assessment. *Educational Research Review*, 36(100451), 1–24. https://doi.org/10.1016/j.edurev.2022.100451.

Richardson, M., & Clesham, R. (2021). Rise of the machines? The evolving role of AI technologies in high-stakes assessment. *London Review of Education*, 19(1), 1–13. https://doi.org/10.14324/LRE.19.1.09

Sambell, K., McDowell, L., & Montgomery, C. (2013). *Assessment for learning in higher education*. Routledge.

Schwartz, D. L., & Arena, D. (2013). *Measuring what matters most: Choice-based assessments for the digital age*. MIT Press.

Selwyn, N. (2021). *Education and technology*. Bloomsbury.

Shute, V. J., Dennen, V. P., Kim, Y., Donmez, O., & Wang, C. (2010). *21st century assessment to promote 21st century learning: The benefits of blinking*. A report for Digital Media and Learning network. [Online]. https://clalliance.org/wp-content/uploads/files/val_big_pic_FINAL.pdf

Shute, V., & Ventura, M. (2013). *Stealth assessment: Measuring and supporting learning in video games*. MIT Press.

Sternberg, R. J., & Lubart, T. I. (1998). The concept of creativity: Prospects and paradigms. In R. J. Sternberg (Ed.), *Handbook of creativity* (pp. 1–14). Cambridge University Press.

Thomson, P., & Sefton-Green, J. (Eds.) (2011). *Researching creative learning: Methods and issues*. Routledge.

Tight, M. (2021). Twenty-first century skills: Meaning, usage and value. *European Journal of Higher Education*, *11*(2), 160–174. https://doi.org/10.1080/21568235.2020.1835517

Timmis, S., Broadfoot, P., Sutherland, R., & Oldfield, A. (2016). Rethinking assessment in a digital age: Opportunities, challenges and risks. *British Educational Research Journal*, *42*(3), 454–476. https://doi.org/10.1002/berj.3215

Trilling, B., & Fadel, C. (2009). *21st century skills: Learning for life in our times*. Jossey-Bass.

Walen, S., & Gericke, N. (2023). Transferring makerspace activities to the classroom: A tension between two learning cultures. *International Journal of Technology and Design Education*, *33*(5), 1755–1771. https://doi.org/10.1007/s10798-022-09799-2

Walland, E., & Shaw, S. (2022). E-portfolios in teaching, learning and assessment: Tensions in theory and praxis. *Technology, Pedagogy and Education*, *31*(3), 363–379. https://doi.org/10.1080/1475939X.2022.2074087

Weller, M. (2020). *25 years of ed tech*. AU Press. [Online]. https://www.aupress.ca/books/120290-25-years-of-ed-tech/

Whitelock, D., & Watt, S. (2008). Reframing e-assessment: Adopting new media and adapting old frameworks. *Learning, Media & Technology*, *33*(3), 151–154. https://doi.org/10.1080/17439880802447391

Wiliam, D. (2011). What is assessment for learning? *Studies in Educational Evaluation*, *37*(1), 3–14. https://doi.org/10.1016/j.stueduc.2011.03.001

Winsor, P. J., & Ellefson, B. A. (1995). Professional portfolios in teacher education: An exploration of their value and potential. *The Teacher Educator*, *31*(1), 68–81. https://doi.org/10.1080/08878739509555100

Yeung, K. L., Carpenter, S. K., & Corral, D. A. (2021). Comprehensive review of educational technology on objective learning outcomes in academic contexts. *Educational Psychology Review*, *33*, 1583–1630. https://doi.org/10.1007/s10648-020-09592-4

Chapter 11

Feedback

Creatively promoting desirable affective engagement in Higher Education

Maria Tsapali

Introduction

Emotion or affect plays an important role when seeking, giving, receiving, and using feedback (Molloy et al., 2012). Assessment feedback is a significant aspect of the learning experience in Higher Education (HE), having an impact on students' achievement and enabling them to become independent learners (Ryan & Henderson, 2018). Studies suggest that the HE sector struggles to fully understand the purpose of feedback and provide it in an appropriate way (Carless et al., 2011). For instance, in their analysis of the results of national surveys conducted in the UK on student satisfaction in HE, Bell and Brooks (2018) state that assessment and feedback rank among the factors exerting the least influence on student satisfaction. Although there has been extensive work looking at feedback practices in different global HE contexts (see Henderson et al., 2019), little attention has been given to the role that emotion plays in the way the learner will interpret and receive feedback. Indeed, although the emotional dimensions of learning and teaching in HE have been problematised in the literature (see Quinlan, 2016), one area that remains overlooked is the role of emotion in feedback processes.

Principally through an exploratory review of the literature, this chapter serves two main aims:

- To examine the role of emotion in feedback in HE settings, and
- To identify strategies, both established and creatively inspired, that can promote affective engagement in feedback processes for HE students around the world.

By way of a brief overview of the chapter content, an academic discussion is initially facilitated in which different empirical findings on the relationship between feedback and emotions, and potential factors affecting this relationship, are explored. Then, different strategies that have been suggested to promote desirable affective engagement in feedback processes are categorised and reviewed. Given that this edited book is focused on creative practice, the chapter

DOI: 10.4324/9781032633534-15

will explore how lecturers can creatively provide feedback to HE students that take into account their emotional state, so as to facilitate affective and effective engagement with feedback and learning. This approach to feedback can be seen as creative as it is both novel and useful (Williams et al., 2016). To achieve this, the notion of 'creative touches' (Brownhill, 2024; see Chapter 1) will be embraced, exploring how HE staff can creatively provide adaptive feedback through a selection of *energising* ideas, suggestions, and recommendations, whilst at the same time being mindful of students' emotions. The chapter opens with an exploration of the role of feedback in HE practice.

The role of feedback in HE practice

Effective and high-quality feedback is a key element of quality teaching practice in HE, this being highly valued by students (Biggs & Tang, 2007). Through formative feedback (think assessment *for* learning [AfL]; see Sambell et al., 2012), instructors offer guidance and support students' progress during a unit/the term, while summative feedback (think assessment *of* learning [AoL]; see Wood & Jones, 2020) typically includes a grading process and is carried out at the end of a unit/year (Rowe et al., 2014). In HE settings, feedback can be delivered through written comments in a report or a grade (these could be alphabet letters, percentages, or numbers), or verbally in a group/one-to-one context (such as during a workshop or a supervision). Research shows that feedback serves a variety of functions for students; these include the clarification of instructional expectations and processes, praise, demonstration of care and interest in students, wellbeing and academic progress, and an opportunity for the development of interpersonal relationships between instructors and students (Rowe, 2011).

Emotional responses to feedback

Although the role of emotion in feedback is not well researched and understood as compared to cognitive or motivational aspects, emotion is important as it can affect students' willingness to engage with feedback (Goetz et al., 2018; Olave-Encina et al., 2021; Pitt & Norton, 2017). Research confirms that HE students experience a range of positive and negative emotions when they receive feedback (Doloriert et al., 2012; Hill et al., 2016, 2021a, 2021b, 2021c; Mahfoodh, 2017; Trisdayanti et al., 2019). For instance, Rowe et al. (2014) identified a range of basic emotions – positive (joy/happiness, relief, interest/excitement, and love) and negative (anger, fear, boredom, and disgust) – that students feel in response to feedback. Olave-Encina et al. (2021) explored international students' emotional responses to feedback and identified a set of complex and dynamic emotional responses that were associated with the self, the information on feedback messages, and the lack of familiarity with feedback practices. The authors state that the emotions triggered by the feedback students received influenced the construction of a new identity in the academic environment. Hill et al. (2021a) report that many of the undergraduate students participating in their research struggled to receive negative feedback and act upon it, especially in the first and second years of their programme when feedback was often linked to a sense of failure. Mahfoodh (2017) examined the relationship between the emotional responses of university students with English as a second language (ESL) towards teacher written feedback and their [students'] success with revisions. They found that students experience a range of responses such as acceptance and rejection of feedback, surprise, happiness, (dis)satisfaction, disappointment, and frustration. Moreover, Trisdayanti et al. (2019) report that undergraduate students in Indonesia experienced a range of emotions as a response to written feedback from their thesis supervisor, corroborating the findings of previous studies.

The role of emotion in feedback is also evident in the supervision of doctoral students. Studies suggest that a healthy relationship between the student and the supervisor, as well as good emotional management on both sides, are key aspects of effective supervision (Hockey, 2007). For instance, Doloriert et al. (2012) looked at the role of emotion in doctoral supervision with students and supervisors in the UK, reporting that students are often unaware of their emotions and demonstrate low levels of emotion management. Feedback literacy training for both students and supervisors could foster a healthy relationship and contribute to effective supervision practices, an activity which will be explored later on in the chapter.

It should be noted that, in some cases, certain negative emotions experienced as a result of exposure to feedback can have positive organisational and interpersonal outcomes (Johnson & Connelly, 2014). In their experimental study with a sample of 260 undergraduate students, the researchers looked at students' reactions to feedback associated with a fail mark; they found that when students experienced guilt in response to disappointed displays of feedback, they were more likely to display beneficial behaviours and attitudes, with an enraged response to an angry display of feedback being socially detrimental. Moreover, Värlander (2008) argues that emotions are a natural part of learning and should not be considered as barriers.

Factors affecting students' emotional response to feedback

Different factors can affect how university students will respond to feedback. Some of the identified factors in the literature include grade expectations and emotional maturity (Pitt & Norton, 2017). Ryan and Henderson (2018) conducted a large-scale survey with over 4500 students in two Australian universities. As part of the survey, students had to rate their own levels of sadness/happiness, shame/pride, and anger/contentment in response to specific feedback comments (i.e., those received on the students' most recent assessment task). The results indicated that for the item relating to *feedback comments often being upsetting*, 19.8% (n = 265) of international students and 12.5% (n = 396) of domestic students 'agreed' or 'strongly agreed'. The difference between the two groups was found to be significant. Different emotional responses were also found among students who received grades that were lower or higher than expected, a finding that is corroborated by Kahu et al. (2015) who found that students' pre-conceived conceptions of their achievement level can affect their ability to process the feedback.

Pitt and Norton (2017) introduce students' emotional maturity as a factor influencing their emotional responses to feedback. In their study with third-year undergraduate students, the researchers found that some students reported adaptive skills in responding to and utilising feedback, while others reported maladaptive behaviour when they were dissatisfied with the feedback received. It is hard to identify what makes a student react in a positive or negative way, but the relevant literature seems to suggest that it might be a combination of emotional maturity, self-efficacy, and motivation interacting with each other (Kahu et al., 2015; Nash et al., 2015). More factors that could be relevant, and should be investigated further, include the emotional state of the student when receiving the feedback, the type of relationship with the supervisor, previous educational experiences, and levels of self-efficacy.

Strategies

This section considers a range of suggestions, recommendations, and ideas found in the literature, these being stimulated by Brownhill's (2024) 'creative touches', which can collectively help HE staff alter the way they provide feedback whilst taking into account students' emotions to facilitate effective emotional responses to feedback. The strategies are divided into two categories:

1 Pedagogical strategies, and
2 Feedback literacy training.

The first category includes the different pedagogical strategies that have been empirically tested or creatively stimulated in relation to when feedback is delivered: *before*, *during*, and *after* the strategy implementation. The second category addresses those strategies regarding feedback literacy training for both *instructors* and *students*.

Pedagogic strategies

Before feedback is given

The reviewed studies suggest different strategies before the delivery of feedback that can be helpful in acknowledging and managing students' emotions (Pitt & Norton, 2017; Ryan & Henderson, 2018; Värlander, 2008). Hill et al. (2021a) suggest that supervisors or instructors should be well-prepared for the individual meeting with the student by reviewing, beforehand, the strengths and weaknesses of the work and have specific action points to discuss. They also stress the importance of creating a welcoming and warm environment for the students by considering things in advance like the physical context (room/ learning space), their body language, tone of voice, and verbal expression. Through this, students can feel welcome and supported, especially if instructors embrace one or more of the following practical ideas:

- Ensure that students have access to water (for hydration purposes), tissues (in case they get emotionally upset), a power socket for their electronic device (if making notes on a laptop), and potentially a treat like chocolate or candy for emotional support.
- Use traffic light highlighting (digital; pen) to visually indicate select aspects of strength and consideration in students' written work, e.g., green for 'Good – keep going!', yellow for 'In need of minor tweaking' and red for 'Stop and think'.
- Ask students to predict what positive and negative feedback they think they will receive based on their own honest evaluation of their writing *before* their instructor discusses their work – *how accurate were they?*

Värlander (2008) suggests that feedback preparation activities can help students to reflect on the role of feedback, and instructors can become more aware of students' concerns and anxieties regarding feedback situations. Värlander (Värlander, 2008, p. 152) poses the following questions:

- What is the role of feedback?
- Why do we use it as an assessment method?
- What are the objectives and the advantages of feedback?

These questions could help students and instructors to be in alignment in relation to feedback by briefly exploring their thoughts, using these as a springboard into a productive meeting. Although these questions can be helpful at the beginning of a supervisor-student relationship (doctoral level or for first-year undergraduate students), they could potentially become repetitive if they are used overtime. As such, readers are encouraged to work with students to creatively generate new questions using Jasper and Mooney's (2013, p. 34) 5WH cues – *What…?, Why…?, When…?, Where…?, Who…? and How…?* – offering these on sticky labels which are randomly referred to/selected and answered as appropriate. Alternatively, the instructor could start with questions that aim to identify students' expectations with regard to the feedback they will receive – *will it all be positive? Will it all be negative? Will it reflect the* Sh*t Sandwich *technique of giving feedback, e.g., positive [bread]/negative [filling]/positive [bread]?*

As mentioned previously, students who have high expectations are more prone to experience negative emotions if the feedback is not to the level they expected compared to students who had lower expectations to begin with

(Ryan & Henderson, 2018). Identifying students' grade expectations before the delivery of the feedback (*'What grade do* you *think this piece of work should be awarded? Why?'*) can help the instructor support the student in a more targeted way, acknowledging that they might experience negative emotions if the feedback is not what they were hoping for. Through reflection, Pitt and Norton (2017) call for instructors to carefully consider the students' emotional maturity level and any emotional backlash they might experience before delivering the feedback – *might they need a supportive peer, a personal tutor, or a member of Student Services to be in the room with them if negative feedback is to be given?* Ryan and Henderson (2018) argue that operational mechanisms should be in place before the feedback is given to identify students who might have different needs and require more support (e.g., student support documents, emotional maturity, and high expectations) both *during* and *after* the feedback is delivered.

During feedback delivery

There is a consensus in the literature that dialogic feedback processes are characterised by open communication and a dynamic exchange of ideas, a fostering of feelings of respect, confidence and trust, and can have positive effects in managing emotions (Carless, 2018; Hill et al., 2021a; Smith & Lowe, 2021; Värlander, 2008). Carless (2006) stresses that instructors who fail, through dialogue, to identify whether they are in alignment with their students can negatively affect learning. Moreover, Juwah et al. (2004) suggest moving beyond conceptualising feedback as a transmission process – the transferring of information from the instructor to the student – as it ignores the student as playing an active role in constructing meaning from the feedback message. Thus, feedback should be conceptualised in a creative way as a dialogue during which the student has the opportunity to *discuss* the feedback with the instructor (Värlander, 2008). This could either take place in individual meetings (e.g., a PhD supervision meeting), paired tutorials, or larger group meetings (e.g., unit feedback), these taking place face-to-face or online. A dialogic approach to feedback that is enabled through both curriculum design and assessment policy can help students develop their academic judgment on their own work (Carless, 2018; Smith & Lowe, 2021), thus promoting self-assessment.

Although there is a good number of studies offering useful suggestions for strategies that can promote desirable affective engagement in feedback processes (see Ryan & Henderson, 2018; Värlander, 2008), there are only a few recent studies that have empirically tested relevant feedback interventions. Hill et al. (2021a) conducted a qualitative evaluation of the relational feed-forward[1] intervention that included dialogue about ongoing assessment

---

1 For an accessible discussion about feed-forwards at the HE level, see Hine and Northeast (2016).

between student and instructor, thus aiming to manage student anxiety, enable productive learning attitudes, and promote well-being. The data were collected from 19 undergraduate students taking two units in a US and a UK university. The one-to-one meetings between the instructor and the students included the following main elements:

1 The instructor 'setting the scene' for honest conversations about feedback, exhibiting respect and empathy, and positioning themselves as student allies,
2 The instructor asking the student to summarise the strengths and weaknesses of their work in relation to the assessment criteria, and
3 A conversation about how to discern the key aspects of the assignment, and apply the appropriate knowledge and skills to improve their performance.

The study findings confirmed that anticipating the instructor's feedback can be a stressful time for the students, with a second-year undergraduate student stating that '*I felt a bit nervous, kind of vulnerable ... my tutor was going to judge me and tell me face-to-face what she thought about my work*' (Hill et al., 2021a, p. 7). Moreover, the findings indicate that the relational feed-forward intervention has a positive impact on student feedback literacy (for example, appreciating the value of feedback and managing affect) and that students were keen to have instructors help them manage their emotional responses to assessment in order to promote their wellbeing. According to the researchers, the positive impact on student emotions appeared to derive from a suite of central aspects of the intervention (Hill et al., 2021a, p. 8) – see Figure 11.1.

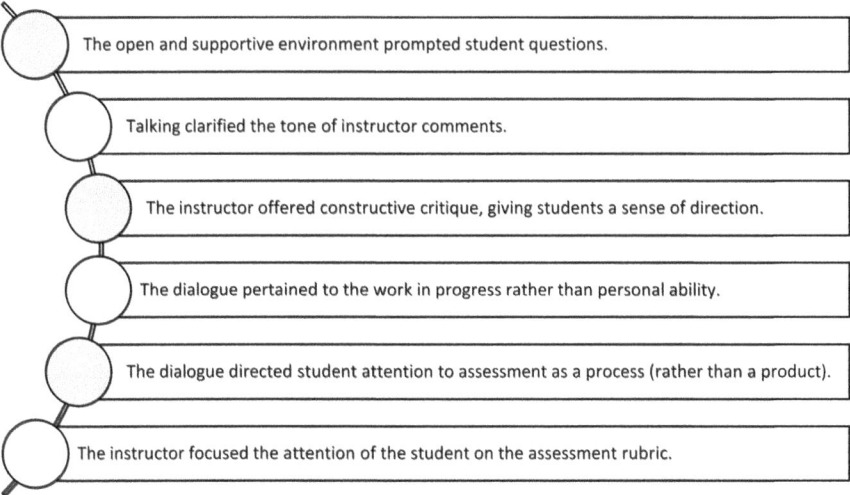

The open and supportive environment prompted student questions.

Talking clarified the tone of instructor comments.

The instructor offered constructive critique, giving students a sense of direction.

The dialogue pertained to the work in progress rather than personal ability.

The dialogue directed student attention to assessment as a process (rather than a product).

The instructor focused the attention of the student on the assessment rubric.

Figure 11.1 The six central aspects of the intervention (adapted from Hill et al., 2021a, p. 8).

In addition, the one-to-one interaction with the instructor seemed to positively affect the instructor-student relationship, with some students stating that '*she* [the instructor] *made me feel like she truly cared and wanted the best for me*' and '*During the meeting it wasn't just about the assignment, it was more like building a bond between us ... I feel like I am more connected to her*' (Hill et al., 2021a, p. 9). Based on these findings and their previous work (Hill & West, 2020; Hill et al., 2016, 2019, 2021b, 2021c), the authors suggest that assessment practices need to be evaluated, especially for the first year of university, by either embedding one-to-one meetings with students or making feedback literacy part of the first year curriculum so that students learn how to approach and manage feedback. Other stimulating strategies which could be embraced include:

- Using a creative combination of written, audio, and video feedback, drawing on this as part of the feedback delivery (McCarthy, 2015),
- Encouraging students to make use of digital technology to capture (record; transcribe) the points raised as part of the feedback discussion,
- Suggesting students use 'Teach Back' – a quality practice in the field of healthcare – as a way of helping instructors ascertain if students are understanding the feedback and feed-forwards they are offered (please visit https://tinyurl.com/24er3vzn for a short overview of the method which can be easily adapted to the university context).

A body of empirical evidence suggests that promoting positive emotions during feedback exchanges can enhance students' engagement with and understanding of feedback, and also reduce negative emotional responses such as anxiety (Fredrickson, 2001; Fredrickson & Cohn, 2008). For instance, Rowe et al. (2014) report that caregiving aspects of feedback such as feelings of closeness with the instructor and concern were associated with love-related emotions experienced by students. Moreover, students experienced positive emotions such as happiness and comfort when receiving personalised feedback from their instructors, and when instructors were persistent and willing to support students (Rowe et al., 2014).

After feedback is delivered

A number of researchers agree that reflection activities that take place after feedback has been given can help students and instructors acknowledge any emotions related to feedback in a positive way, collaboratively thinking about how the feedback process can be improved in creative ways (Rowe et al., 2014; Yorke, 2003). Värlander (2008) argues that feedback-on-feedback activities can be helpful as they allow active dialogue between the instructor and the students about how the emotions associated with giving and receiving feedback are perceived by both parties. Some questions that could be

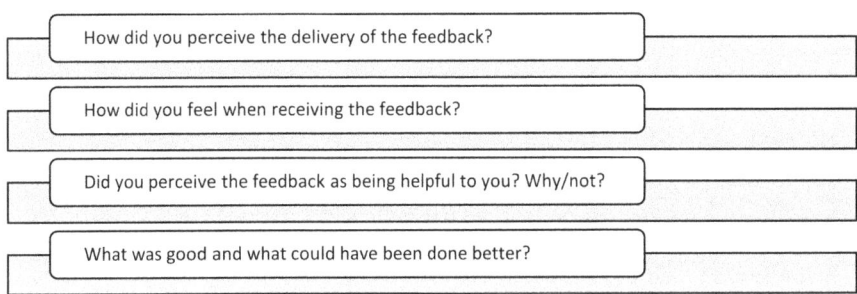

How did you perceive the delivery of the feedback?

How did you feel when receiving the feedback?

Did you perceive the feedback as being helpful to you? Why/not?

What was good and what could have been done better?

Figure 11.2 Suggested questions that could be used for reflection on the delivery of feedback (adapted from Värlander, 2008, p. 153).

used for reflection, and responded to verbally or in written format, are offered in Figure 11.2.

Alternatively, students could share their thoughts non-verbally using facial expressions, hand gestures (thumbs up/thumbs down), or showing a certain number of fingers on one hand that indicate their feelings on a five-point Likert-scale (1 being 'very unhappy', 5 being 'very happy'). Moreover, Yorke (2003) suggests that it is important to have students contribute to the instructors' reflections about feedback by asking them how the feedback process and its delivery could be improved. This could be creatively sought through emails, handwritten notes in comment boxes, quick online surveys, and recorded voice messages. However, as Rowe et al. (2014) note, it might be difficult for instructors to design and implement such pedagogical activities if they do not themselves first have an understanding of emotions and their influence on feedback processes. Thus, it is important to design feedback literacy training that equips both instructors and students with the appropriate knowledge and creative skills to acknowledge and manage their emotions in feedback situations.

Feedback literacy training

Instructor training

Researchers such as Cekiso et al. (2019) and Rowe et al. (2014) have called for HE teaching training to be reconceptualised and include targeted training on the promotion of positive student-instructor relationships and awareness of the role of emotion in feedback. Instructors would benefit from understanding the triggers of certain emotions in feedback processes, modifying their practice accordingly (Rowe et al., 2014). For instance, in a teaching training environment, instructors can learn that delivering timely feedback can reduce students' anxiety, and delivering detailed feedback can promote the feeling of gratitude in students (Rowe et al., 2014). This could be creatively learned through puppet play, simulations, or one of the following activities taken from the work of Denton and Brownhill (2018):

- Spot the mistake – get instructors to spot the mistake in a piece of text about timely feedback (see p. 57),
- Graphic representation – invite instructors to create a 2D or 3D version of a feedback theory or innovative model that underpins the new knowledge being shared (see p. 73),
- Game play – play guessing games, simple board games, dice games, or online games to explore students' feelings in relation to feedback (real and imagined) (see p. 125).

However, it should be acknowledged that applying this knowledge and understanding 'in practice' can be challenging in the current global HE context in which class sizes appear to be getting bigger, and staff reporting being overworked, often struggling to meet marking and other administrative deadlines (see Jayman et al., 2022). Other elements that could be included in instructor and, more specifically, supervisor training include clear communication guidelines in feedback situations, the clarification of roles and responsibilities of both supervisors and students, and the importance of supervisor availability, either face-to-face or online (Cekiso et al., 2019).

Another aspect of instructor training could be the understanding of the different factors that can influence students' emotional responses to feedback (see the section on *Emotional responses to feedback* in this chapter). This could be creatively facilitated through case studies, song lyrics in which the factors are embedded/stressed, and self-made animations (think *Canva*). Ryan and Henderson (2018) argue that instructors should have in place operational mechanisms to identify students who need support and modify feedback practices accordingly to be sensitive to different student cohorts (e.g., lower versus higher grade expectations, different educational backgrounds). Moreover, Pitt and Norton (2017) state that instructors should be able to acknowledge the feedback audience and the individual differences they have in terms of emotional maturity to communicate feedback in a sensitive way and mitigate any negative emotional reactions.

Overall, fostering positive emotions, and carefully considering students' needs and individual differences in emotional responses in a positive way can foster deeper engagement with feedback, facilitate positive student-instructor relationships, and enhance student feelings and perceptions about feedback (Rowe et al., 2014). Creatively, this could be achieved through role-play activities, text messages, and the creation of *TikTok* videos. However, the extent to which HE instructors see the creation of emotionally positive and emotionally aware learning environments as part of their role needs to be discussed and debated further (Moore & Kuol, 2007). Moreover, addressing these goals is unlikely to be easy, particularly without creating an additional workload for already overloaded HE staff (Ryan & Henderson, 2018).

Student training

Creative feedback literacy training that is designed for students should focus on helping them manage and regulate their emotions in feedback contexts (Carless & Boud, 2018). Cognitive reappraisal theory offers some valuable insight towards this direction (Rowe et al., 2014). Cognitive reappraisal is the re-interpretation or changing of the meaning of an event – in this case, it would be the giving of feedback – in a way that changes its emotional impact (Gross & John, 2003; Rowe et al., 2014). People who use cognitive reappraisal compared to suppression experience greater positive emotion/less negative emotion, better interpersonal functioning, and better wellbeing (Gross & John, 2003). Other strategies to help students manage and regulate their emotions include the use of stress balls, taking part in individual/paired/group physical activity, breathing exercises, and practically using adapted ideas from the *Developing Engagement with Feedback Toolkit*[2] (Winstone & Nash, 2016), along with the associated case study by Winstone and Winstone (2018).

Mixed training

Many authors who have argued for better feedback literacy training have suggested that both students and instructors would benefit from targeted training (Cekiso et al., 2019; Doloriert et al., 2012; Gray & Crosta, 2019). Both students and instructors/supervisors should be trained to acknowledge and manage their emotions and their evolving relationship at the same time (Doloriert et al., 2012). Mixed workshops, where both students and instructors participate in creative activities driven by the energetic thinking of Denton and Brownhill (2018), could prove to be a productive environment for them to learn how to communicate effectively and build a healthy relationship, this being especially important for master's and doctoral supervision relationships (Gray & Crosta, 2019). Värlander (2008) offers some good suggestions about the content of the training and activities that could be included (Figure 11.3). The instructor or the supervisor could, for instance, share with the students their own experiences of receiving and handling feedback from peer review (journal article writing), and stress that emotions of frustration, anxiety, and joy are part of the process, and are related to learning and improving one's work (Värlander, 2008). Moreover, it is important to discuss good and bad examples of feedback in small groups with a focus on the language used, politeness, and constructiveness. Some prompt questions to be used could include.

---

2 Of personal interest is the 'Feedback flowchart' on p. 21.

Is this a good or bad feedback situation? Why/why not?	What could have been done better? How? Why?
How would you feel in this situation? Why?	What does an ideal feedback situation look like? Why?

Figure 11.3 Suggested prompts that could be used in feedback literacy training (adapted from Värlander, 2008, p. 153).

These questions could be used as a starter for conversations on the role of emotion in feedback and learning between instructors and students as both parties could relate to the examples in an effective manner. Additional creative suggestions, especially those that promote self-reflective thoughts in instructors and students, can be found in the work of Brownhill (2022a, 2022b, 2023) – personal favourites include *Self-Reflective Shapes*, *poetry slams*, and a *self-reflection walking route*. Overall, it is important for both students and instructors to become feedback literate (Hill et al., 2021a) and recognise the role of emotion in the feedback process.

Concluding comments

This chapter has reviewed the literature on the role of emotion in feedback processes in HE, recognising strategies that can facilitate students' desirable affective engagement with feedback. The literature suggests that students can experience a range of positive and negative emotions in response to feedback that can be mediated by different factors such as grade expectations and emotional maturity. A range of established and creatively inspired pedagogical strategies have been categorised that manage emotional responses to feedback, with suggestions for feedback literacy training also being identified. More research is needed to explore the efficacy of these strategies and their potential to help students engage with feedback in a positive and productive way, which can, in turn, influence students' creative thinking (see Howard-Jones, 2008).

Acknowledgements

The author would like to generously thank the editor of this book for his numerous suggestions that have energised the 'creative content' of this chapter.

Suggested further reading

Crisp, B. R. (2007). Is it worth the effort? How feedback influences students' subsequent submission of assessable work. *Assessment and Evaluation in Higher Education*, *32*(5), 571–581. https://doi.org/10.1080/02602930601116912

Fong, C. J., & Schallert, D. L. (2023). "Feedback to the future": Advancing motivational and emotional perspectives in feedback research. *Educational Psychologist*, *58*(3), 146–161. https://doi.org/10.1080/00461520.2022.2134135

References

Bell, A. R., & Brooks, C. (2018). What makes students satisfied? A discussion and analysis of the UK's national student survey. *Journal of Further and Higher Education*, *42*(8), 1118–1142. https://doi.org/10.1080/0309877X.2017.1349886

Biggs, J., & Tang, C. (2007). *Teaching for quality learning at university*. McGraw Hill.

Brownhill, S. (2022a). Asking key questions of self-reflection. *Reflective Practice*, *23*(1), 57–67. https://doi.org/10.1080/14623943.2021.1976628

Brownhill, S. (2022b). Asking more key questions of self-reflection. *Reflective Practice*, *23*(2), 279–290. https://doi.org/10.1080/14623943.2021.2013192

Brownhill, S. (2023). Asking *additional* key questions of self-reflection. *Reflective Practice*, *24*(3), 400–412. https://doi.org/10.1080/14623943.2023.2190578

Brownhill, S. (2024). *Surprise, surprise!* (Re-)grabbing the attention of students in the university classroom through creative touches. *Journal of Education & Language Studies (OAJELS)*, *1*(4), 555568 (1–7). [Online]. https://juniperpublishers.com/oajels/pdf/OAJELS.MS.ID.555568.pdf

Carless, C. (2006). Differing perceptions in the feedback process. *Studies in Higher Education*, *31*(2), 219–233. https://doi.org/10.1080/03075070600572132

Carless, C. (2018). Feedback loops and the longer-term: Towards feedback spirals. *Assessment and Evaluation in Higher Education*, *44*(3), 705–714. https://doi.org/10.1080/02602938.2018.1531108

Carless, D., & Boud, D. (2018). The development of student feedback literacy: Enabling uptake of feedback. *Assessment and Evaluation in Higher Education*, *43*(8), 1315–1325. https://doi.org/10.1080/02602938.2018.1463354

Carless, D., Salter, D., Yang, M., & Lam, J. (2011). Developing sustainable feedback practices. *Studies in Higher Education*, *36*(4), 395–407. https://doi.org/10.1080/03075071003642449

Cekiso, M., Tshotsho, B., Masha, R., & Saziwa, T. (2019). Supervision experiences of postgraduate research students at one South African higher education institution. *South African Journal of Higher Education*, *33*(3), 8–25. [Online]. https://hdl.handle.net/10520/EJC-18b055cb25

Denton, A., & Brownhill, S. (2018). *Becoming a brilliant trainer: A teacher's guide to running sessions and engaging learners*. Routledge.

Doloriert, C., Sambrook, S., & Stewart, J. (2012). Power and emotion in doctoral supervision: Implications for HRD. *European Journal of Training and Development*, *36*(7), 732–750. https://doi.org/10.1108/03090591211255566

Fredrickson, B. L. (2001). The role of positive emotions in positive psychology: The broaden-and-build theory of positive emotions. *American Psychologist*, *56*(3), 218–226. https://doi.org/10.1037/0003-066X.56.3.218

Fredrickson, B. L., & Cohn, M. A. (2008). Positive emotions. In M. Lewis, J. M. Haviland-Jones & L. F. Barrett (Eds.), *Handbook of emotions* (3rd ed., pp. 777–796). Guilford Press.

Goetz, T., Lipnevich, A. A., Krannich, M., & Gogol, K. (2018). Performance feedback and emotions. In A. A. Lipnevich & J. K. Smith (Eds.), *The Cambridge handbook of instructional feedback* (pp. 554–574). Cambridge University Press.

Gray, M. A., & Crosta, L. (2019). New perspectives in online doctoral supervision: A systematic literature review. *Studies in Continuing Education, 41*(2), 173–190. https://doi.org/10.1080/0158037X.2018.1532405

Gross, J. J., & John, O. P. (2003). Individual differences in two emotion regulation processes: Implications for affect, relationships, and well-being. *Journal of Personality and Social Psychology, 85*(2), 348–362. https://doi.org/10.1037/0022-3514.85.2.348

Henderson, M., Ryan, T., & Phillips, M. (2019). The challenges of feedback in higher education. *Assessment & Evaluation in Higher Education, 44*(8), 1237–1252. https://doi.org/10.1080/02602938.2019.1599815

Hill, J., Berlin, K., Choate, J., Cravens-Brown, L., McKendrick-Calder, L., & Smith, S. (2021a). Can relational feed-forward enhance students' cognitive and affective responses to assessment? *Teaching and Learning Inquiry, 9*(2), 1–21. https://doi.org/10.20343/teachlearninqu.9.2.18

Hill, J., Berlin, K., Choate, J., Cravens-Brown, L., McKendrick-Calder, L., & Smith, S. (2021c). Exploring the emotional responses of undergraduate students to assessment feedback: Implications for instructors. *Teaching and Learning Inquiry, 9*(1), 294–316. https://doi.org/10.20343/teachlearninqu.9.1.20

Hill, J., Healey, R. L., West, H., & Déry, C. (2021b). Pedagogic partnership in higher education: Encountering emotion in learning and enhancing student wellbeing. *Journal of Geography in Higher Education, 45*(2), 167–185. https://doi.org/10.1080/03098265.2019.1661366

Hill, J., Thomas, G., Diaz, A., & Simm, D. (2016). Borderland spaces for learning partnership: Opportunities, benefits and challenges. *Journal of Geography in Higher Education, 40*(3), 375–393. https://doi.org/10.1080/03098265.2016.1144728

Hill, J., Walkington, H., & Kneale, P. (2019). Borderland spaces: Moving towards self-authorship. In T. Bilham, C. Hamshire, M. Hartog, & M. Doolan (Eds.), *Reframing space for learning: Excellence and innovation in university teaching* (pp. 88–101). UCL/IoE Press.

Hill, J., & West, H. (2020). Improving the student learning experience through dialogic feed-forward assessment. *Assessment and Evaluation in Higher Education, 45*(1), 82–97. https://doi.org/10.1080/02602938.2019.1608908

Hine, B., & Northeast, T. (2016). Using feed-forward strategies in higher education. *New Vistas, 2*(1), 28–33. [Online]. https://core.ac.uk/download/pdf/96570274.pdf

Hockey, J. (2007). United Kingdom art and design practice-based PhDs: Evidence from students and their supervisors. *Studies in Art Education, 48*(2), 155–171. https://doi.org/10.1080/00393541.2007.11650097

Howard-Jones, P. A. (2008). *Fostering creative thinking: Co-constructed insights from neuroscience and education.* Higher Education Academy. [Online]. https://tinyurl.com/4w7z2zjc

Jasper, M., & Mooney, G. (2013). The context of professional development. In M. Jasper, M. Rosser, & G. Mooney (Eds.), *Professional development, reflection and decision-making in nursing and health care* (2nd ed., pp. 6–40). John Wiley & Sons, Ltd.

Jayman, M., Glazzard, J., & Rose, A. (2022). Tipping point: The staff wellbeing crisis in higher education. *Frontiers in Education, 7*(929335), 1–7. https://doi.org/10.3389/feduc.2022.929335

Johnson, G., & Connelly, S. (2014). Negative emotions in informal feedback: The benefits of disappointment and drawbacks of anger. *Human Relations, 67*(10), 1265–1290. https://doi.org/10.1177/0018726714532856

Juwah, C., Macfarlane-Dick, D., Matthew, B., Nicol, D., Ross, D., & Smith, B. (2004). *Enhancing student learning through effective formative feedback*. The Higher Education Academy. [Online]. https://www.advance-he.ac.uk/knowledge-hub/enhancing-student-learning-through-effective-formative-feedback

Kahu, E., Stephens, C., Leach, L., & Zepke, N. (2015). Linking academic emotions and student engagement: Mature-aged distance students' transition to university. *Journal of Further and Higher Education*, 39(4), 481–497. https://doi.org/10.1080/0309877X.2014.895305

Mahfoodh, O. H. A. (2017). "I feel disappointed": EFL university students' emotional responses towards teacher written feedback. *Assessing Writing*, 31, 53–72. https://doi.org/10.1016/j.asw.2016.07.001

McCarthy, J. (2015). Evaluating written, audio and video feedback in higher education summative assessment tasks. *Issues in Educational Research*, 25(2), 153–169. https://www.iier.org.au/iier25/mccarthy.pdf

Molloy, E., Borrell-Carrio, F., & Epstein, R. (2012). *The impact of emotions in feedback*. Routledge.

Moore, S., & Kuol, K. (2007). Matters of the heart: Exploring the emotional dimensions of educational experience in recollected accounts of excellent teaching. *International Journal for Academic Development*, 12(2), 87–98. https://doi.org/10.1080/13601440701604872

Nash, G., Crimmins, G., & Oprescu, F. (2015). If first-year students are afraid of public speaking assessments what can teachers do to alleviate such anxiety? *Assessment and Evaluation in Higher Education*, 41(4), 586–600. https://doi.org/10.1080/02602938.2015.1032212

Olave-Encina, K., Moni, K., & Renshaw, P. (2021). Exploring the emotions of international students about their feedback experiences. *Higher Education Research and Development*, 40(4), 810–824. https://doi.org/10.1080/07294360.2020.1786020

Pitt, E., & Norton, L. (2017). 'Now that's the feedback I want!' Students' reactions to feedback on graded work and what they do with it. *Assessment and Evaluation in Higher Education*, 42(4), 499–516. https://doi.org/10.1080/02602938.2016.1142500

Quinlan, K. M. (2016). How emotion matters in four key relationships in teaching and learning in higher education. *College Teaching*, 64(3), 101–111. https://doi.org/10.1080/87567555.2015.1088818

Rowe, A. (2011). The personal dimension in teaching: Why students value feedback. *International Journal of Educational Management*, 25(4), 343–360. https://doi.org/10.1108/09513541111136630

Rowe, A. D., Fitness, J., & Wood, L. N. (2014). The role and functionality of emotions in feedback at university: A qualitative study. *The Australian Educational Researcher*, 41(3), 283–309. https://doi.org/10.1007/s13384-013-0135-7

Ryan, T., & Henderson, M. (2018). Feeling feedback: students' emotional responses to educator feedback. *Assessment and Evaluation in Higher Education*, 43(6), 880–892. https://doi.org/10.1080/02602938.2017.1416456

Sambell, K., McDowell, L., & Montgomery, C. (2012). *Assessment for learning in higher education*. Routledge.

Smith, M., & Lowe, C. (2021). DIY assessment feedback: Building engagement, trust and transparency in the feedback process. *Journal of University Teaching and Learning Practice*, 18(3), 1–16. https://doi.org/10.53761/1.18.3.9

Trisdayanti, I., Marlina, N., & Dewi, N. S. N. (2019). "My feelings": Undergraduate students' emotional responses towards supervisors' written corrective feedback in their thesis writing. *TLEMC: Teaching and Learning English in Multicultural Contexts*, 3(1), 43–51. https://jurnal.unsil.ac.id/index.php/tlemc/article/view/1125

Värlander, S. (2008). The role of students' emotions in formal feedback situations. *Teaching in Higher Education*, *13*(2), 145–156. https://doi.org/10.1080/13562510801923195

Williams, R., Runco, M. A., & Berlow, E. (2016). Mapping the themes, impact, and cohesion of creativity research over the last 25 years. *Creativity Research Journal*, *28*(4), 385–394. https://doi.org/10.1080/10400419.2016.1230358

Winstone, N. E., & Nash, R. A. (2016). *The developing engagement with feedback toolkit (DEFT)*. Higher Education Academy. [Online]. https://www.advance-he.ac.uk/knowledge-hub/developing-engagement-feedback-toolkit-deft

Winstone, N., & Winstone, N. (2018). *Developing engagement with feedback toolkit 16-19*. Godalming College. [Online]. https://www.surrey.ac.uk/sites/default/files/2018-10/deft-16-19.pdf

Wood, C., & Jones, G. (2020). Evaluating the nature of summative feedback on electronically submitted work at a UK University: implications for post-compulsory education. *Research in Post-Compulsory Education*, *25*(4), 420–444. https://doi.org/10.1080/13596748.2020.1846314

Yorke, M. (2003). Formative assessment in higher education: Moves towards theory and the enhancement of pedagogic practice. *Higher Education*, *45*, 477–501. https://doi.org/10.1023/A:1023967026413

Conclusion

Simon Brownhill

In the proposal that secured our book contract with Routledge, we originally set out to offer readers a concluding chapter that was entitled *Looking back to look forwards: Concluding comments, recommendations, and next steps*. The descriptive text below recognises the chapter's anticipated content:

> The main conclusion of the book will *look back* by reviewing the aims of the book and synthesising the main ideas generated from the chapters in an effort to help the reader appreciate the coverage of the book and its content. *Looking forwards*, the conclusion will consider new and exciting developments in the HE arena, signposting readers to cutting edge/contemporary research for reading and personal reflection. Support for readers to embrace creativity in their pursuit to engage adult learners will be offered in the form of bullet point/tabular guidance, signposting them to a suite of valuable websites, professional organisations, and *YouTube* videos.

However, by way of a *surprise* (see Brownhill, 2024, p. 2), not just to the reader but also to the contributing authors of this volume, the publisher, and the author himself (!), the ending to this edited book has been creatively revised to stimulate both activity and action in those who choose to engage with it. Table 12.1 offers readers a grid that is separated into two parts: 'Flick or Scroll back' (Part 1; activity) and 'Action forwards' (Part 2; action). To effectively engage with the grid, readers are encouraged to sequentially follow the set of numbered instructions offered below and on p. 197.

1 **Part 1:** 'Flick or Scroll back' – for readers who have a physical (paper) copy of this edited book, they are encouraged to *flick back* through its pages, skimming and scanning them for anything of personal/professional interest. For those readers who have an e-book copy of this edited volume, they are encouraged to *scroll back* through the digital pages, again, skimming and scanning them for anything of personal/professional interest. In Part 1 (Table 12.1), paper readers are invited to physically make a personal note in

DOI: 10.4324/9781032633534-16

Table 12.1 A 'Flick or Scroll back'/'Action forwards' grid

Part 1: 'Flick or Scroll back'

Part 2: 'Action forwards'

the grid ('jot down') anything that serves as a reminder (prompt) for them, e.g., a page number, a key word, a sub-heading, a figure number, a phrase, a cited surname, or a practical idea. For digital readers, they are invited to make their personal notes in a format that suits them, e.g., handwritten notes in a physical jotter, text typed into a word processing package of their choosing, or verbally recorded in a digital speech-to-text app. Readers are recommended to note down as many or as few personal notes as they wish [given that they are personal to you, there is no set number of notes to make a record of, the hope being that you make a note of at least one thing!].

2 **Part 2:** 'Action forwards' – readers are asked to identify one personal note from Part 1 (Table 12.1). They should then consider what action they are going to take based on the note they have chosen. Actions can be varied, illustrative examples of which include the following:

a talking to a colleague about what has been read,
b undertaking some desk research to learn more about an advocated strategy, or
c integrating an idea into an upcoming lecture/workshop.

In Part 2, readers should record in written or digital form their planned action, this being offered in the form of a goal. To achieve this, I advocate that readers develop SMART goals. By SMART, this refers to a goal which is specific, measurable, attainable, realistic, and time-bound. Ogbeiwi (2017, p. 335) suggests that '[w]riting SMART goals is fundamental to planning effective results-oriented action'. To support readers who are unfamiliar with SMART goals, the following resources are recommended:

• *Website (blog post)*: https://post.edu/blog/what-are-smart-goals/
• *Downloadable PDF*: https://tinyurl.com/2h6e3p5t
• *Journal article*: 'Being smart about writing SMART objectives' by Bjerke and Renger (2017).

By way of an example, here is an illustrative SMART goal (based on a reading of Chapter 1):

> *By the end of March, integrate a silent voting task using coloured voting cards* (see Table 1.1) *into the taught input for* Assessment in Schools 6,[1] *reviewing its effectiveness with a short online student survey (email), post-session.*

3 Implement the action-led goal, celebrating its completion and reader success.

Without reader commitment to point 3, there is likely to be little change to their thinking or their practice with those they have the good fortune of

---

1 Name of a postgraduate taught unit, along with a session number.

working with. Readers are reminded of the title of this edited volume: *Creative Practice in Higher Education: Engaging Adult Learners through Theory and Pedagogy*. Creative practice can only be implemented in the Higher Education arena by those readers who are brave, take a chance, and purposefully use theoretical ideas and pedagogical practices advocated in this book to energise and enrich what they do with adult learners. With this in mind, it is my intention to leave readers with the following adapted advice from Brownhill (2024, p. 6):

> … readers are encouraged to embrace an enthusiastic attitude towards [creativity and its associated practice], recognising that its impact on [adult learners] can only be known if lecturers creatively experiment with it as part of their impending/future practice.

So, kindly go forth and be creative!

References

Bjerke, M. B., & Renger, R. (2017). Being smart about writing SMART objectives. *Evaluation and Program Planning*, *61*, 125–127. https://doi.org/10.1016/j.evalprogplan.2016.12.009

Brownhill, S. (2024). *Surprise, surprise!* (Re-)grabbing the attention of students in the university classroom through creative touches. *Journal of Education & Language Studies (OAJELS)*, *1*(4), 555568 (1–7). [Online]. https://juniperpublishers.com/oajels/pdf/OAJELS.MS.ID.555568.pdf

Ogbeiwi, O. (2017). Why written objectives need to be really SMART. *British Journal of Healthcare Management*, *23*(7), 324–336. https://doi.org/10.12968/bjhc.2017.23.7.324

Index

www.ingramcontent.com/pod-product-compliance
Ingram Content Group UK Ltd.
Pitfield, Milton Keynes, MK11 3LW, UK
UKHW022137040325
455759UK00006B/14